THE MODERN CHRISTMAS IN AMERICA

The American Social Experience Series

GENERAL EDITOR: JAMES KIRBY MARTIN

EDITORS: PAULA S. FASS, STEVEN H. MINTZ,

CARL PRINCE, JAMES W. REED & PETER N. STEARNS

*1. The March to the Sea and Beyond: Sherman's Troops in
the Savannah and Carolinas Campaigns*
JOSEPH T. GLATTHAAR

2. Childbearing in American Society: 1650–1850
CATHERINE M. SCHOLTEN

3. The Origins of Behaviorism: American Psychology, 1870–1920
JOHN M. O'DONNELL

4. New York City Cartmen, 1667–1850
GRAHAM RUSSELL HODGES

*5. From Equal Suffrage to Equal Rights: Alice Paul and
the National Woman's Party, 1910–1928*
CHRISTINE A. LUNARDINI

*6. Mr. Jefferson's Army: Political and Social Reform
of the Military Establishment, 1801–1809*
THEODORE J. CRACKEL

*7. "A Peculiar People": Slave Religion and
Community-Culture Among the Gullahs*
MARGARET WASHINGTON CREEL

*8. "A Mixed Multitude": The Struggle for Toleration
in Colonial Pennsylvania*
SALLY SCHWARTZ

9. Women, Work, and Fertility, 1900–1986
SUSAN HOUSEHOLDER VAN HORN

*10. Liberty, Virtue, and Progress: Northerners and
Their War for the Union*
EARL J. HESS

11. Lewis M. Terman: Pioneer in Psychological Testing
HENRY L. MINTON

THE MODERN CHRISTMAS IN AMERICA

A Cultural History of Gift Giving

WILLIAM B. WAITS

NEW YORK UNIVERSITY PRESS

NEW YORK AND LONDON

NEW YORK UNIVERSITY PRESS
New York and London

Library of Congress Cataloging-in-Publication Data
Waits, William Burnell.
The modern Christmas in America : a cultural history of gift
giving / William B. Waits.
p. cm.—(The Anerican social experience series ; 26)
Revision of thesis (doctoral)—Rutgers University, 1978.
Includes bibliographical references (p.   ) and index.
ISBN 0-8147-9251-0 (cloth : acid-free paper)
1. Christmas—United States—History. 2. Gifts—United States—
History. 3. United States—Social life and customs. I. Title.
II. Series
GT4986.A1W35 1993   92-28974
                                            CIP
394.2′68282′0973—dc20

New York University Press books are printed on acid-free paper,
and their binding materials are chosen for strength and durability.

Manufactured in the United States of America

c 10 9 8 7 6 5 4 3 2 1

To
Nancy Ellen Waits, Wonderful Wife,
and to the memory of
Warren I. Susman, Extraordinary Teacher

Epigraph

Considerable difficulty and bad feeling will be avoided on Christmas morning if the donors of Christmas presents will hereafter mark clearly on the outside of each package just what it contains, how it works and what it is for.

As a result of the present confusion, families are forced to spend endless hours classifying their mysterious gifts and solving the puzzle of what they are meant to be. For example, Mother will be up half the night trying to decide whether that cunning object from Aunt Emma is a chafing dish or a mustard foot bath, and, if so, why it is filled with salted almonds.

Grandma will wear the worsted nightcap which she received from Aunt Ettie for a full week before she discovers that it is really a hot water bottle cover.

Father will swallow half a pint of gasoline under the impression that his new patent cigar lighter is a pocket flask.

As if to add to these difficulties, every Christmas is made even more involved by the artistic relative who makes her own Christmas presents.

In order to aid the harassed student in understanding these Christmas presents, therefore, we have devised a system of tests.

Test 1: The first test is to try to wear it. If you can get your hand into it, it's mittens. If you can get your feet into it, it is probably a pair of bed socks. If, on the other hand, it seems to fit down over your ears, it is a skating cap. If you can pull it down as far as your waist, it is a slip-on sweater, and if it will not fit over your head at all, it is probably a lettuce bag.

Test 2: If you cannot wear it, then see if you can wind it up. If you wind it up and it runs, it is a clock. If you wind it up and it does not run, it is a pencil sharpener. If it runs without being wound up, it is a Ford. If it does not choose to run, don't you believe it.

Test 3: Next try to drink it. If you can swallow it, it is liquor. If you can swallow it and stay conscious, it is good liquor. If you can't swallow it yourself, try it on your guests.

Test 4: Now put it on the floor and jump up and down on it. If it does not smash, it is a pogo stick. If it does smash, so much the better.

Test 5: If the gift responds to none of these tests, however—if you cannot wear it, drink it, wind it up, ride it, smoke it, or use it in any conceivable way—then it undoubtedly is a Work of Art. Replace it reverently in the box, pack the excelsior around it again, and give it away the following Christmas.

—Corey Ford, "Breaking Even on Christmas," *Collier's*,
80 (17 Dec. 1927): 49

Like this article, this book tries to unravel the mysteries of Christmas gifts.

Contents

Preface

Most Americans believe that our way of celebrating Christmas is old, that we have observed the Yule season in essentially the same way for centuries. Although the celebration has become commercialized over time, they say, its core—centered around the Christmas tree, family togetherness, and church services—has always been much as it is today. But in fact we have had no single form of celebration and have enjoyed several types of Christmases during our history. Moreover, our current form of celebrating is not very old, dating only from about 1880.

When Europeans first began to settle the Atlantic seaboard, the English Christmas was the celebration familiar to most of them. It had as its central symbols the Yule log, the boar's head, and the wassail bowl, and was characterized by adult revelry with peers rather than adult gratification of children's desires. However, in North America, responses to this form of celebration diverged sharply. The Southern Atlantic colonies embraced it, thereby becoming the New World locus of the transplanted English Christmas, while Calvinist New England held it in disfavor and even outlawed the celebration of Christmas between 1659 and 1681. The Puritans' antipathy was consistent with their theology as there was no affirmative command in the Bible to celebrate the birthday of Jesus. Moreover, the prospect of unrestrained revelry made them uncomfortable. Although today we are graced every season with nostalgic accounts of sleigh rides over New England hillsides to Grandma's house for Christmas, such accounts are contrary to historical fact: good New England grandmas through the first half of the nineteenth century disliked Christmas. The public sector was in accord; for example, December 25 was not a school holiday in the antebellum Northeast and children were required to attend classes.

Although these two responses to Christmas characterized most of the seaboard settlements before 1800, neither served as the model for the modern celebration. The Christmas of the Middle Atlantic colonies—wedged between New England's suspicions of the revelrous English celebration and the South's embracing of it—was the type of Christmas that became favored. The Dutch in New Amsterdam and the Germans in Pennsylvania introduced a northern European celebration guided by Lutheran rather than Calvinistic doctrine. They needed no affirmative biblical command to engage in the festivities, only an absence of prohibition, so they did not display the Puritan reservations about Christmas. Indeed, Martin Luther himself had participated in, and encouraged, Yule festivities. In tone, the northern European celebration was more child-centered than the English one, and the revelry, although present, was subdued. The Christmas tree, adopted from neighboring Scandinavia, was the central symbol of the festivities rather than the Yule log or crèche. Before 1800 the scale of the celebration, whether in the Southern, Middle Atlantic or New England region, remained small.

After 1800 Americans began to celebrate Christmas on a somewhat larger scale, with the Middle Atlantic region and its northern European style of Christmas, leading the way. As New York rose to economic and cultural predominance in America following the opening of the Erie Canal in 1825, its Yule celebration also prospered. Soon the South, and later New England, fell under its sway and adopted the northern European forms. This was the Christmas of Washington Irving and Clement Moore, and even today it is the subject of nostalgic descriptions placed in rural settings. Gifts were usually handmade, and many of them were for children or the poor, with other types of exchanges being less frequent than they are today.

During the nineteenth century, as the United States expanded into Florida, the Louisiana Purchase, and the Southwest, it added yet another form of celebration, the Latin Christmas. Settlers in these parts of North America had brought from Spain and France Yule customs guided by Catholic doctrine. They placed more emphasis on the family, the crèche (manger), and the Epiphany (the adoration of the Magi on January 6) than did the English, and less on adult revelry. Although this Latin Christmas was overshadowed by the dominant northern European celebration, it contributed to more frequent use of manger scenes and a strengthened emphasis on the family.

During the late nineteenth century, America was transformed economically and socially. Factories expanded their output dramatically and drew millions of rural dwellers into cities as laborers. On the foundation of these startling developments, the nation developed not only a modern culture, but also a modern Christmas. It was during these years that the celebration achieved its present gargantuan scale. Gift giving became pervasive, with new categories of givers and recipients participating in exchanges, and with many new types of items considered suitable as gifts. Although this modern celebration followed northern European forms and came from the Middle Atlantic states—much as the Christmas of the first eighty years of the nineteenth century had—it was urban, not rural, in tone and was typified by the exchange of manufactured rather than handmade gifts. The emergence of this modern celebration and its subsequent history are the focus of this work.

What kinds of sources must one examine to get the best descriptions and representations of the modern Christmas? I relied heavily on the documents of mass culture, in particular on mass-circulation periodicals, because they document the celebration that was most typical of the nation as a whole and expressed core American values. In large part, periodicals expressed these values because of the way in which they were financed. In the late nineteenth century, Frank A. Munsey and Cyrus H. K. Curtis devised a new way of financing periodicals. Unlike earlier magazine publishers, they earned most of their income from sales of advertising space to businesses rather than from newsstand sales of magazines to readers. In order for advertising revenue to support the magazine, they set their advertising rates much higher than was industry custom. Munsey and Curtis justified these higher rates because their magazines had much larger circulations than their competitors. For example, by the early twentieth century, Curtis had achieved the hitherto-unheard-of circulation of one million readers for each of his two major magazines, the *Ladies' Home Journal* and *The Saturday Evening Post*. In contrast, magazines that were financed by newsstand sales and subscriptions—magazines such as *Scribner's*, *Harper's*, and *Atlantic*—had readerships of about 150,000. With Munsey and Curtis, mass circulation periodicals had arrived.

Munsey and Curtis achieved their circulations through two devices. First, they made the selling price very low, about five or ten cents a copy, compared to the thirty or so cents a copy which other magazines cost. This low selling price did not produce a profit, but it defrayed the costs of publication. Second, they made the content of their magazines reflect the most widely held attitudes in the nation. Publishers of mass circulation periodicals were compelled to adopt this policy by the strongest of financial considerations. If they had discussed controversial topics, they would have alienated readers, and that would have required them to lower the all-important advertising rates. In order to prevent the serious economic results of declining readership, publishers and editors made sure their magazines mirrored attitudes already held by the largest possible segment of the public, thus making them a highly valuable source for discovering what these widely held attitudes were.

Recognizing the special reflecting quality of mass-circulation periodicals, I made them my main body of source materials. I analyzed 1,720 articles related to Christmas-gift giving from these periodicals. In addition to articles, I also analyzed Christmas gift advertisements from two of the most widely circulated—and typically American—magazines published during the period: the *Ladies' Home Journal* and *The Saturday Evening Post*. I did a content analysis of 1,270 advertisements, which I selected at random from five three-year periods: 1900–1902, 1911–1913, 1920–1922, 1928–1930, and 1936–1938.

Finally, I analyzed 460 articles from trade journals. These articles, written for the use of businessmen, were very helpful as historical sources. Most contained forthright arguments, supported by good evidence and specific examples. Although the articles almost always encouraged profit-making, they exhibited few other biases or value judgments.

My analysis of these primary sources revealed that the modern Christmas celebration had a significant internal diversity—most importantly, diversity based on the social roles played by individual celebrants such as husbands, wives, parents, children, community members, the poor, employees, and friends. No doubt there were other dimensions of diversity, but I leave those to subsequent scholars.

Scholarly secondary literature on the American Christmas celebration is sparse; historians, for example, have virtually ignored the festival. The general lack of scholarly effort in analyzing the Christmas celebration is ironic when one considers the enormous effort Americans (scholars included) have expended in celebrating Christmas since 1880. Each winter the public energetically shops, wraps presents, prepares holiday foods, and performs the multitude of other tasks that are necessary for a proper celebration. Economically, this event usually causes months of financial anxiety. Fortunate, indeed, have been those who are able to meet holiday expenses as they arose; more commonly, however, the holiday season generates sheaves of bills that are paid off over subsequent months. All told, the finances of millions of Americans have operated in the shadow of holiday expenditures for a full quarter of each year.

The sizable effort the public puts into celebrating Christmas has been matched by the efforts of American manufacturers, retailers, and advertisers. As early as 1880, the prescient among the nation's businessmen saw that they could use the emerging custom of Christmas gift giving to increase their sales. Ever since, they have moved purposefully to expand gift giving in America and have enjoyed the rewards of their effort. Indeed, they have been so successful that many businessmen have come to rely on end-of-the-year sales for a substantial percentage of their yearly profits. Remarkably, none of this activity by businessmen and the public attracted much scholarly interest.

Although secondary works on Christmas are sparse, secondary works on various subjects related to Christmas are plentiful and useful. For example, there are histories of periodicals, advertising, the economy, festivals, the family, labor, charity, and urbanization, as well as anthropological and sociological studies of gift giving and festivals. I frequently relied on these works, without which my own study would have been much more difficult.

Acknowledgments

I researched this book at the libraries of Rutgers and Princeton universities, at the New-York Historical Society, and at the New Brunswick, Newark, Trenton, New York City, and Philadelphia public libraries. In particular, the Free Library of Philadelphia and the New York Public Library graciously permitted me to photograph from their archives the advertisements that appear in the book. I am grateful for the kind assistance of the staffs of all of these institutions.

Frank Lyons photographed the ads with care and high standards. Early in my work on the book, Susan Tiller and Janice Bernardo provided clean typed copies on which I scribbled revisions.

Colin Jones and the staff of New York University Press offered valuable advice about putting the book into a finished form. Their professionalism made the labor of preparing it for press a pleasure.

I am grateful to James W. Reed, Dean of Rutgers College, for his encouragement of this project, which began with his service on my dissertation committee. He has not only made many specific recommendations that have improved this book, but also provided wise counsel. I am also grateful to Tilden D. Edelstein and Angus K. Gillespie, who offered helpful comments on this work at its early stages.

Mark Thomas Connelly offered valuable observations on the manuscript and sharpened my thinking and writing throughout. I have also treasured his friendship.

My greatest intellectual debt is to the late Warren I. Susman, who guided this work as a dissertation. His tutelage made my world—like the worlds of so many others who studied with him—a much richer place.

I thank my parents for their tolerance of my graduate study, and for their ample and timely supplements to my fellowships and earnings from part-time teaching. I also thank my late aunt Edith Turley for her warm and steady encouragement. I thank my stepdaughter Valerie for her admirable sense of responsibility, and my late mother-in-law, Doris Maher, for her kind comments. I thank my son, Martin, for being patient beyond his years during those times when his oldest playmate was occupied.

My deepest debt is to my wife, Nancy, who has been the closest of companions throughout the writing and revision of this work. She has been constant in her support, clearheaded when I was not, and gracious regarding time that was the book's rather than ours.

CHAPTER I

Introduction

This book tells the story of the emergence of the modern form of Christmas celebration. How has the Yule festival come to dominate our minds and pocketbooks each winter? Before 1880 the scale of the celebration was small by present-day standards. The volume of commerce generated by the festival was not a significant part of the total national economy, not only because fewer presents were exchanged but also because those presents were usually handmade. The handmaking of the gift items fit well into the yearly cycle of the predominantly agrarian economy. After the harvest of their crops in the fall, farmers had free time in which to handmake Christmas gifts as well as other items. In addition, the nation's industrial capacity was not large enough to allow for the production of many seasonal fripperies.[1]

However, during the late nineteenth century, America industrialized and urbanized rapidly. Rural dwellers swarmed into the nation's metropolises from the American and European countrysides in the hope of securing employment in one of the new factories. At the same time, the expanding industrial sector of the American economy achieved sufficient size to make America the world's greatest industrial power. The economic and social transformation of the nation was the basis for a new American culture, a culture we label "modern" and associate with the twentieth century. It is a culture dominated by urban values and symbols, and it is a culture in which consumption values loom large for the first time in the nation's history. High status attaches to the purchase and possession of certain items, rather than to previously esteemed traits such as moral virtue, thriftiness, and productive capacity. In the twentieth century, Americans have been encouraged to spend rather than to save, and high consumers, such as movie stars and sports figures, have become our cultural heroes.

The modern form of celebrating Christmas emerged as an integral part of this modern culture and soon drew virtually everyone under its influence. Even those sections of the country that had historically resisted the celebration, most notably New England, joined in the festivities. So, to a limited extent, did non-Christian groups such as Jews, even though they had no doctrinal connection to the nativity symbols that were the ostensible core of the festival. By 1912 journalist Margaret Deland observed that "there can be no possible doubt that the Christmas folly which causes 'swearing' is increasing. By the first of December the very air seems to tingle with the mad compulsion of giving. Contrast the number of gifts we feel we must make with the number we made ten of fifteen years ago." No other celebration came close to demanding the level of effort, money, and attention that Christmas did. When we consider the magnitude of the modern celebration, its emergence should be considered one of the significant developments in recent American history.[2]

The questions raised by this development are many. What were the causes for the rise of the festival at this time? How are developments in the history of Christmas related to developments in American culture generally? Was the modern festival foisted on the public by avaricious businessmen, or did the festival rise on a groundswell of public favor? Did the modern Christmas assume its present form from the beginning of its emergence, or did it change over time? Why did it assume the form it did? How much diversity existed within the festival, and how does it affect our generalizations about Christmas?

Although the characteristics that have typified the modern celebration are challenging to identify, it is still clear that some of the most popular concepts used to describe the modern festival are not very helpful. For example, I have avoided the term "commercialization"—that most popular of all words for describing the development of the celebration—because it is overly vague. Does it mean that there was an increase in the use of money in connection with the celebration, that there were larger sales volumes, that there was more promoting of sales at Christmas, that buying and selling came to assume a larger role in the celebration of the holiday, or that the celebration was related to a surrounding consumption culture? All of these developments—and more—tend to get subsumed under the label of "commercialization" when it is important for analytical purposes to keep them separate. Hence, the absence of the word "commercialization" in this book, although there is much about matters that are usually subsumed under that term.

This book does not discuss the religious aspects of Christmas. The reason is simple. Religion has not played an important role in the emergence of the modern form of the celebration. This may come as a surprise —even a shock—to those who think of Christmas as being predominantly religious. However, in practice, the secular aspects of the celebration, such as gift giving, the Christmas dinner, and the gathering of family members, have dwarfed its religious aspects in resources spent and in concern given. Although celebrants may have had meaningful Christmas experiences in church or in other religious settings, they have spent much more time during the holiday season on such secular matters as selecting presents, then wrapping and presenting them, and making arrangements for holiday visits and feasts. One cannot escape the conclusion that the secular aspects of the modern celebration have been more central than the religious aspects. The safest way to determine what is most important to people is to look at how they spend their time, money, and effort, and in the case of the modern Christmas celebration, they have spent it on secular matters. One must not confuse the rationale for the celebration (the celebration of the birthday of Jesus) with what is central to the celebration as indicated by the behavior of celebrants.

Because the modern Christmas cannot be adequately described in terms of commercialization or in terms of its religious aspects, two other themes will run through this study: the rapid industrialization and urbanization of America during the late nineteenth century and the effort to reform the celebration during the early twentieth century.

The urban industrial setting provided a new context for prominent social relationships. Americans were struck by the visibility of the urban poor, the presence of a prominent urban working class employed in factories, and their continual observation of strangers in America's cities. At Christmas, their problem was how to express these relationships. Could the new manufactured gift items appropriately symbolize them, and should the same types of items be used to express the more intimate relationships of the family? How wide should one's circle of recipients be in a city that contained mostly strangers?

Celebrants commonly spoke of social roles when they talked about their Christmas gifts. What was the appropriate item to symbolize the relationship with one's husband in modern American society? With one's wife? Children? The poor? With one's employer or employees? Friends? Fellow community members? The role played by a particular recipient was crucial, as givers tended to search for gifts that were appropriate for that role. Consistent with this emphasis on social roles of recipients, when commentators wrote about the appropriateness of items for those in particular social roles they inevitably expressed their view about the meaning of those roles in the culture.

This study emphasizes the rich mosaic of social roles—the diversity— within American society. It is only after one identifies the major roles that one can understand property exchanges in a society. For example, in examining a gift exchange, on the surface one may only see the item passing from person A to person B. Lost are the layers of meaning of the exchange based on the roles that the two parties see themselves playing. To the parties, the gift is not simply a gift from A to B but a gift from a husband to a wife, or from an employer to his or her employee, for example. Therefore, the roles of the two parties—and the relationships between those two roles in the society—not only provide the context for the presentation of the gift, but also account for much of the significance of the exchange for the participants.

Because social roles are very significant in gift exchanges, in this book I examine the most important roles separately. The reader will find separate chapters on gifts between friends, between husbands and wives, from parents to their children, between community members, from the prosperous to the poor, and from employers to their employees. Each of these roles has had its own history and has responded to its own unique combination of historical forces. We must appreciate these separate histories before we can safely generalize about the celebration as a whole. Unfortunately, many recent commentators on Christmas blithely generalize about the celebration "as a whole" without giving sufficient attention to the internal diversity within it.

The second major theme which runs through this book is the reform of the celebration, a theme which was particularly prominent during the Progressive period. The efforts to reform Christmas took many forms: nostalgic, empassioned, and ideological, to name a few. However, the most important and prominent strain in the reform efforts was rationality.

Generally, reformers educated themselves about the celebration, identified problems associated with it, formulated plans to address those problems, and took appropriate action to bend the festival to their liking. They generally based their conclusions on data and analyses rather than on belief or speculation, and avoided mystical or magical solutions. They made efforts to counter urban alienation, reassessed what were appropriate gifts to present to friends, developed new ways to express the relationships between employers and employees, helped ameliorate the harsh working conditions of women and children, and increased the efficiency of charity for the poor. Their efforts to rationalize the celebration were by and large successful.

This book tells how the modern Christmas emerged by focusing on gift giving. The analysis of this aspect of the celebration provides a valuable perspective on the changing social relationships that accompanied the emergence of modern America, a perspective that would have been difficult to obtain any other way. Gifts symbolize the relationships between the exchanging parties and are therefore a valuable aid in elucidating social relationships. Although anthropologists have used gift exchanges and other property exchanges in this way since Marcel Mauss and Bronislaw Malinowski, historians have remained curiously oblivious to the possibility of using gifts to understand societies. In one sense, this study is an effort to apply to American history some of the insights and sensitivities gleaned from anthropology.

I intend that this be an entertaining book, one that conveys some of the joy and excitement Americans brought to the celebration. Good spirits have been very much a part of Christmas, and to exclude the flavor of these sentiments would not do justice to the history of the festival. Moreover, the humor of the celebration is itself a source of insight, a fact that should not surprise us given the insights of Freud and others on the significance of humor.

However, just as the good spirit of the celebration is expressed in this book, so too is the celebrants' concern over the symbolic messages that their gift giving conveyed. Because gifts symbolized the relationships between the exchanging parties, and frequently told recipients what the giver thought of them, picking appropriate gift items was not a petty matter. We all know from personal experience that the selection of gifts is serious, and that the presentations are frequently tense.

Moreover, many gifts symbolize relationships that have strong strains of dominance, or even of exploitation—serious matters indeed. One need only think of the relationships between husbands and wives, parents and children, employers and employees, or the prosperous and the poor. What was the appropriate way to express these unequal relationships at Christmas? What aspects of them should be emphasized and deemphasized? And what would be the effects on the social order?

The givers' deep concern with the symbolic messages conveyed by their gifts prompted them to comment about the meaning of those gifts in mass circulation periodicals and trade journals. Because gifts said much about social roles, Christmas became the principal time during the year when Americans reflected on the meaning of social relationships. Thus the characteristics of gift exchanges make them a most useful window through which we can view and understand American society.

CHAPTER 2

Fundamental Themes: Annual Festivals and Gifts

Christmas has been America's major annual festival. As December approached, celebrants anticipated their return to the special festive atmosphere of the holiday, a return that promised escape, of a sort, from everyday problems. How was this atmosphere created? What was the nature of the escape? In short, how did Christmas work symbolically?

First, Christmas worked through annual repetition. Its ritualized and memorable recurrence marked the turning of another yearly cycle as surely as New Year's Day or birthdays. The period of the celebration thus became set apart from the rest of the year, which was neither ritualized nor especially memorable. It became a special time: festive, conflict-free, and imbued with a mystical glow. Its memorableness was heightened by its special position within the annual cycle of time at the end of one year and at the beginning of another. Christmas is positioned in the juncture between two units of time, a position which sets it apart from both the period before it and the one that follows it. Thus, time itself was of a different sort during Christmas.

The time in the juncture, festival time, had an unmistakable cyclical quality to it, because celebrants returned to it and experienced it afresh each year. As the renowned mythologist Mircea Eliade has characterized it, there was an "eternal return." This cyclical time contrasted with the regular, straight-line progression of time (that is, historical time) used to mark off most of the year, as well as the cumulative passage of the years themselves. Historical time proceeds in one direction, with unique units being added continually—units that will never be returned to again. In its cyclical quality, Christmas was similar to the conflict-free golden ages which the mythologies of most cultures say preceded the creation of the Earth.[1]

Even for those who thought in terms of historical time, the result was much the same because Christmas preceded the beginning of the next calendar year, the point at which historical time began its inexorable progression through a new unit of time, a year. Thus Christmas was a time which, symbolically, preceded a "creation," the beginning of historical time.[2] These times were idyllic in most mythologies, such as in our own Garden of Eden story.

In being a special time between the end and beginning of yearly cycles, Christmas was similar to two other winter events: New Year's and the winter solstice. The historical relationship between Christmas and both of these is very close. Christmas and New Year's have been so intertwined over the centuries that for many purposes we should regard them as parts of a single festive season. For example, the early Christmas celebrants simply copied many of the observances of an already existing pagan celebration, the Roman Kalends (or Calendar) festival, which marked the arrival of the new calendar year. In addition, after Christians had generally reached a consensus to celebrate the birth of Jesus on December 25, the Church, in order to add further importance to the day, designated it as the first day of the Church calendar.

In more recent times, the relationship between Christmas and New Year's has remained close. For example, since 1800 New Year's Eve has become the accepted date for engaging in the revelrous behavior that had, in earlier times, taken place on Christmas Eve or on Christmas Day. In substantial part, the overflowing wassail bowls of the old English Christmas dinner find their historical descendants in the overflowing glasses of champagne at countless New Year's Eve celebrations.

The close relationship between the two festive days goes beyond this transfer of the culturally accepted time to become intoxicated. Most celebrants merged Christmas and New Year's, making them two high points within a single extended holiday season. Millions of cards sent each year unite the two days in this way when they wish their recipients "Merry Christmas and a Happy New Year" or "Season's Greetings." For all of these reasons, New Year's should be regarded as a part of the celebration of Christmas.

Christmas has also been closely associated with the winter solstice, the annual beginning of a new solar cycle that recurs every year on either December 21 or 22. Indeed, in the early centuries of the Christmas celebration, most people believed that the two events coincided exactly, as astronomers then thought that the solstice occurred on the 25th. Moreover, probably because pagans were already celebrating the solstice on December 25 in the Solar Invictus festival (the Festival of the Unconquerable Sun), early Christians also chose that day to celebrate the birth of Jesus.

But why was the solstice important enough to both pagans and Christians to become the occasion of large annual festivals? Why have many cultures around the world held festivals at about this same point in the annual cycle? The key lies in the most basic characteristic of the solstice: it was the exact time at which the seasons turned back from the deepest part of winter toward the planting season of spring, the growing season of summer, and the harvesting season of fall. It marked the much desired turn back toward larger food supplies and warmer weather. It is certainly not surprising that most cultures associate winter, the season of dead and dormant plants, with death, while they associate spring, the season of verdant plants, with life. On this symbolic level, the solstice represents the victory of lifeward trends over deathward trends. This powerful life-over-death message inherent in the change of seasons has exerted a strong —almost irresistible—appeal for humans concerned about their own individual paths toward death and about the continuance of the societies in which they live.[3]

Thus Christmas Eve and Christmas Day have been part of a cluster of special days during the winter that composed a single festive season. This season has been our own golden age, similar to the golden ages in mythologies around the world. It should therefore not surprise us that the same themes and cultural forms that have appealed to celebrants in annual festivals around the world have had a similar appeal for Americans.

Cyclical time appealed to celebrants because it allowed them to escape both their pasts and their futures, those two haunting features of historical time. They found comfort in escaping the past because their pasts contained memories that caused discomfort. Although memories might evoke pain, regret, or guilt, a respite was offered by a symbolic sojourn in cyclical time. In returning to the beginning of a cycle of time, celebrants drew a line of demarcation between that cycle and the cycle that preceded it. The events of the previous cycle of time were automatically severed from the present, giving celebrants a new start. The New Year's resolution custom, with its emphasis on making a fresh beginning, is the most common modern expression of this basic human need.

Cyclical time also relieved Christmas celebrants from the specter of their own futures—futures that not only contained the possibility of illness or separation from loved ones, but also the certainty of their own deaths. At the end of each cycle, they returned to a new beginning rather than plunging ahead. By participating in Christmas festivities celebrants symbolically relived the previous Christmases they had experienced. This return created a sense, however illusory, that they were not progressing along a straight-line path into the future. Thus, in providing an escape from both a guilt-ridden past and an ominous future, cyclical time was frequently more comforting than historical time and was one of the most powerful attractions of Christmas.

To help themselves escape, celebrants used various symbolic mechanisms, for example, reproducing earlier Christmases by repeating its elements, that is, by ritualizing it. Most Christmas celebrants placed considerable importance on repeating such holiday activities as putting the same decoration on the top of the tree or distributing the presents in the same manner. The restaging of past Christmases went beyond repeating certain activities: it also required participation by the same group of celebrants year after year. The ritual gathering of the same family members each year helped create the sense that they were once again back at the time when they all lived together. Symbolically, this served to mitigate the pains that separations had brought, and also helped to reassure family members that they could re-create the gathering again in the future. The comfort the celebrants gained from such gatherings was the foundation of the belief that all family members should be home during the holidays.

The desire to escape straight-line time at Christmas does much to explain the popularity of nostalgic Christmas articles in mass periodicals. These nostalgic articles contained either the writers' warm, idealized recollections of the Christmases during their own childhoods, or accounts of the celebration in the nation's past. Invariably, they bemoaned the

transformation of a simple, predominantly rural society into a complicated, predominantly urban one. Through their glowing descriptions of
the past, the writers invited their readers to return briefly through their
imaginations to an idealized earlier age, and thereby to transcend straight-
line time. Just as participation in the New Year's celebration gave a sense
of returning to the fresh and innocent beginning of a yearly cycle, reading
nostalgic articles imparted a sense of returning to the fresh, innocent
beginning of one's own life or the nation's life.

The sense of returning to the beginning during the Christmas celebration was strengthened by the use of infants—humans just beginning their
lives—as major symbols in the holiday festivities. The most important of
these symbolic infants was, of course, the baby Jesus. It is significant
here to remember that it was not only Jesus's individual beginning that is
honored at Christmas, but also, according to Christian doctrine, the
beginning of a new period in human history.

The symbol for the arrival of the new calendar year was also an infant:
the Baby New Year. The youth of Baby New Year was emphasized by
contrasting him with the the aged Father Time, the symbol of the year
just ending. Similarly, the winter solstice—the third major component
of the holiday season—was at the exact point at which the seasons turned
back from winter, symbolized by Old Man Winter, toward spring, symbolized by baby rabbits and eggs.

Christmas celebrants also heightened their sense of returning to the
beginning of time by constructing small, scale models of scenes that they
believed occurred at that beginning. Two of the most important models
in the American celebration were Christmas trees and manger scenes.
The trees were symbolic descendants of the Tree of Life—Yggdrasil—
in Scandinavian folklore, while the mangers of course portrayed the birth
of Jesus.

In order for celebrants to reap the maximum symbolic benefit from
these models, it was important for them to be present when they were set
up each year. The importance of setting up the models was reflected in
its ritualization in many homes. The acquisition and decoration of the
Christmas tree frequently marked the beginning of the holiday season
and, as any four-year-old could testify, the season lasted as long as the
tree was in place.

The act of constructing microcosms, such as mangers, transported the
celebrants back to the original time of creation. The construction was, at

its core, a symbolic reenactment of God's original act of creation, and thereby put celebrants in the role of the creator of the universe. Their act of placing the small figure of the baby Jesus in the manger scene was symbolically analogous to God's act of placing Jesus in the manger at Bethlehem.

As an aid in helping celebrants to assume the role of the creator, it was important that the models were scaled smaller than life-sized. Because the models were smaller, the celebrants—by imagining that the models were actually life-sized—could easily make themselves, by comparison, seem larger than life, just as most people envision the creator as being. They looked down on a small manger scene and put themselves in the place of the larger-than-life God they believed looked down on the small manger in Bethlehem.

Once celebrants regarded themselves as being creatorlike in their size relative to the models, it was but a short step to regard themselves as being creatorlike with regard to time—in other words, to believing that they could transcend earthly straight-line time. As long as the Christmas tree and manger were displayed, celebrants were not subject to regular time but existed in the special timeless world of the creator. Thus our four-year-old is right: as long as the tree was up, the time was special.[4]

The purpose of all of this ritual effort was to promote the celebrants' escape into a golden age analogous to the ones most mythologies say preceded the original act of creation. Golden ages are characterized by an absence of the usual societal tensions, and Christmas celebrants have historically placed great emphasis on eliminating tensions and unhappiness during the holidays. All were supposed to forget personal animosities, avoid contentious situations, and maintain a pleasant demeanor throughout the season.

During the Christmas season special attention was given to making sure that all celebrants were happy. Consider, for example, the provision of foodstuffs. In most homes, women prepared the special dishes their families particularly enjoyed, and in larger-than-normal quantities. In addition, the general Christmas "right" to gastronomic happiness motivated large annual donations to organizations dedicated to providing poor families with the traditional Christmas dinner foods so that they too could participate in the annual ritual feast.

One of the major ways in which Christmas celebrants tried to create a conflict-free golden age during the holidays was by softening social relationships that traditionally were tense. Usually these relationships were characterized by inequalities in power between the parties, for example, the rich and the poor, men and women, and parents and children.

To soften the tensions between economic classes, prosperous celebrants made charitable contributions at Christmas that lessened the economic distance between themselves and the "have-nots," with the goal of giving everyone the means to celebrate at least minimally. To ameliorate the tensions between marital partners, husbands customarily gave their wives more expensive gifts than vice versa. Finally, tensions between parents and their offspring were reduced by the special liberties and presents that parents bestowed during the holidays.

Other types of unequal relationships followed a similar pattern. During various periods, celebrants favored such egalitarian notions as automatic respites for debtors from repayments that fell due on Christmas Day. In the antebellum South, slaves were given extra food, presents, and certain liberties during the Yule season. In numerous areas, students exercised a special seasonal license by locking their teachers out of their schoolhouses. More recently, employers in many companies have given their employees some sort of Christmas bonus or time off. And any number of overly indulgent or rowdy celebrants have appreciated the special leniency shown by police during the season toward those who have committed minor offenses.

The modern Christmas celebration is not only an annual event, but it is also a celebration that is centered around the exchange of gifts. Gift exchange is found in all cultures, and has certain common characteristics.

First, gift exchanges must be distinguished from market exchanges, the other major way of transferring property. Anthropological investigations have shown that gift exchanges express the personal bonds between givers and recipients, bonds that may be based in affection, respect, or kinship, for example. The wish of the parties to preserve and foster these ties takes precedence over their concern with the value of the items exchanged. In gift exchanges, some form of reciprocation is almost invariably expected, though it is usually not requested explicitly or expected immediately.

Market exchanges, on the other hand, relegate the personal bonds between the parties to a distinctly secondary position, after the primary concern for the market value of the items. This makes market exchanges distinctly cold, in some cases to the point of haggling over the cost or expressing overt hostility. Those involved in such exchanges try to get at least equal value, with anything more that much to the good. The return exchange (that is, the payment for the goods) is usually explicitly required by clearly defined terms and is made immediately.[5]

Since the studies of Mauss and Malinowski, we have known that gifts symbolize personal bonds between the exchanging parties. However, any further generalization about what gifts symbolize is difficult to formulate because they can symbolize many different aspects of relationships. For example, some gifts represent one of the parties involved, such as a husband's gift of fine silverware to his refined wife (in which case the silverware symbolizes the recipient), or a baker's gifts of fruitcakes to his close friends (in which case the cakes symbolize the giver). Items can also symbolize the relationship between the parties, that is, their common area of interest, such as a presentation of sports equipment between playing partners.

Gift items may symbolize not only individuals or their relationship in the present, but also a course of future development desired for the recipient, such as a father's gift of a Gilbert erector set to his son to prod him toward engineering. Finally, gifts can symbolize a desire that the recipient return to a past that was supposedly better than the present; for example, a gift of college tuition to a drop-out would convey this message.

Either the giver or the recipient can provide the impetus for the selection of a particular gift item. To use the above example of the father's gift of an erector set, it is clear that the set symbolizes the giver's wishes. However, the same gift item can also symbolize the recipient's wishes to become an engineer—wishes that may even conflict with the father's desire that, say, his son take over the family mercantile business. The issue here is who dominates the symbolic message conveyed by a particular gift.

These categories are very basic and do not exhaust the richness and complexities of the symbolic messages conveyed by gift exchanges. Some exchanges do not fit neatly into any of the categories, while others fit into several of them. For example, if both father and son hope that the son will become an engineer, then the erector set expresses the wishes of both the giver and the recipient.

When one tries to unravel the symbolic messages conveyed by gifts, one's first inclination is to focus on the individuals; after all, most presentations are private matters. However, the most important messages conveyed by gifts are social. The parties are members of social groups; for example, individual fathers are members of the social group of fathers and are expected to act roughly in conformity with the behavior expected of fathers in their culture. Thus a gift item that is symbolic of an individual father is also, in part, symbolic of all fathers. These broader social meanings are the meanings that will concern us in the remainder of this book.[6]

CHAPTER 3

The Gifts Everyone Wanted: The Rise of Manufactured Gift Items

During the first eighty years of the nineteenth century, Americans usually handmade the items they exchanged at Christmas. Needlework, wooden toys, and baked goods were typical gifts, and all of these required the givers' efforts to bring them to their finished, presentable form. Both men and women were involved, because some of the processing tasks were almost always done by men, while others were almost always done by women. For example, men usually fashioned the wooden toys, while women sewed and did needlework. A writer in 1912 recalled that "my father, with tools and an amateur hand, had spent his winter evenings in fashioning [my new rocking-horse]. . . . Every stitch in the woolen scarf that went twice around my neck . . . was worked by my mother's patient hands." Generally speaking, men were more active than women in acquiring raw materials, while women were more active than men in transforming these raw materials into finished products.[1]

Before 1880 Americans, regardless of where they lived, tended to present handmade gift items, although handicrafts were somewhat more popular in nonurban settings. Rural and small-town Americans had a strong tradition of handmaking items they needed to carry on their lives. After the industrial revolution, many remained isolated from the manufacturing centers that produced and distributed machine-made goods. In his classic monograph, *The Transportation Revolution, 1815–1860*, George

Rogers Taylor describes the prevalence of handicraft production in isolated upstate New York before the opening of the Erie Canal in 1825, and its sharp decline after the canal's opening.[2] This same general process was repeated at numerous times and in various places as the country developed. Americans who remained isolated had to rely on handicraft production and were able to obtain manufactured goods only as the nation's transportation system developed.

These isolated Americans, who generally relied on agriculture for their livelihoods, were not overly burdened by the demands of handmaking the Christmas gifts they presented. Each fall they enjoyed substantial amounts of free time after they had gathered and preserved the harvest. They had few chores to do until they prepared for planting in the spring, allowing them more free time to handmake their Christmas gifts than city dwellers had.

The custom of presenting handmade Christmas gifts began to change after 1880 because of rapid industrialization and the dramatic expansion of the country's transportation system. These developments promptly lessened the popularity of handmade gift items for several reasons. First, manufactured items became more available to isolated Americans, and they, too, could now enjoy the fruits of the industrial age. Second, industrialization sharply expanded the number of wage laborers and concentrated them in cities, where manufactured items were most available and easily purchasable for holiday presentation. Third, industrial laborers, unlike farmers, did not have free time before Christmas, which made it difficult for them to make their holiday gifts. Purchasing gift items rather than making them was a highly appealing solution for laborers at the end of their long workdays.[3]

Another reason for the decline in the popularity of handmade gifts after 1880 was the appearance of many attractive new types of manufactured items on the national market such as bicycles and household appliances. During the Christmas season, gift givers were naturally lured by these fascinating items. The productive capacity of the industrial sector of the American economy expanded significantly following the Civil War, so that, by the turn of the century, the nation's industries—together with the mechanized farms of the interior—could produce more than enough to meet the nation's basic needs for food, shelter, and clothing. Consequently, manufacturers were able to make items designed to meet needs other than the basic ones. For the most part, the manufactured items that Americans began to present as Christmas presents after 1880 were from this category.[4]

The shift from handmade to manufactured gifts occurred gradually between 1880 and 1920. During those forty years, some givers chose to present items that symbolized this transition, a type of gift I call a "halfway" item. Such goods were partially processed by manufacturers but required further handwork by givers to finish them. Some popular examples were furniture kits, pictures outlined for coloring, ready-drawn embroidery patterns, cloth cut for hemming into handkerchiefs, and blank Christmas cards to be decorated with seasonal symbols.[5]

The millions of Americans with rural backgrounds who had recently moved to the cities liked the halfway items because, in requiring finishing, the halfway items were similar to the handmade items they were used to presenting. They also liked them because they had been partially completed by their manufacturers and therefore required less effort to complete than if they had to be made from scratch. Thus, they could be completed after the workday.

The halfway items were also popular with another urban group, the ladies of leisure of the middle and upper-middle classes. These women not only had the necessary time to make Christmas gift items, but more importantly, gifts that were at least partially handmade advertised their leisured life style, which, in turn, attested to their husbands' earning power.[6]

In spite of the appeal of halfway items to wage laborers and affluent women, their popularity waned as the country became even more thoroughly industrialized. The halfway items were only the products of a transitional period, as their dual nature aptly symbolized. They are noteworthy for their reflection of a shift in American culture from domination by rural, agrarian values to domination by urban, industrial values, a shift that was largely completed by the end of World War I. Since 1920 virtually all of the presents Americans have given at Christmas have been machine-made, purchased in their finished form, and ready for presentation. The age of handmade gift items, and even the halfway items, was over. Americans were very conscious of the shift from handmade to manufactured gifts between 1880 and 1920, and they commented at length on its significance.[7]

The writers of the ads and articles agreed that handmade gifts were

2. Herrick Designs Co. Christmas cards, *LHJ*, 28 (Dec. 1911): 82.

1. Potter's Silks and Stamped Goods, *LHJ*, 20 (Dec. 1902): 56.

3. G. Reis & Bros. Foundation [embroidery] letters, *LHJ*, 28 (Dec. 1911): 72.

Plate 1. I call items such as these "halfway items" because they were halfway between the handmade items of the pre-1880 Christmas and the manufactured items of the modern Christmas. They were sold in partially completed form and finished by givers before presentation. Halfway items were especially appealing to those who had grown up in rural settings—where the handmaking of gifts was common—but had moved to urban settings, where wage-labor jobs made it difficult to find time to handmake items from start to finish.

better than manufactured gifts, all other things being equal. Or, stated more formally, they believed that the symbolic messages conveyed by handmade gift items were intrinsically superior to those conveyed by manufactured ones. Why should the writers—almost unanimously—

have come to this conclusion? What were the characteristics of the hand-made items that led writers to favor them?

First, each handmade item was unique. It differed not only from all other handmade items, but also from the highly uniform, machine-made products with which the handmade items were always compared. Many givers purposely designed each handmade gift to meet the individual needs or desires of the recipient; for example, a quilt could be made in the recipient's favorite color or pattern, or with any number of other special characteristics. In short, the handmade items were made "just for" their recipients. In the writers' opinions, the one-of-a-kind nature of these gifts and their potential for personalized design appropriately symbolized the wish of the exchanging parties that their relationship be unique and distinctive from all others.[8]

The second characteristic intrinsic in handmade gift items which convinced writers they were superior was the gift of time—something that was absent in manufactured products. The time it took givers to hand-make an item was almost always longer than it would have taken to shop for a similar manufactured one. As a writer in 1908 put it, "Gifts which are the product of one's own handiwork are generally the most highly prized, for they carry with them the sweet assurance of many moments of painstaking effort and loving thoughts with every stitch and stroke." If we remember that gifts symbolize the relationship between the exchanging parties, the significance of the gift of time becomes clear: it indicated that the giver was willing to donate some of his or her time to the recipient in the future if the recipient was in need of it.[9]

Time gave special weight to a gift item: it was irreplaceable. Each person had only a finite amount of it. This fact distinguished time in a fundamental way from the material value of gifts, because material value was replaceable, unit for unit. Once a giver had spent time hand-making a gift item, the recipient could not return the time that was involved. The closest that recipients could come to it was to spend some of his or her own time handmaking a gift in return, thereby symbolizing that the recipient was also willing to devote some irreplaceable time to the relationship. The parity attained by this choice was that of an equal loss of time rather than an exchange of positive material value.

The final characteristic of handmade gift items that, according to the writers, made them superior to manufactured ones was that they were free from contamination by the impersonal values of the marketplace, since givers generally did not have to go to the market to acquire them. Because the gifts were handmade, they did not carry the symbolic messages associated with the market, particularly the message that the value of the items outweighed the personal relationships between the exchanging parties.[10]

Between 1880 and 1920 these unfavorable assessments of manufactured gift items differed fundamentally from the behavior of givers, who clearly preferred to buy gifts ready-made. In the realm of values, virtually everyone regarded manufactured gift items as inferior, in the abstract, to handmade ones: they were inferior symbols of the personal relationships that tied givers to most of their recipients. However, in the realm of behavior, an ever larger percentage of Americans chose to give manufactured products rather than handmade ones. Americans "voted with their pocketbooks" in favor of the new machine-made goods. This contradiction between stated values and behavior created tension for Americans who were uncomfortable avowing a preference for the symbolic messages conveyed by handmade gifts while presenting more and more machine-made gifts.

One solution to the contradiction was to make manufactured items seem more like handmade items. This could be accomplished through a variety of devices—for example, by symbolically "decontaminating" the manufactured items from any taint of marketplace values. Businessmen, who were intensely interested in marketing manufactured items as Christmas gifts, sought to find ways to distinguish their manufactured items intended for Christmas gift exchanges from their usual manufactured items intended for purchase throughout the year. After 1900, they devised many such mechanisms.

One way of decontaminating mass-produced products was to make them—or merely claim to make them—especially for the Christmas trade, thus differentiating them from year-round products. This could be done simply by adding the word "Christmas" or "holiday" in the advertising copy. Their furs became "Christmas furs," and their handkerchiefs "holiday handkerchiefs." Businessmen began to use this device with frequency during the early twentieth century.[11]

The most common complaint leveled against these "specially made" Christmas items was that they were gaudy and of poor quality. For example, in 1922 a merchant recalled the following:

Christmas Furs

When you buy a Christmas present for yourself or for your friends, you want something that bears the marks of QUALITY. This is especially true in regard to furs. Nothing else can so reflect the good taste of the wearer or of the giver.

We are the only exclusive fur house in Chicago.

The foundation of our business is the confidence of the most exacting fur buyers in the country.

Every-thing in *Furs*

Satisfaction guaranteed or money refunded.

This beautiful Blue Wolf and Near-Seal Garment, $18.00.   *Write for Beautifully Illustrated Catalogue, Free.*

L. S. BERRY, Manufacturer of Furs exclusively.

121 Michigan Boulevard, Cor. Madison St., CHICAGO

4. L. S. Berry Christmas furs, *LHJ*, 18 (Dec. 1900): 47.

Holiday Handkerchiefs

No. 30—This Box contains 6 Ladies' Pure Linen Handkerchiefs. Hemstitched and beautifully embroidered. 6 different designs in Box. . . . . . Price **$1 50**

Buy your Handkerchiefs direct from the Importers and save several profits

Send for our new Catalog, No. 30, Illustrating the finest line of Handkerchiefs in America.

Newcomb-Endicott Company *Detroit: Mich.*

5. Newcomb-Endicott holiday handkerchiefs, *LHJ*, 28 (Dec. 1911): 74.

Plate 2. After 1880, Americans began to purchase gifts rather than make them by hand. However, this purchasing linked gifts with the impersonal values of the market, thereby making them seem cold and inappropriate as symbols of intimate personal relationships. In an effort to make some manufactured items seem more giftlike, advertisers simply labeled them as special Christmas gift items, hoping this would decontaminate them from the coldness of the market.

When I went into the retail business years ago we were obliged, if we wanted extra holiday business, to stock special Christmas merchandise. . . . Most of this merchandise was manufactured solely for the Christmas trade. The line included such articles as celluloid collar and cuff boxes, plush photograph albums with mirrors set in the centre of the cover, specially bedecked necktie holders made out of wooden towel rings, moustache cups for papa and numerous other things of like nature.[12]

The poor quality of these items most probably contributed to the decline in their popularity after World War I.

Businessmen also decontaminated their manufactured items by simply stating that they were suitable for presentation as Christmas gifts. By making such assertions, they hoped to create an image of gift acceptability —a gift vogue—for certain items among American gift givers. As a trade-journal writer observed in 1925, "Whether a manufacturer makes any other efforts or not to get his product in the gift class, he cannot succeed as he should unless he tells the customer that his product makes a good gift."[13]

This relatively simple mechanism for transforming everyday manufactured items into gift items was especially popular during the 1920s. Indeed, the mechanism was so popular that businessmen began to debate among themselves about whether there were any manufactured items that were inappropriate for transformation into gift items. Some of those who believed that almost anything could be made into a gift pointed approvingly to the ad campaign of the Walworth Pipe Wrench Company, begun in 1920, in which Walworth had successfully persuaded givers to present their Stillson wrenches as Christmas gifts. Walworth went so far as to wrap the wrenches in special holiday packaging.[14]

Others were not so sanguine about this expansive notion of what was acceptable for gift presentation. In 1928 a businessman took umbrage at some of the suggestions he had seen in recent Christmas gift ads: a can of paint, a cooperative apartment, a Class A 6 percent participating investment trust certificate, a set of six handsome tarpaper clothes bags, and a hair mattress. Another writer in the same year was appalled by ads he had seen suggesting potatoes and floor wax as Christmas gifts. Businessmen who remained unmoved by the satirical edge of these articles were reminded by a trade journal writer in 1929 that they might sell more products by simply continuing their regular sales approach throughout the month of December than by disrupting it in pursuit of a share of the Christmas gift trade.[15]

Businessmen often instructed their salesmen to emphasize the gift potential of the items when they called on merchants. They mailed promotional material directly to merchants, reassuring them that the items were indeed appropriate for gift presentation.[16] More frequently, however, businessmen made their arguments for gift acceptability in advertisements. According to the texts of the ads, items were "suitable," "appropriate," "acceptable," "perfect," or "ideal" as Christmas gifts. Indeed, this strategy was so popular that such phrases became the most common phrases in Christmas gift ads. Businessmen also used a variety of less explicit devices to make their point. They placed illustrations of

6. Beehler folding umbrellas, *SEP*, 184 (2 Dec. 1911): 61.

Plate 3. After 1880, Americans could choose their Christmas gifts from many new manufactured items recently marketed in the nation's stores. But, because of their novelty, the items lacked settled meanings as gifts, which made givers anxious about whether the items conveyed the messages they intended. To help alleviate givers' anxiety, some advertisers boldly asserted that their items were "ideal" gifts.

the items near illustrations of common holiday symbols, such as sprigs of holly, Christmas trees, and poinsettias, hoping that proximity would bring purification.[17]

Advertisers portrayed many "special gift consultants" to recommend their items for Christmas presentation. Although they often drafted store clerks and movie stars for this role, their favorite choice, by far, as a decontaminator of manufactured items was Santa Claus. Santa's ability to cleanse away market values was reflected in a comment by a trade-journal writer in 1922: "People will not buy a thing for presentation purposes unless it has a gift vogue. The article has to be approved by Santa Claus before it is acceptable as a gift." During the 1920s ad writers began to invoke Santa more frequently than before. In the following decade, his presence increased to the point that fully 20 percent of Christmas-gift ads in the *Ladies' Home Journal* and *The Saturday Evening Post* contained illustrations of him, whereas early in the century, he had been present in no more than 6 percent. In the 1930s Santa appeared so frequently that advertisers, in a commendable act of self-reflection, began to question whether he was being overused.[18]

Which of Santa's characteristics made him particularly effective in disassociating machine-made products from the values of the market-place? In large part, Santa was effective because, according to his myth, he did not use money and was not engaged in making profit. In his North Pole shop, he and his elves handmade all of the items that he distributed around the world. He made no trip to the toy store to buy the toys, nor even a trip to purchase raw materials. Santa's motivation for his monu-mental undertaking was free of market considerations: Santa trying to turn a profit? His gargantuan giveaway was antithetical to pecuniary self-interest, and its only reward was the satisfaction of making recipients happy. No wonder Santa was a valuable decontaminator of manufactured items.

The ads described above were published in periodicals, but they often also appeared in special holiday gift catalogues. All of the items in these catalogues were, by virtue of their inclusion, specially separated from the secular world and labeled as being acceptable for presentation as Christ-mas gifts. Businessmen first began to use this decontaminating mecha-nism with frequency toward the end of the nineteenth century, and they have continued to use it freely to the present day.[19]

Businessmen and gift givers turned some manufactured items into gift

The World's Greatest Traveler
Recommends
Interwoven
Socks for Christmas

7. Interwoven socks, *SEP*, 201 (8 Dec. 1928): 162.

Plate 4. With many new items to choose from in the economy of abundance, how could gift givers know which ones would please their recipients? Usually they couldn't, but for psychological comfort they could turn to Santa Claus, who, according to the myth, always chose perfect gifts for his recipients. No wonder that advertisers found him to be a highly useful marketing symbol.

items simply by giving them special, festive wrappings. And what an effective decontaminating device it proved to be. It identified the item as a gift even before the recipient could tell what it was. It literally encased the item with the message that it was a gift, clearly setting it apart from other products that were destined for ordinary purchase and use. A festively wrapped item was certainly not a part of the normal flow of goods: someone had preordained it with a future as a gift item. Because the gift-wrapped item was singled out as special, it was not as contaminated by the market as were unwrapped items.[20]

During most of the nineteenth century, gift givers wrapped only very few of their presents. For example, parents did not wrap gifts to their children, but simply placed them, unwrapped, in the children's Christmas stockings. It was not until the end of the century that gift wrapping became the norm. Givers not only wrapped more of their presents, but after 1900 the wraps became more elaborate. A writer in 1912 invited her readers to "contrast the elaboration of ribbons, paper, boxes, labels, and what not, with the casual bundle we used to leave at a neighbor's door." By the second decade of the century virtually all Christmas gifts presented in America were wrapped in festive coverings.[21]

The effect of gift wrapping in decontaminating manufactured items could be striking. A merchant recalled fondly how the technique had worked for him:

In our store one memorable year, we ran out of mustache cups and like plunder several days before Christmas. We had to have something to offer the multitude who were storming at counters for gifts for Suzie and Mama and Uncle Joe, so we hied ourselves to a neighboring department store, where we bought all the holly boxes we could get. In these we boxed sets of aluminum and china salts and peppers, crumb trays, cake plates, neckties, jabots, men's shirts, baby rattles, etc. All of these things sold like hot cakes. We ran out of boxes and could get no more, so we wrapped up things in holly paper. This stunt was just as successful. Soon the paper gave out. Next we tied Christmas tags to aluminum tea kettles, carpet sweepers, fireless cookers, and such merchandise and found that the touch was just enough to put these articles in the gift class.[22]

The new custom of gift wrapping went through four distinct stages. First, about 1880, individual gift givers began to wrap the items they presented, but without any significant involvement of businessmen in the emerging gift-wrapping custom. Indeed, only those businessmen who made and marketed the wrapping materials were directly affected by its use. However, during the second stage, which began about 1890, retail merchants, in an effort to attract shoppers, offered to gift wrap the items purchased from their stores during the holiday season. This step directly involved businessmen for the first time in wrapping Christmas presents on a large scale.

The third stage in Christmas-present wrapping began about 1900 and was marked by manufacturers' packaging of some items in gift boxes at their factories. One businessman recalled that, around the turn of the century, "manufacturers began to dress their regular merchandise in Christmas regalia. This perhaps more than anything else is the trick that tied up hundreds of different products with holiday buying. The holly box, the spray of artificial holly and the Christmas tag soon accomplished marvels in winning holiday patronage for industries that had never received much of it."[23]

With each of the first three stages in the appearance of gift wrapping, items became wrapped at progressively earlier stages in the production process. First, individual gift givers wrapped their own gift items just before presenting them. Then, merchants, as a customer service, wrapped items in their stores at the time of their purchase. And finally, manufacturers packaged items in special holiday boxes before they were shipped out to retailers.

Manufacturers also played a crucial role in bringing about the shift during the 1910s and '20s to the fourth stage of gift wrapping: from packaging items in special seasonal gift boxes to packaging them in their regular boxes but putting removable holiday sleeves or other seasonal decorations around them. This type of packaging is still prevalent today.[24]

The removable decorations had great advantages over previous styles in gift wrapping. As a businessman said in 1925,

The special gift box . . . has certain disadvantages. After the Christmas season is over, the dealer is apt to be stuck with a quantity of packages on his hands. These packages have lost their timeliness and are a detriment to sales. . . . Walworth, in selling its wrenches as Christmas gifts, furnishes a special slip-on that goes over the regular package. It may be removed by the dealer right after Christmas. . . . The special wrapper idea gives the dealer a chance to turn Christmas stock into regular stock, his only expense being the time spent in removing the Christmas wrapper.[25]

No matter how ingenious shoppers were in devising mechanisms for decontaminating selected manufactured items from market values, it was difficult to escape all connections with one major symbol of the market: money. They still had to purchase their gift items with money before giving them away. To escape this source of contamination, Americans became interested in devising mechanisms that made the money used to purchase Christmas gift items seem special, that is, different from the ordinary money of the market.

During the 1910s, Americans became particularly attracted to one such mechanism: Christmas Club savings accounts. The money put into these accounts was set aside specifically for holiday purchases. Depositors thereby symbolically removed this "special" money from other funds used to purchase everyday items throughout the year. Christmas Club accounts were originated in Carlisle, Pennsylvania, in 1905, by a local shoe factory owner who encouraged his workers to deposit a prescribed amount of money each week, with the total being returned to the depositors two weeks before Christmas. This plan did not spread beyond Carlisle until 1910, when Herbert F. Rawll, a dynamic young salesman of loose-leaf ledgers got involved. Rawll was enthusiastic about the Christmas Club idea and persuaded bank after bank that it was an effective device to attract new depositors. For his part, he turned a handsome profit selling the patented coupon sheets designed to simplify the bookkeeping for the many small deposits.[26]

Rawll's considerable promotional abilities, together with the desire of bankers to attract depositors, fueled a dramatic rise in the popularity of Christmas Clubs during the 1910s. By 1912 he had established clubs in over eight hundred banks. Two years later he incorporated his venture under the name "Christmas Clubs, a Corporation." By 1924 his corporation was servicing six thousand banks and this number rose to a peak of eight thousand during the late 1920s. But the rise of Christmas Clubs was brought to a halt by the Depression, which reduced the number of Christmas Club banks to about fifty-five hundred by 1936.[27]

Rawll's energetic promotion of the clubs, and the bankers' willingness to establish them, would have come to little if the clubs had not struck a responsive chord in the public. Americans hastened to join the clubs and by 1924 the number of club depositors stood at 6 million; by 1931 this total had doubled. Thus, during the early 1930s, in a population of 124 million, one out of every ten Americans had a Christmas Club account.[28]

Under the Rawll plan, banks were free to make their own policies regarding their Christmas Club accounts. After Rawll had sold his bookkeeping forms to the banks, he had no interest in meddling in the banks' pricing of the accounts. As a result, terms varied considerably from one bank to another. For example, there were various policies regarding the amounts of deposits required from club members. During the 1910s many banks used systems requiring graduated deposits, whereby depositors submitted regularly increasing, or regularly decreasing, amounts each week. These systems proved to be burdensome for bookkeepers and depositors alike and, as a result, most banks shifted toward systems requiring uniform deposits throughout the year. Whichever system a bank used, depositors were supposed to leave their funds in the clubs until early December, at which time their banks would release them. Some banks simply prohibited withdrawals during the year, while others permitted them but sometimes penalized depositors for them.[29]

One of the most important policy decisions the banks faced concerned interest: should the banks pay interest on the Christmas Club accounts and, if so, what should the rate be? The policies ranged from paying the same rate of interest as on regular savings accounts to paying no interest at all and charging club depositors a service fee for handling the accounts. Between these extremes, most banks paid club depositors interest at a rate between zero and two percent, although after the 1910s the trend was to eliminate interest entirely.[30]

These rates of interest were, in the vast majority of banks, significantly lower than the rates paid on regular savings accounts. Bankers argued that this was necessary because club accounts were, at best, only marginally profitable: club members deposited relatively small amounts in the accounts; they kept them on deposit for relatively short periods of time; and they utilized a lot of teller time to record their numerous deposits during the year. The bankers' arguments doubtless have some validity, although record keeping was a fairly simple matter with Rawll's coupon system, and tellers did not have to spend much time recording withdrawals from accounts because depositors were not supposed to remove funds during the year.

If, as bankers contended, Christmas Club accounts were not very profitable, why did they agree to establish them? The most important appeal of the clubs was that they promised to attract additional customers to the bank, specifically members of the middle and lower classes who had made little use of banking services. Even if Christmas Club accounts were not very profitable, bankers hoped that new depositors would open regular savings accounts after having established the habit of saving. They wanted Christmas Club depositors simply to shift some of the funds in their holiday accounts into regular savings accounts when the banks released the club funds in December. This hope was borne out by Rawll's carefully compiled statistics on the uses to which club members put their money.[31]

Bankers also liked Christmas Clubs because they allowed institutions to improve their public image. Banks had primarily serviced the upper class, and as a result were viewed as stuffy, reserved, and elitist establishments. Bankers did not need to be reminded that they had been the target of great outbursts of resentment from the American people at numerous times in the past. They wished to change their image, and they hoped that Christmas Clubs, by drawing in middle-class and lower-class depositors, would help them do it.

Although the clubs appealed to bankers, they would doubtless have foundered if they had not also appealed to the general public. Many Americans joined them because they encouraged them to save. The highly structured nature of the clubs provided the last measure of discipline needed by those who had always found it too difficult to save. To them, living in the middle or lower levels of the economic order, the benefits of having a stash of money saved for Christmas became readily apparent when holiday bills waited to be paid.

In addition, the clubs were popular because they were effective decontaminators of money, helping celebrants to "cleanse" the money they used for their holiday purchases from the values of the market. Christmas Club accounts accomplished this feat, in part, by labeling. Bankers emphasized that club accounts were Christmas accounts, not regular savings accounts. Christmas symbols adorned the clubs' promotional materials, and, by its intended use for Christmas items only, holiday club money was further segregated from market money.

The funds in Christmas clubs were also decontaminated through the policy of bankers regarding the payment of interest on the accounts. Depositors received either no interest or a very small amount. Therefore, in using club accounts, the members had eschewed the profit motive— that fundamental element of market economies. And, if club account money was not governed by the profit motive, it was thus purified of at least one market element and distinguished from the depositors' other money.

Viewed from this perspective, if bankers had paid substantial interest to their Christmas Club depositors, they would have negated one of the important symbolic attractions of the clubs—decontamination, which was apparently very important to celebrants. Indeed, the decontamination was so important that when those banks which paid interest on their Christmas Club accounts adopted a policy of paying no interest, they lost very few club depositors.[32]

The cultural significance of the shift to manufactured gift items is tied up in the fundamental shift in the American economy that occurred during the late nineteenth century, a shift from scarcity to potential abundance. Throughout history, to the end of the nineteenth century, the great majority of people existed in a condition of scarcity and want. They spent most of their waking hours trying to fill their stomachs and protect themselves from the elements. The increased productivity stemming from the industrial revolution after 1830 provided greater supplies of some necessities, but until the end of the century, there were still simply too few goods to meet existing demands. It is certainly not surprising that, in this economy of scarcity and high needs, businessmen directed most of their efforts toward increasing their output, confident that the needs of consumers would absorb it. The shortest road to profits lay in making larger quantities of goods.[33]

If greater output was the shortest road to profits, the safest road was through concentrating on the most basic human needs: the needs for food, shelter, and clothing. Why should businessmen speculate about consumer demand for nonessential items when they knew that there was a demand for essential items? They followed this reasoning during most of the nineteenth century, concentrating their efforts on increasing their output of basic products. They were strikingly successful: for example, they expanded food production by inventing new farm machinery and by opening up the fertile Midwest to cultivation and husbandry. Their interest in the technology of agricultural production produced more patents between 1790 and 1900 than the number of patents related to nonagricultural production. Food processing also loomed large in the nation's economy: for example, flour milling was the nation's largest single industry in 1860. Taken as a whole, the advances in agricultural production and food processing during the nineteenth century were dramatic enough to merit a special label from historians: the agricultural revolution.

Businessmen were also effective in expanding production to meet the basic human need for shelter. By 1860 they had made the lumber industry the nation's third largest producing business. Not only did lumbermen turn out a large quantity of lumber, they also made their product more usable. During the 1830s lumbermills began to standarize the size of lumber, a practice that significantly facilitated building design and construction. Furthermore, builders learned how to join the lumber together by the recently devised balloon-frame method of construction. These techniques enabled the relatively easy construction of sturdy shelters for both people and animals.

Dramatic advances were also made during the nineteenth century in meeting people's need for clothing. Certainly the expansion of the production of textiles was one of the most important achievements of the industrial revolution. This expansion was based on a series of inventions, mainly in England and America, which, taken together, enabled the efficient production of large quantities of good quality cloth. The quantity of cloth consumed by the nation was immense; for example, in 1860 the production of cotton textiles was the nation's second largest industry, and the manufacture of men's clothing was the nation's fifth largest. The prospect offered by the industrial revolution was that, for the first time, masses of people could enjoy inexpensive, quality clothing.[34]

During the nineteenth century, producers of the most important basic goods were able to make their factories, farms, and forests produce rivers of goods. By 1890 they had acquired the capacity to satisfy the needs of the whole population for food, shelter, and clothing, and soon thereafter they had significant excess capacity. Still, many citizens were faced with serious economic deprivation, but, since 1890 this has been the consequence more of an unequal distribution of goods than an inadequate productive capacity.[35]

The existence of excess productive capacity produced important changes in the American economy that transformed Christmas gift giving. It allowed businessmen to manufacture items that met a wide variety of consumer needs beyond the most basic ones. Indeed, it not only allowed businessmen to begin producing nonessential items, it impelled them to do so in order to keep their share of the market. They responded to the imperatives of the new order with vigor, and turned some of their energies to producing new goods, such as appliances to make housekeeping easier, and better-quality clothing to enhance the appearance of the wearer.

Although these items were not intended to meet basic needs, many of them were still practical and useful.[36]

Because consumers' basic needs were already being met, they began to purchase products because they met other, less fundamental needs. The buyers' individual subjective desires loomed larger in influencing the selection of goods as the more universal basic needs became less important. This shift in the focus of purchases was adopted by Christmas gift givers as well as other purchasers, and it significantly increased the difficulty of gift selection.

Christmas shopping was now harder because gift givers often could not discover what the innermost, often secret, longings of others were. Some writers despaired of even trying. A writer in 1904 cautioned her readers that

the giving of gifts, even in the right spirit, is a difficult business, for who can tell what other people want? How many sighs are breathed on Christmas morning: "Oh dear, I did want a ring, but I hate opals." "Well, there, I'm sure it was very kind of William—but I should so much rather have had a really handsome card-case than this purse. Not but that it's very nice, I'm sure, only—" and then a sigh. "Yes, I did want books. But—well, I hate poetry. Still, this is very interesting, of course,—" and so on.[37]

How much easier it had been to present the relatively simple gifts of the nineteenth-century economy of scarcity such as edible treats or small knitted items, both of which virtually everyone needed. Earlier gifts had almost always been chosen from a few acceptable types of goods which, in comparison with later gift items, said fairly little about the nature of the relationship between the exchanging parties: they had relatively little definitive power and were, therefore, vague symbols. For example, gifts of food merely acknowledged that recipients got hungry, and the knitted items, that they got cold. Such conclusions were easier for givers to reach than speculating whether a recipient wanted a card-case more than a purse.

In contrast, manufactured gift items produced in the new economy of abundance were very diverse. From the wide variety of available items givers could, for the first time, select gifts that fairly precisely symbolized their relationships with recipients. As a result, gifts increasingly carried the weight of "what someone really thinks of you." For many, the possibility of increased accuracy of gift items as symbols of relationships heightened the anxieties of both parties to the exchange.

8. Hamilton watches, *SEP*, 211 (10 Dec. 1938): 85.

Plate 5. In the modern Christmas celebration after 1880, givers were anxious about choosing gift items to present. This ad played on these anxieties by having "Mary" set forth in painful detail her anguish at having selected an uninspired gift for her husband the previous Christmas. Of course, she avoided this unhappy result this year by giving him a Hamilton watch.

Manufactured items were not only more accurate symbols, they were also new. Most of them were types of items that had never before appeared on the market, for example, fountain pens and radios. This quality of newness affected the significance of the items when Americans exchanged them as Christmas gifts. They did not have the established (though vague) meanings attached to nineteenth-century gifts. Therefore, givers could not be sure about how recipients of the new items might interpret them. Givers lost that comfortable certainty of knowing the message they were conveying, a loss that increased their anxiety when gift giving.[38]

But why did people choose to give these new items if selecting them increased their anxiety? The answer seems to lie in the strong attraction of Americans for new products. The intense desires of gift givers to present new manufactured goods outweighed the anxieties generated by giving them. We know that Americans preferred new items by looking at their behavior. Beginning in the 1880s, as soon as new types of manufactured items began rolling off the nation's assembly lines, Americans purchased them and presented them in large numbers, foregoing the handmade gift items or older types of manufactured goods. Still, they continued to say they preferred handmade items for about thirty-five years thereafter, creating a cultural lag until the expressed values of the citizenry began to reflect its new pattern of behavior. During this period, Americans exchanged manufactured items at Christmas, but they did not yet regard their newness or stylishness as positive qualities, as they would begin to do in the 1920s.

The ready acceptance of the products of the new industrial order is telling about turn-of-the-century American culture. It implies at least a partial acceptance of the industrial order that produced the desired products. While one might expect city dwellers to be fairly tolerant of factories, it is particularly noteworthy that rural Americans were also accepting of them. Such tolerance was based in a yearning for the comforts and amenities promised by an industrial society. Farmers aggressively sought the newest manufactured goods, especially after 1890.[39]

The desire for new manufactured products not only underlay an acceptance of factories, but also a tolerance of the cities in which they were located. Americans associated factories with urban settings and believed that cities were the natural loci of the industrial system. Thus, they were inclined to tolerate—even like—cities.[40]

Around the turn of the century, Americans began to devise numerous mechanisms to reduce the anxieties generated by the new gift items. One of the most important of these was the hint. Whatever form a hint took, it always involved the transmission of the recipient's desires to the giver, enabling the giver to select and present the hinted-for items with the comforting expectation that they would be well received. Of all the mechanisms, the hint probably provided the most direct relief for givers' anxieties about what to present to their recipients.

Beginning early in this century, magazine writers began to encourage hinting, and their encouragement became steadily stronger through 1940. They prodded recipients to make suggestions about what they wanted to receive, while prodding givers to solicit hints from their prospective recipients. Some writers went beyond encouraging hinting in general terms to devising specific mechanisms. For example, a 1911 ad for Caloric fireless cookstoves instructed housewives who wanted a stove for Christmas to turn down the corner of the page on which the ad was printed. The ad also contained the following note:

To Husbands: If you find your wife has folded the corner of this page, take it as a hint that a Caloric Fireless Cookstove would be genuinely acceptable at Christmas in your own home.

An ad for Gilbert mixers in 1936 was even more aggressive. It encouraged wives to "tear this ad out and put it in your husband's pocket." In the same year, an ad for Hamilton watches told readers to fill in the conveniently provided blank space with the name of the Hamilton model they wanted, and then to show the ad to the "right person" before Christmas. This tactic, the reader was assured, would overcome "Santa Claus's inability to read minds."[41]

Some of the hinting mechanisms devised during the first forty years of this century were more complicated than the rather straightforward techniques suggested in these ads. For example, in 1933 Bamberger's department store of Newark, New Jersey, interviewed hundreds of Garden State residents in an effort to discover the holiday wishes of typical citizens from such social groups as policemen and teachers. The store then ran ads with pictures and biographical sketches of those interviewed, at the same time revealing their Christmas wishes. The implication was that whatever one policeman in his thirties, or one schoolteacher in her twenties, wanted was what other policemen and schoolteachers of similar

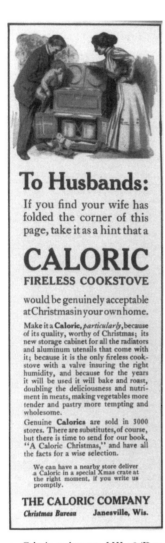

9. Caloric cookstoves, *LHJ*, 28 (Dec. 1911): 80.

10. Gilbert Kitchen-Kit mixers, *SEP*, 209 (5 Dec. 1936): 93.

Plate 6. Gift givers knew they could pick perfect gifts if they could only discover what their recipients really wanted. Therefore, they liked to get hints by which recipients let their wishes be known. While the Caloric ad encouraged women to hint for a cookstove by turning down the corner of the page, the Gilbert ad prompted women to take an even more aggressive tack by putting a copy of the ad in their husbands' pockets.

11. Hamilton watches, *SEP*, 209 (12 Dec. 1936): 117.

Plate 7. In the post-1880 economy of abundance, givers had to remind readers to know the particular items their recipients wanted from the wide variety that were available. Not only were there many new types of items, but also various models for each type. This advertiser sought to ease givers' difficulties in selecting among models by providing recipients with a blank space in which they could "hint" for the exact Hamilton watch model they wanted.

ages would want. Gift givers who were puzzled about their selections could simply give whatever a similar person in the ads wanted.[42]

The next year, 1934, Bamberger's established an even more complex mechanism by which their gift-giving customers could discover their recipients' innermost desires. The store first mailed letters to ten thousand residents in the area, telling them that Bamberger's would help them find out what their recipients wanted for Christmas if they would send the store the names and addresses of those recipients. After the store received this information, it sent letters to those who had been listed, telling them that someone wished to give them a Christmas present but didn't know what they wanted. The potential recipients were to write down their Christmas wishes and mail the lists back to the store. The store then sent the wish lists to the appropriate givers, along with information about where in Bamberger's the givers could find the items.[43]

Another way to reduce gift-selection anxiety was to shift the task of selection from giver to recipient by giving money. This way recipients could use the cash to purchase what they really wanted, and the givers need not worry whether they had correctly fathomed the subjective desires of their recipients. Money presentations attracted some interest in the early twentieth century, encouraged by a few magazine articles offering advice on the best way to go about it.[44]

At first glance, presenting gifts of money would seem to be an ideal way for givers to relieve some of their gift-selection anxieties. Yet such gifts often presented serious symbolic problems, and therefore received only lukewarm support from magazine writers and the public. Money is the medium of exchange for market transactions and provides the unit in which the value of almost all items can be expressed. As a gift item, it ascribed a certain numerical value to relationships but did not define the quality of the relationships. No wonder it struck many Americans as being too impersonal as a gift item. Thus even the advocates of money giving frankly acknowledged the coldness of the act and focused their efforts on describing ways to personalize it.

Americans hoped a new type of item, gift certificates, would retain many of the anxiety-reducing aspects of money gifts while avoiding the message of impersonality. The certificates originated with specialty shops such as those selling millinery, but by the mid-1930s many large department stores, such as Famous-Barr of St. Louis, had begun to offer them.[45]

The certificate idea was simple. Givers surveyed promising stores,

GIVE *HIM* A *STETSON* FOR *CHRISTMAS* AND LET *HIM* SELECT IT *HIMSELF*

A *man can never have too many hats . . . . The Stetson Gift Card received on Christmas morning gives him his own choice of the best hats made*

✦ ✦ ✦

FOR your father, husband, brother, or friend, here is a gift to bring certain happiness on Christmas Day, and for many days thereafter.

The Stetson Gift Card may be secured from Stetson dealers . . . that is to say, at the better stores. The hats are priced from $8.50 upward. Pay the dealer for the grade you wish to give, and the card will be sent for you. The recipient will present the card and choose his Stetson himself.

Stetson hats are the first choice of those who are most careful about their appearance, of those who dress primarily for ease and comfort, and of those who select each article for its excellence and wear.

Stetson has been making hats since 1865 . . . hats that are recognized everywhere as the finest that can be made . . . hats that are worn by the best-dressed men the world over. John B. Stetson Co., Philadelphia.

STETSON HATS

12. Stetson hats, *SEP*, 202 (14 Dec. 1929): 199.

Plate 8. One way givers could be sure their presents matched their recipients' heartfelt desires was to have their recipients select the presents themselves. Shifting the burden of gift selection from givers to recipients could be neatly accomplished through such devices as gift certificates.

determined which of them offered the certificates, and then selected the particular stores at which they thought their recipients would like to shop. They purchased certificates of a certain value, presented them as Christmas gifts, and recipients later went to the stores that had issued them and redeemed them for their designated value in merchandise.

In the stores, the certificates functioned like money. They allowed recipients to satisfy their own desires within the limits of the values of the certificates and within the limits of the stores' selections of merchandise. Because of the relatively wide variety of items made available to certificate recipients, givers could be reasonably certain that their recipients would find something that would make them happy. Their anxiety was thereby reduced.

The certificates as symbols had the advantage of appearing less "monetary" than money simply because they were not currency. In addition, they were publicly labeled as *gift* certificates, and the recipient's name was on them, making them appear more personal than currency. Finally, at the very least the giver had made a judgment about the type of store the recipient would probably like to shop in.

Unfortunately, even with their positive symbolic qualities, gift certificates retained some of the undesirable qualities of gifts of money. Like money, they did not clearly define the relationships between the exchanging parties. The certificates lacked definitive power for the very reason that they were able to function as a medium of exchange within the limited economy of the store. Because a recipient could apply the certificate toward the purchase of *any* item in the store, the certificate did not *specify* the item, and it therefore did not define the relationship. Thus certificates did not make qualitative statements about relationships, only quantitative ones—expressed by the face value of the certificates.

We can be sure that all recipients took account of the value of the certificates. It was the shortest of mental steps from a five-dollar gift certificate to a five-dollar bill. Gift certificates were therefore still not an ideal solution to the problems of symbolism raised by gifts of money. However, their popularity indicates that many Christmas celebrants at least regarded them as being more personal than cash.

Another way to relieve the anxieties of gift givers in the economy of abundance was through the mechanism of reassurance. If gift givers were reassured that the items they were planning to give would make their recipients happy, they could present them with less anxiety. Without question, the most important conduit for the mechanism of reassurance was advertising. Christmas gift ads in periodicals were replete with sweeping assurances that the items described would make whoever received them happy. Hundreds of items became "ideal gifts" and "perfect gifts" for readers' prospective recipients.

But there were even more specific themes of reassurance. One was to reassure prospective givers that their recipients longed for the items being advertised. Advertisements pictured recipients, or prospective recipients, expressing their desire for the items being promoted; for example, in 1901 an ad depicted a boy wishing—with the help of a large wishbone in the background—for an Ingersoll Dollar watch for Christmas. Some ad writers carried this theme a step further by showing people whose desires had moved them to action, to hint for items. In 1920 an ad showed a young woman hanging an Onyx stocking on the mantle while saying in earshot of her father, "I do hope Santa takes the hint."[46]

Another device used by advertisers to reassure gift givers was to generalize—indeed, overgeneralize—about recipients. Advertising copy was full of sweeping assertions that every person within very large social categories would be pleased by the items shown: "Every man will like these ties"; "Women love our perfumes"; "For Him"; "Perfect for her." In making such sweeping assertions, advertisers simply ignored individual differences and preferences which invariably exist among members of any large group. It only mattered that potential givers were reassured that their gifts would meet the expectations of their recipients.

A 1930 ad made ample use of the pronouns "he" and "him" to argue for the wide desirability of Krementz jewelry. It portrayed a woman holding a gift-wrapped package marked "For Him." The text invited the reader to imagine "what a joy [it will be] to watch *him* open it!" and provided further reassurances to potential givers that all male recipients would like gifts of Krementz jewelry:

Will you be there when he opens your gift? Dare you watch his face during that unguarded instant when he first sees what you have bought for him—that telltale moment when his expression shows what he *really* thinks of your gift. Give him Krementz and you will see his face light up with pleasure before his lips find the words to express it—for a gift of Krementz jewelry gladdens the heart of every man![47]

Potential givers were assured of the gift acceptability of certain items through ads that portrayed recipients joyfully receiving them. For example, a 1911 ad for Conklin pens showed "Tom" beaming at his new

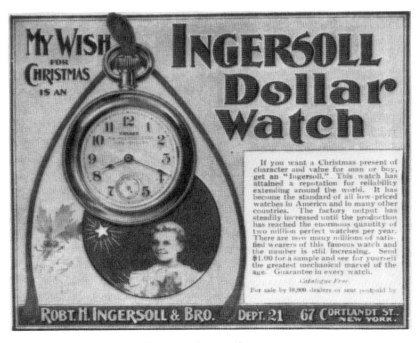

13. Ingersoll Dollar watches, *SEP*, 174 (7 Dec. 1901): 32.

Plate 9. Readers of periodicals saw many illustrations of prospective recipients, such as this young boy, wishing for gifts. Readers were encouraged to conclude that, because the recipients in the ads wanted the items, their own recipients would be similarly pleased, a conclusion that was surely comforting to anxious gift givers.

pen as he exulted, "Now that's what I call class! And just what I wanted, too. Either I talk in my sleep or Alice is a mind-reader." Readers were led to conclude that Conklin pens would make their own recipients just as happy.[48]

Finally, advertisers reassured potential gift givers about the gift acceptability of certain items by having Santa Claus recommend them. Because of Santa's reputation as an infallible gift selector, his reassurance carried great weight. He, more than any other gift giver, had the knack for knowing exactly what everyone wanted. Furthermore, his recommendation implied that he had already, in previous years, given the items, and we know from the Santa myth that because he had presented them, they had made their recipients happy. Presumably, they would be just as happily received when given by the readers of the ads.

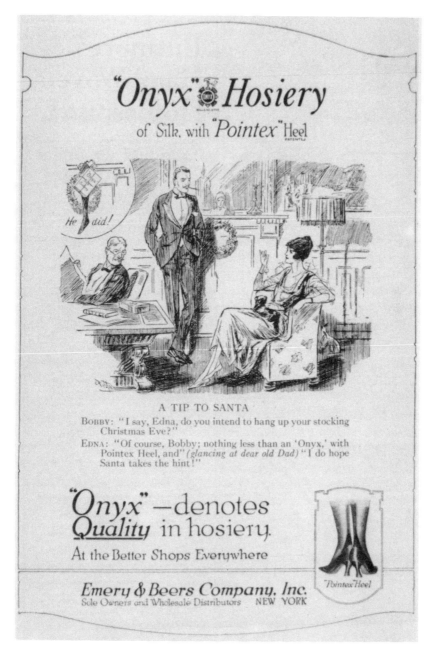

14. Onyx hosiery, *LHJ*, 37 (Dec. 1920): 150.

Plate 10. "Edna's" coy hint to her father that she wanted Onyx stockings as a Christmas present suggested to readers that their own female recipients would also want them. Anxious givers were led to believe that Edna's fictional desire reflected reality.

15. New Haven Clock Co. Junior Tattoo clocks, *SEP*, 184 (2 Dec. 1911): 45.

Plate 11. How were givers to know whether an item would meet the heartfelt desires of the recipient? This ad provided some comfort by assuring givers that Junior Tattoo clocks were "for everybody's stocking," a sweeping assertion that ignored significant differences in personal preferences.

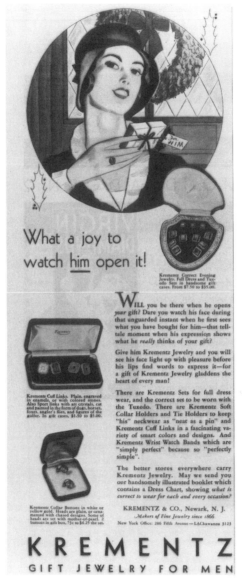

16. Krementz jewelry, *SEP*, 206 (6 Dec. 1930): 180.

Plate 12. It might well be "a joy to watch *him* open it," but which "him"? Preferences varied substantially from man to man. This ad glossed over the complex reality by assuring readers that Krementz jewelry "gladdens the heart of every man." Those who were convinced could ignore individual preferences.

Dec. 10th

ALICE:—*"A Conklin Pen! The very thing I'll get Tom! Won't he be tickled! And it's such a sensible, practical gift, too."*

Dec. 25th

TOM:—*"Fine! Now that's what I call class! And just what I wanted, too! Either I talk in my sleep or Alice is a mind-reader."*

Jot down on YOUR Christmas List

Conklin's
Self-Filling
Fountain Pen

The original Self-Filler—never equalled.   Sold for 13 years. 1,000,000 satisfied users

It will bring a delighted smile of sheer joy to his face on Christmas morning. He can use it in his *work*—and every day, too.

The Conklin *fills itself* and *cleans itself;* 14K iridium-tipped gold pens that *never* scratch or blot. All styles and sizes. Exchangeable after Christmas if point doesn't suit. Sold by stationers, druggists, jewelers everywhere. Write for booklet—*Pleasing "Him" for Xmas.*

The Conklin Pen Manfg. Co.,   261 Conklin Bldg., Toledo, Ohio

17. Conklin's fountain pens, *LHJ,* 28 (Dec. 1911): 90.

Plate 13. By exulting in his new Conklin pen, the "Tom" of this ad alleviated readers' anxieties about pleasing their own recipients. The ad inferred that, if readers gave them Conklin pens, they were sure to be as delighted as Tom.

After 1880 gift givers shifted from giving handmade gift items to giving the new manufactured items that were beginning to appear in the American marketplace. Handmade gift items had many special qualities that had made them particularly suitable for expressing personal relationships through gift exchanges. They were unique and variable in their form in contrast to standardized manufactured items. Inherent in them was the giver's gift of time, and they were not contaminated by the market. In spite of these advantages, new manufactured items proved to be the item of choice for gift givers from 1880 on. The tensions created by the shift from handmade to manufactured items gave rise to a wide variety of anxiety-reducing and decontaminating mechanisms. The appearance of these mechanisms strongly suggests that the new order, although preferred by the American people, imposed new burdens.

CHAPTER 4

Gimcracks, Appliances, and Silverware: A Survey of Manufactured Gift Items

Since Americans shifted from giving handmade Christmas gifts to manufactured ones around 1880, the choice of gifts has become very wide. In this chapter we will look at the changes in givers' preferences among the many machine-made goods that were available.

First there were the "gimcracks," to use the most common contemporary name for them (others were "doodads," "geegaws," and "tomfoolery"). Gaudy figurines, cheap paintings, and poor-quality jewelry were examples of these. Gimcracks had three distinguishing characteristics: they were low-priced compared to most gift items, ranging between twenty-five cents and two dollars apiece; they were of obvious poor quality; and they served no practical function. Gimcracks made aesthetic claims only, although by most standards they were almost invariably tacky.[1]

Families and friends alike were given gimcracks. The items served to continue a rural custom within a new urban setting. Before 1880 rural Americans had given small handmade items to both family members and neighbors throughout the year, thereby reaffirming family and friendship ties. While some of these presentations were made at Christmas, it is the constancy of the presentations throughout all times of the year that is most significant. Rural Americans who moved into cities during the late

Christmas Favors

China Bald Head Match Holder. China Scratch Me Match Holder. Above two figures 35c each including mail. China Dutch Kiss Figure 15c. Broom Pencil 5c. U. S. Mail Bag 5c. Miniature "Cold Feet" Bag 10c. Celluloid Bird Card Holders, assorted designs, 15c. Christmas Stockings filled with good Toys 5c, 10c, 25c, 50c, $1.00. Red Flannel Stockings, holly trimmed, to put presents in, 19 inches, 25c. Holly Jack Horner Pie, 12 Ribbons, $4.00. Crêpe Paper Holly Salted Nut Cases, 90c doz. Holly Ice Cream Cases, $1.20 doz. Christmas Snapping Mottoes 25c, 50c, $1.00 per box of 1 dozen. We make up $2.00, $5.00 and $10.00 assortments of Christmas Tree or Table Favors. *We positively do not pay mail charges.* B. SHACKMAN & CO., Dept. 19, 812 Broadway, New York.

18. B. Shackman & Co. Christmas favors, *LHJ*, 28 (Dec. 1911): 78.

A Pleasing Christmas Gift

What shall I buy the folks for a Christmas present? One of the most pleasing and acceptable gifts you can make Pan-American Exposition Souvenir Coffee Spoons made especially for will be a set of the Lake Shore & Michigan Southern Railway by the Oneida Community. They are made of best material, carefully and handsomely finished and fully guaranteed. They are serviceable and will last for years. Like quality spoons sold at Exposition at 50 to 75 cents each.
The set consists of six spoons. A different Exposition subject is engraved in the bowl of each spoon.

In ordering: Remit by express or post-office money order to ONEIDA COMMUNITY Niagara Falls, N. Y. Complete Set in Satin-lined Box, postpaid to any address for $1.00

For comfortable, enjoyable travel between the cities of Chicago, Toledo, Cleveland, Buffalo, New York and Boston, use the famous through trains over the Lake Shore & Michigan Southern Railway. For any particulars about travel via this route, address A. J. SMITH, G. P. & T. A., Cleveland, Ohio.

19. Oneida Pan-American Expo souvenir spoons, *SEP*, 174 (7 Dec. 1901): 30.

Beautiful for Christmas Gifts. Order To-Day
Easily sent by mail. Suitable for all ages. Inexpensive. Reproductions of the world's great paintings. Each 5½x8 inches. Send 25c in stamps for 25 art subjects, or 25 Madonnas, or 25 for children, or 25 kittens, or $1 for the 4 sets, no two alike. Send $1 for Art Set of 100, or for 21 pictures, each 10 x 12.
CATALOGUE of 1000 small illustrations and 2 pictures for 3 two-cent stamps. It ought to be in your home. The Perry Pictures, 15 to 25 times as large as this Baby Stuart, cost only **ONE CENT EACH** for 25 or more. 2250 subjects. *Awarded Four Gold Medals.*
THE PERRY PICTURES COMPANY, Box H. J., Malden, Mass.

THE PERRY PICTURES

20. Perry Pictures Co. reproductions, *LHJ*, 28 (Dec. 1911): 70.

Plate 14. "Gimcracks" such as these were the most popular type of Christmas gifts from 1880 to 1910, the first thirty years of the modern celebration. Their hallmarks were low cost, low utility, and low aesthetic merit.

nineteenth century continued to give small gifts as tokens of friendship, and gimcracks now perpetuated this old custom involving a wide circle of recipients.

Gimcracks were commonly marketed as special holiday items. For example, some were decorated with Christmas symbols such as holly wreaths, Christmas trees, and pictures of Santa Claus. Although these festive decorations served to decontaminate them from market values, they also precluded their sale during the rest of the year. Certainly a coffee cup bearing Santa's smiling face would not sell in July.

Gimcracks were closely tied to Christmas in other ways. Ads assured potential purchasers that gimcracks had been manufactured expressly for holiday presentation. The close association of these trinkets with the holidays made it difficult to sell them during the rest of the year, and made it difficult as well for mundane items to gain a share of the Christmas trade. Thus, within the holiday appeal of the items lay the seeds of their disfavor. Gimcracks are most significantly related to exchanges between friends, so they are discussed at greater length in chapter 5.

Although gimcracks were the gifts of choice at American Christmases between 1880 and 1910, by the latter year they began to experience serious competition from two new types of gift items: Christmas cards and expensive, useful items such as household appliances. Each of these was presented to a different group of recipients. Celebrants gave cards to their friends while reserving the expensive gifts for members of their immediate families and perhaps a few close friends. This practice contrasted with the earlier custom of giving one type of item—gimcracks—to friends and relatives alike.[2]

The shift around 1910 from gimcracks to cards in exchanges between friends substantially reduced the time givers spent on Christmas remembrances for their friends, because cards were usually acquired in bulk and could easily be "wrapped" in their envelopes. Giving cards also saved givers money as their cost was almost negligible in comparison with other items. Therefore, Christmas cards were a less substantial gift than gimcracks had been and were generally considered to be a more honest symbol for all but the closest friendship relationships in the new urban setting. It was better to give a simple card to an acquaintance than to present a gimcrack that suggested that the relationship meant more than it actually did. Commentators favored card giving over gimcrack giving, a custom they believed had become too burdensome and unwelcome.

21. A. M. Davis Quality cards, *SEP*, 185 (7 Dec. 1912): 51.

Plate 15. Around 1910, Americans began to present cards rather than gimcracks to their friends at Christmas, a shift that was an important part of the Progressive reform of Christmas gift giving. Cards moved to a higher plateau of popularity following World War I when they were promoted by the new Greeting Card Association, and to an even higher level during the 1930s, because of the Depression.

While givers began to present inexpensive cards to their friends, they began to present expensive, useful items to their immediate family and a few close friends. The cost of these items ranged between two dollars—the approximate sum required for tools, gadgets, and small appliances—and several hundred dollars required for major appliances and automobiles. The new items were practical and facilitated the accomplishment of daily tasks for their owners, bringing comfort and ease to living. For example, household appliances helped wives prepare meals and raised the standards of household cleanliness. To say that they were useful is not to say that they were essential. Ease in preparing meals and ease in cleaning one's house were matters of comfort and choice and therefore were not as basic as the needs for food, shelter, and clothing that had guided manufacturing production during the nineteenth century.

Some of the new gift items were already familiar to Americans, having been available for some time—for example, hardware, pipe wrenches, and towels. Others were newcomers, such as vacuum cleaners, electric stoves, and electric irons. Descriptions of items in Christmas gift ads varied depending on how long they had been marketed and how familiar they were to the public. Ads for familiar products assured readers that it was acceptable to present them as gifts. For example, a 1912 ad for Utica pliers claimed that the tool would be well received because of its helpfulness to the recipient, even though it might seem inappropriate; its functional merits would overcome its mundane associations. Echoing this sentiment, an ad writer in 1920 suggested that his readers present Belber luggage because "thoughtful people are giving, not less generously, but more intelligently. They realize that fripperies are out of date." Although the arguments for the already existing items were delivered in earnest, the tone of the ads was apologetic. In contrast, ads for newly marketed items such as household appliances contained no apologies. They extolled the new technology represented in the items as a basis for presenting them as gifts. Technology, therefore, was not inherently secular or mundane. Rather, it could be an important element in Christmas gift giving without raising significant cultural tensions.[3]

According to the ads, the new items brought an ease of living to those who used them. In reality, they merely raised standards of household cleanliness without lessening housekeepers' work. A 1920 ad argued that Bissell carpet sweepers and vacuum cleaners were appropriate Christmas gifts because they kept rugs and carpets clean "without the old drudgery,"

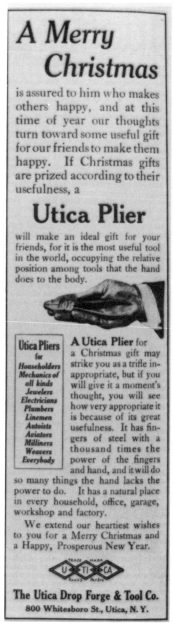

22. Utica Drop Forge & Tool Co. pliers, *SEP*, 185 (7 Dec. 1912): 58.

23. Nicholson File Co. files, *SEP*, 201 (8 Dec. 1928): 154.

Plate 16. A hallmark of gimcracks had been their lack of utility. However, around 1910, tastes in gift giving took a practical turn and gimcracks fell out of favor. Useful gift items, such as appliances and these tools, dominated gifts to family members and very close friends during the 1910s and remained popular through 1930.

thus "the pleasure of receiving a Bissell's on Christmas Day is multiplied 365 times during the year for the home manager." The technology of the new items was a positive characteristic that promised more comfortable living. It was only a short step from embracing technology to promoting the newness of an item for its own sake, and by the late 1920s this step had been taken. Christmas gift ads, such as those for appliances, emphasized style and fashion. Advertisers transformed some types of appliances, such as toasters, carpet sweepers, and refrigerators, into consumption items when they shifted the emphasis from the usefulness of their technology to their fashionableness and modern design. Utilitarian items became status symbols.[4]

Three social groups were instrumental in bringing about the change in gift-giving customs around 1910: manufacturers, retailers, and shoppers. All acted to bring about the shift, not only because it was in their economic self-interest to do so, but also because they believed that doing so constituted a desirable reform of gimcrack giving.

Manufacturers objected to the custom of gimcrack giving because most of them did not profit from it. Only a few manufacturers—mainly those who made ceramic pieces, handkerchiefs, jewelry, and cigars—produced the gimcracks that celebrants exchanged during the holidays. While this small number of manufacturers did a brisk business at Christmas, others merely watched. Those in closely related industries doubtless considered shifting part of their capacity to making gimcracks in order to cash in on Christmas-season sales, but in most cases, such seasonal shifts in production were prohibitively expensive.[5]

After 1910, with the new public acceptance of useful gift items, the prospects of industrialists improved. Manufacturers of useful items— who until now could only envy the Christmas sales of the gimcrack makers—were now able to compete for holiday profits. All they had to do was to create a "gift vogue" for the products they already made, an easy enough task, and certainly easier than the previous challenge of shifting production to gimcrack-making. In 1922 a trade journal writer noted that in that year's gift market "many products not customarily offered as gifts have been introduced for this purpose. . . . Few, indeed, are the manufacturers who did not make some sort of an attempt to get their wares into Santa Claus's pack." The trend toward useful gifts expanded the types of manufacturers who could compete for holiday

A Bromide

is one who gives use-
less Christmas pres-
ents — just to "hold
his end up."

Don't Be
a Bromide

Give your friends Christ-
mas presents they want—
not presents they're going
to wrap up and give to
someone else a year hence.

ANY friend will *appreciate* a year's subscription to some good magazine. There's real pleasure in store for him. Fifty-two times
a year the postman will remind him that last Christmas you thought of
him — and weren't a bromide.

Send us the names and addresses of the friends you mean to favor.
Inclose your remittance of $1.50 each ($1.75 in Canada). Tell us
the subscriptions are Christmas gifts.

Then, to reach each of them on Christmas morning, we will mail
one of the beautiful Maxfield Parrish announcements, stating that *The
Saturday Evening Post* will be sent for a year — at your request. The
copies will follow weekly. Address your letter to

THE CURTIS PUBLISHING COMPANY, PHILADELPHIA, PENNA.

24. *Saturday Evening Post* magazine ad, *SEP*, 186 (6 Dec. 1913): 64.

Plate 17. Gimcracks appealed to givers on the basis of low price and (dubious) aesthetics
rather than usefulness. Although they dominated Christmas gift giving between 1880 and
1910, during the Progressive period, they alienated many celebrants. The Progressive
antipathy to useless items inspired the creation of the Society for the Prevention of Useless
Giving (SPUG) as well as this 1913 ad for *The Saturday Evening Post*.

sales, so it is not surprising that manufacturers enthusiastically supported
—and sometimes spearheaded—the new penchant for useful gift items.[6]

Retailers also embraced the new trend because it helped them in the
same way it helped their manufacturing brethren: it significantly expanded the types of retailers who could share in the seasonal sales. For
the first time, merchants who sold such useful products as hardware,
groceries, and appliances could look forward to increased business in
December. A writer in 1922 observed:

> The bulk of Christmas buying used to be largely concentrated on a limited
> number of retailers. But . . . this has all been changed. Now practically every
> type of store and business participates in the holiday melon. . . . Take the
> hardware store, for instance. In the old days the hardware dealer got very little
> holiday business. But today the hardware man is in a splendid position to reap a
> rich Christmas harvest.[7]

Retailers also liked the shift to useful gift items because it lessened the
business risks of pursuing the holiday trade. During the heyday of gimcracks, merchants who sold these special Christmas items had to predict
as accurately as possible the volume of sales during that particular Yule
season. Their goal was to have their store shelves become empty at the
end of the last shopping day before Christmas. Only this precise timing
gave maximum profits to the merchants; understocking meant lost sales,
while overstocking meant that the leftover—and now unsalable—merchandise had to be carried in the stores' inventories for a year. In 1922 a
businessman recalled the stocking problems of the gimcrack sellers:

> The merchants who stocked up heavily on these articles in anticipation of a brisk
> Christmas trade spent an uneasy December. A snowstorm set solar plexus quiv-
> ering. An unexpected change in the temperature caused him to pace the floor
> worriedly. The worst of it was that in trying to dispose of his Christmas jiggum-
> bobs he was forced to neglect his regular merchandise. In many cases in order to
> give his Christmas stuff adequate display and to impart a holiday atmosphere to
> his place of business, the retailer found it necessary to remove his regular goods
> to his stockroom or to shove them into a heap in the back of his store. Customers
> who asked for anything other than holiday knickknacks were frowned upon.

All of this uncertainty and disruption of business was caused by "stuff
that would sell for only two or three weeks prior to the visit of old St.
Nick. If we did not get rid of it then, we were obliged to carry it over for
another year."[8]

With the shift to useful gift items, merchants could sell the same items during the holidays that they sold year-round. They no longer had to fear being stuck until the following Christmas with unsalable seasonal gimcracks. Retailers brought these advantages to the attention of manufacturers, thereby fostering a powerful, symbiotic relationship. About 1910, at the behest of retailers, manufacturers of useful items began to package their products in special holiday boxes, a practice that made them seem more giftlike and therefore more salable. By 1920 manufacturers went a step further by decorating their regular packages with removable frills or festive sleeves. Packaging with removable decorations was even more helpful to merchants than the gift boxes had been because, after each December 25, merchants could keep unsold items in stock by merely removing the decorations. Without question, the shift to useful gift items, together with their packaging in boxes with removable decorations, gave merchants much greater margins of error than they had had with seasonal gimcracks. As a result, merchants could safely place orders large enough to meet holiday demand.[9]

Manufacturers and merchants had ample economic reasons to support the shift from gimcracks to useful gift items. Economic factors also motivated the public to support such a shift, even though the useful items were, item for item, more expensive than gimcracks. First, they were given to a much smaller circle of recipients, only to members of the givers' immediate families plus a few close friends. Second, celebrants concluded that the purchase of useful items—even though expensive—was ultimately thriftier than purchasing less expensive but useless gimcracks. While the cost was higher, the waste was less.

The useful items were thriftier in another way. Celebrants who gave them had usually been planning, even before the holidays, to buy them for their recipients and merely used the occasion to make the purchases. Consider, for example, a husband who was planning to buy his wife a new refrigerator and selected the holidays as the time to do so. Presenting the refrigerator at Christmas saved him the expense of buying it for her at some unceremonious time during the year, and then having to buy her another Christmas gift item during the holidays. The presentation of the useful item at Christmas resulted in a lower total expenditure by allowing givers to get "gift credit" for items they were going to purchase anyway.

Changes in the styles of home interiors also encouraged Americans to support the shift to useful gift items. Around 1910 Americans became disenchanted with the cluttered interiors of the Victorian era. As simpler

25. Frigidaire refrigerators, *SEP*, 202 (14 Dec. 1929): 93.

Plate 18. Indeed, why not give your wife a Frigidaire for Christmas if you were planning to buy her one anyway sometime during the year? Why not get "gift credit" for giving it at Christmas—and avoid the expense of purchasing other Christmas presents? Although this Frigidaire and other useful items that became popular with gift givers after 1910 were more expensive than gimcracks had been, in the long run gift givers realized savings by giving them at Christmas.

rooms with fewer knickknacks became preferred, the tacky "ornamental" gimcracks lost popularity: they were fundamentally incompatible with the new aesthetic values of simplicity and function. Even if gimcrack manufacturers had responded to changing tastes by offering simpler, more modern items, they could not have maintained their popularity because gimcracks—whether simple in design or not—were intrinsically nonfunctional and caused clutter.[10]

The shift from gimcracks to useful gift items for presentations to the immediate family and close friends drew broad support from manufacturers, merchants, and shoppers alike. They actively encouraged the change, not only because it was in their economic interest, but also because they believed that useful items were more rational and attractive gifts than gimcracks. However, despite this breadth of support a sizable segment of each of the three groups turned against them after 1925.

The main criticism leveled against useful items was that they were overly practical and did not necessarily make recipients happy. As a writer in 1929 observed,

Each sordid, utilitarian, workaday article—on sale every day in the year—acquires in December a veneer of ribbon, holly, red tissue paper and tinsel, to blossom forth as the ideal Christmas gift for someone near and dear to you—someone who will judge you largely on the originality you have shown.

The Public is urged to forego all gift purchases which might show thought, effort or originality on the part of the giver—and instead, to buy practical gifts. Articles to safeguard the health for more work. Articles with which to earn enough money to buy, next Christmas, articles with which to go back to work. Like the man who works in order to eat in order to work.

In the same year, another writer vented his sharp-edged satire on an ad for electric irons:

There is a broadly smiling Santa Claus in this advertisement, you see, benevolently handing one of the irons in its holiday box to somebody's wife. Does the lady lift her hands in horrified indignation? Does she repel the offering with scorn born of the intimation that she should put in a little extra work during the coming year? Nay, nay, brother, she does not. Instead, her eyes are open in holy admiration of the kindly forethought which suggested such a lovely gift. Both her hands are raised, palm outward, in delighted surprise. Is it possible that we read these facial expressions wrongly and—but, no, the figures have balloons issuing from their lips, à la comic strip. Santa Claus rumbles blithely, "From your husband—a Pushit Electric Iron to bring you pleasure throughout the year." And the enraptured wife breathes happily, "Just what I wanted!"

A character in a 1927 article echoed these criticisms of practical gifts and pointed to the new type of gift item that was winning over gift givers as the ideal type of Christmas gift item:

Frankly, I can't see a washing machine as the ideal gift. My wife would be just a little disappointed if I gave her one for Christmas. She wants something prettier and more luxurious that she can take pride in showing to her friends. A wrist watch, a bale of lingerie, a ring or some furs would be just about 100 per cent with her. But a washing machine in spite of its out and out usefulness fifty-two weeks a year? Never![11]

The gift items of which the character in this ad approved—fine watches, lingerie, rings, and furs—were different from either the gimcracks of the turn of the century or the useful items of the 1910s. They were consumption items and were distinguished by the fact that they were expensive and without much practical value. They were prized for their "show-value," for the envy their display aroused in others, and for the increased status their owners consequently enjoyed. Consumption items became the third major type of manufactured gift item, after gimcracks and useful items, to dominate Christmas gift giving in America. Among these items were silverware, fine perfume, high-quality men's clothing, and various sophisticated, expensive toys for children. Compared to gimcracks, consumption items were expensive and had genuine aesthetic merit; compared to useful items, they were ornamental rather than functional and were intended to increase the recipients' status rather than help them perform practical tasks. In a word, the consumption items were luxuries.[12]

The concept of "luxury" is the key to understanding consumption items. Items are luxurious when they have high monetary value and low utility value; indeed, the extent of their luxuriousness may be measured by the difference between those two characteristics. Take, for example, one of the most prominent consumption items, silverware. The cost of silver utensils is high in proportion to their usefulness. After all, one can eat every bit as well with utensils made from materials costing a fraction of the cost of silver. Yet it is precisely this fact that makes silverware luxurious and justifies our classifying it as a consumption item.

When advertisers and magazine writers promoted consumption items on the basis of their luxuriousness, they did so because they believed that the cost/use gap of the items was a positive characteristic that would encourage their sale. They bet that consumers would rather pay for

26. Royal cameras, *SEP*, 201 (15 Dec. 1928): 74.

Plate 19. The text of this 1928 ad emphasized the appearance rather than the usefulness of the Royal camera, thereby reflecting the consumption values of the 1920s. The focus on "show value" contrasts strikingly with the attention paid to function during the 1910s in ads such as those for Utica pliers and Nicholson files (illustrations 22 and 23).

27. Belber traveling goods, *SEP*, 193 (11 Dec. 1920): 71.

Plate 20. The shift from usefulness to consumption values after 1920 is neatly expressed in these two ads for luggage. The Belber ad of 1920 extols the usefulness of its product, noting that "fripparies are out of date," while the Dresner ad of 1929 highlights beauty and luxuriousness.

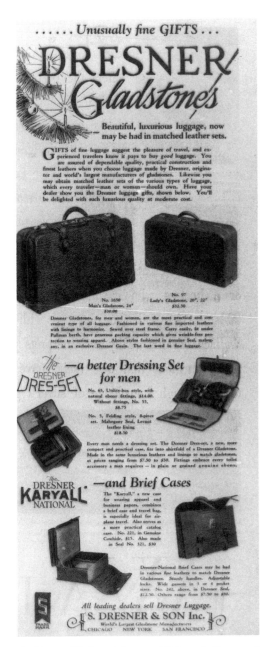

28. Dresner Gladstone's luggage, *SEP*, 202 (7 Dec. 1929): 203.

Happy to own it ... proud to show it

Really, you can't blame her. Who wouldn't drag her friends out into the kitchen to show off her new General Electric? There it stands, gleaming white, strong as a safe, incredibly quiet ... the envy of all who see it.

For a gift that gives all-year usefulness, that makes every-day tasks lighter, that safeguards health, the General Electric is really ideal. It makes a generous supply of ice cubes and, of course, freezes those luscious desserts which every hostess enjoys serving.

When you buy a General Electric you are choosing the one and only electric refrigerator which has an *all-steel* cabinet. It is rust-proof, warp-proof. Its doors are finished with trim black Textolite edges, an attractive contrast to the whiteness of the cabinet. The inside corners are rounded so that they are

most easy to clean. And the graceful legs leave plenty of broom-room under the cabinet. In fact, this refrigerator has every detail that makes for greatest sanitation and cleanliness.

And the General Electric is the only refrigerator which has all its mechanism mounted on top in an hermetically sealed

Prices on the new all-steel models now start as low as $215 at the factory.

steel casing ... out of the way, dust-proof. It never needs oiling and leaves the greatest cabinet area for food storage. It allows the heat to rise *above* the cabinet—not up through it. It has an accessible freezing regulator and it creates absolutely no radio interference.

When you are deciding on the gift that will best serve the whole family, consider the sound value which the General Electric offers. The operating cost is but a few cents a day and not a single owner has thus far paid a dollar for repairs or service. No other refrigerator approaches this record. Conveniently spaced payments can be arranged.

For complete information about all the models, write to Electric Refrigeration Department of General Electric Company, Hanna Building, Cleveland, Ohio. Ask for an illustrated Booklet—S-12.

GENERAL ⊛ ELECTRIC
ALL-STEEL REFRIGERATOR

29. General Electric refrigerators, *SEP*, 202 (14 Dec. 1929): 38.

Plate 21. Before 1920, refrigerators were regarded as utilitarian items, but in this ad of the '20s, usefulness is of only secondary importance to this proud recipient. Rather, she likes the appliance primarily because showing it off, here at a party, secured the approval—even envy—of others. The emphasis on appearance typifies the consumption values that began to dominate American culture during the 1920s.

expensive silverware even though it had no greater functional benefit than other tableware. Consumers proved them to be right as they exhibited a strong preference for consumption items. But why did Americans choose the luxury items when, from a rational perspective, such choices made no sense.

Americans began to like luxury items during the late 1920s, when they began to develop a more favorable attitude toward spending money. Spending became pleasant, even exciting, which represented a change in some long-standing cultural values. At least since Ben Franklin's maxim that "a penny saved is a penny earned," Americans had tried to spend as little as possible, with thrift remaining a dominant cultural value through- out the nineteenth century. Toward the end of the century, however, the great expansion of industrial production laid the groundwork for a new attitude about spending money. It was vital that the large quantity of products surging into the market be purchased or economic ruin would surely follow. A penny saved in this new economic environment meant glutted stockrooms of unpurchased goods and economic stagnation. Dur- ing the 1920s, to forestall this threat, Americans warmed up to spending, increasing demand for the country's burgeoning supply of goods.[13]

In order to purchase luxury items, givers had to be willing to spend freely, because they always spent more than the functional value they got in return. The free expenditure necessary to purchase luxury items gave those items special symbolic messages when they were selected as gift items. For example, because givers of luxurious gifts spent more than rationally necessary they sent the message that they were willing to devote more than a strictly rational amount of their resources to the maintenance of their relationship with their recipients. Spending more than the functional value of the items implied that in the future the giver would not only meet the needs of the recipient if called upon to do so but would also offer resources beyond those needs.

The purchase of luxurious gift items required free spending, and their presentation implied the giver's ability to spend in that manner. Thereby the fact of the giver's prosperity was conveyed to recipients and others, a message that held great attraction for many. By giving luxury items, givers indicated that they were richer than if they had given an equally expensive but useful item. The low utility content of luxury items im- plied that the giver had satisfied all of his practical needs and could spend a considerable sum on items that merely gave pleasure.

"Hi-Lo" Brush Control doubles the brush range and reduces the effort by half.

WHY not a new, improved Bissell for Mother's Christmas? Her old one has been a faithful servant these many years. Let her move it upstairs and enjoy your new Christmas Bissell for general use. The new Bissell sweeps any surface, from heavy, tufted rugs to bare floors . . . easier! A marvelous new "Hi-Lo" Brush Control causes the brush to adjust itself automatically so that it maintains contact with *any surface.* You need scarcely "bear down" on the handle. You really must see the new Bissell to appreciate all this new improvement means. Your leading furniture, hardware, or department store will gladly demonstrate.

A Bissell with "Hi-Lo" Brush Control (on all Cyco models) costs only the price of a few brooms — $5.50 and up (50c more in West and South). "The Bissell Booklet" mailed free. Bissell Carpet Sweeper Co., Grand Rapids, Mich.

The New **BISSELL** SWEEPER with "Hi-Lo" Brush Control

30. Bissell carpet sweepers, *LHJ*, 46 (Dec. 1929): 188.

Plate 22. This 1929 ad suggested moving the old, but still functional, Bissell upstairs to make way for the new improved model. Style and fashion enjoyed higher regard than utility during the 1920s. While this ad suggested that carrying a sweeper from floor to floor was a burden, only nine years earlier Bissell had run an ad that argued that its sweepers could be easily carried from one floor to another, thus obviating the need for one on each floor. Times had changed.

Once Americans had adopted the attitude that the cost/use gap of luxury items was a positive characteristic, it was but a short step to conclude that paying more for gift items was preferable to paying less. By 1925 ad writers had taken this step. For example, they increasingly characterized the prices of items in their ads as "moderate" or "reasonable" rather than as "low," the latter having been by far the most popular price description before 1925. The shift in the choice of adjectives was a direct product of their belief that shoppers would now actually be attracted by the prospect of paying more.[14]

Along with the new approval of free spending came a new emphasis on style. After 1925 Christmas ads regularly assured readers that items they suggested for presentation were fashionable. Gift items had to be new, modern, or "smart." Consistent with this emphasis, ads encouraged Americans to discard any unfashionable items they might have, even if they were still useful. A 1929 ad suggested husbands give their wives a new Bissell carpet sweeper and relegate their old, faithful—but still functional—Bissell sweeper to lesser duties on the second floor of the house. Americans should buy new products because it would keep their households up to date or because everyone else was buying them, not because they needed them. This emphasis on style—and the spending without regard for function which staying in style involved—served to increase demand for goods in the economy of abundance.[15]

Most Americans have a general understanding that Christmas gift items were once handmade but became manufactured at some point in history. We see how much may be learned by going further, asking what types of manufactured items givers preferred and why. The shift from gimcracks to expensive, useful items was effected consciously by manufacturers, retailers, and the public in order to expand those who profited from the Christmas trade and to reform the custom of gimcrack giving. The shift from expensive, useful items to consumption items was a logical outgrowth of the emerging economy of abundance. Thus, the shifts from one type of preferred manufactured item to another, like most other aspects of Christmas, followed a rational rather than a haphazard course.

CHAPTER 5

From Gimcracks to Cards: Gift Giving between Friends

Before 1880, adult friends generally did not exchange Christmas gifts. Those few who did usually chose their remembrances from among hand-made items, or from predecessors to gimcracks, such as books, candy, and small pieces of needlework. They also gave an early variety of Christmas card, though it was not the type that would gain popularity after 1910.[1]

The English originated the Christmas-card custom in the 1840s, and Americans began to exchange these holiday tokens twenty years later. The years between 1860 and 1890 became the "early period" of American Christmas card exchange, during which cards were exchanged by only a small number of prosperous Americans. Their prosperity was reflected in the cards' high quality—and high prices. The finest of them were made by the Prang Company of Boston, a company that came to symbolize high-quality cards.[2]

After 1880 Americans began sending new manufactured gimcracks to their friends. In addition, they began to present remembrances to larger and larger numbers of recipients, not only to close friends but also to acquaintances and business associates.[3] The increase in the popularity of gimcracks coincided with a decrease in the popularity of the Prang cards. By 1890 the slump in card exchanges was dramatically acknowledged in the decision of the Prang company to discontinue their production of cards. After that year, the early high-quality, American-made cards were virtually absent during the holidays, until 1906. The only cards available during the "slump" were "imported cards mostly, of violent colors and vulgar designs," which were sold in even fewer numbers than cards had during the late 1880s.[4]

Between 1880 and 1910, gimcrack-giving between friends—as generally in the society—enjoyed its heyday. By the first decade of the twentieth century, however, many writers in periodicals began to criticize the new dominance of the gimcracks in those presentations. For example, a writer noted in 1904 that, "Twenty-five years ago, Christmas was not the burden that it is now. . . . And each year more presents are being given, more 'debts' are being incurred," while another observed:

That Yuletide has come to be anticipated—with trepidation—is no secret. Each year this becomes more obvious. With midwinter comes the nerve-wrecking realization that before many days all good "Christians" must be prepared somehow to spend money that they cannot afford, to purchase "things" the recipients do not want. The horror of appearing mean tempts the wisest to become a spendthrift, and the spendthrift to become a fool. . . . Happily, there is a growing revolt against this state of affairs.[5]

In this climate, card giving revived as the appropriate symbol for most friendships. Gift givers also began to give expensive, useful items to a restricted group of recipients: family members and a few very close friends. In 1909 a writer argued that "the giving of gifts is a matter so intimate, so personal, that the practice should be discountenanced save between near kinfolk or friends of long standing." Similarly, a writer in 1906 believed that "the giving of gifts in general, and of Christmas gifts in particular, ought to be confined strictly to members of the same family, unless one feels inclined to bestow simple and inexpensive tokens of good will and friendly feeling upon intimate friends."[6] Viewing the shift away from gimcracks from the perspective of 1927, Charles Ovington, the owner of a large New York gift store, reflected that

there is less swapping of gifts at Christmas than there used to be. . . . I can remember when the majority of our women customers came into the store with a Christmas list which was literally a yard long. Now people spend more on Christmas than they ever did, but they concentrate on members of their immediate families and on a few friends who really count. Glass hatpin holders made out of test tubes wound with baby ribbon have been replaced by the Christmas card. In short, folks are getting more sensible about their giving.[7]

To meet the new public preference for the presentation of cards, businessmen began to produce and market them with vigor. They enjoyed quick success, as indicated by a survey of the mail system made during the Christmas season of 1911, which showed that Americans sent more total pieces of mail—both packages and cards—than they had during previous Christmases, yet the total weight of those pieces was significantly less. The conclusion was inescapable: Americans were sending more cards and fewer packages of gimcracks. A writer elaborated on the reasons for the shift:

Americans gradually for the last two years have been replacing the old method of gift-giving by merchandise with a new method of exchange of attractive Christmas cards. That this new spirit of a saner Christmas will grow there seems no doubt. The gift-giving had become a nightmare with many persons in recent years, and had reached its zenith in 1909. It had been on the increase for many years. It had so grown that one had to keep books against Christmas, and the new year opened with a nervous breakdown and with the poorer persons nearly in bankruptcy. . . . People finally saw that this must stop somewhere. No one believes that we have entirely recovered. But the postmasters, readers of the signs as given by the shipments of mail, tell us that we are on our way, at any rate, to a better appreciation of how Christmas should be celebrated in the giving of gifts.[8]

Christmas cards became more popular than gimcracks because they were a less substantial type of remembrance: they seemed to be honest and rational symbols of most friendship relationships; they were the type of gift that could appropriately express the true weight of the givers' relationships with most of their friends. Cards could be given with peace of mind, whereas gimcracks often made their givers uneasy. As one writer observed, "The Christmas gift without the Christmas significance is indeed a thing stripped of all meaning, a thing dead. . . . Better a small card that can go through the mail, that carries the message of beauty, than this."[9]

The most obvious way in which cards were less substantial than the gimcracks was in their cost. Indeed, the cost of cards was so low that givers tended to think of them as having no economic weight, as being mere symbols of thoughtfulness. Because cards carried no real value, recipients became obligated only to return the thought in the form of return cards. They created no economic debt which a return gift had to set right and they conveyed no willingness by givers to provide substantive economic aid in time of need. They only symbolized givers' classification of recipients as friends. Cards did not indicate the extent of givers' economic commitment to the relationships, whereas the economic value of more substantial gift items was a rough indicator of how much money the giver was willing to commit to the continuance of the relationship.

Gift givers found it useful that cards were a clearly distinguishable type of remembrance. There was simply no confusing cards with other types of gifts. The cards' distinctiveness made it easier for givers and recipients to limit their exchanges to them, a limitation which produced some appealing results. Because cards were priced within a limited range, any agreement to exchange them eliminated the possibility that there would be embarrassing differences in the value of gifts the parties presented. Such an understanding also eliminated the gradual escalation in the cost of remembrances, a common occurrence when givers exchanged substantial items over several years.

Cards were also less substantial gifts than gimcracks because it took less time to shop for them. Givers simply went to a store that had an adequate selection, purchased their favorite style of cards in the correct quantity, and addressed and mailed them. Gimcracks had required much more thought and many more hours of shopping and wrapping, prompting a writer in 1912 to comment on "the pushing, tired women, buying things which very often they do not wish to purchase, for people who cannot conceivably want to own them." But the effort required to buy gimcracks became a part of the gift, and this aspect was not present in card exchanges. According to many periodical writers around 1910, the shorter time in which cards could be purchased made them better symbols of the givers' relationships with their friends.[10] In addition, they displayed higher aesthetic merit and craftsmanship than gimcracks. Cards had relatively superior quality even though they cost less than gimcracks, proof that higher cost does not necessarily translate into higher quality.

Between 1900 and 1920, the criticisms leveled against gimcracks became serious in tone. For example, a writer in 1913 described them as "only tawdry and gaudy gimcracks, flimsy gewgaws, ephemeral and unbeautiful; purchased often with lassitude, received with distaste, and soon relegated to the limbo of attic or ash heap." In the late 1910s and in the '20s, some writers began to use humor to attack the cheap garishness of many Christmas gifts. For example, William Rose Benet directed some his wry barbs at paintings he had seen during his Christmas shopping:

Some of them were very moving, of course: the picture of the young man, in a degenerate topper, pink tail-coat and jockey boots, kissing the girl with curls and a blue-satin directoire, in the rose arbor, with the fox terriers in the foreground.

Or, there was one of "Baby's First Lesson." All the frames were prettily gilded. I was quite attracted by them myself.[11]

Benet's criticism, based largely on aesthetic grounds, was echoed by others who criticized gimcracks as being unimaginative and inappropriate. As with the aesthetic critiques, commentators were at first serious and then became humorously satirical during the late 1910s and '20s. Compare Margaret Deland's observation of 1904 that "the giving of gifts, even in the right spirit, is a difficult business, for who can tell what other people want?" with Will Cuppy's description in 1926 of his friend Egbert's gift-giving habits:

Each Christmas Egbert sends me some of these abalones. . . . Not that Egbert is so lacking in imagination as to send me cuff links every time. His system involves vest buttons, stick pins and cuff links in regular rotation. The year 1918, for instance, is forever fixed in my memory as Vest Button Year. The Christmas of 1937, I find by rapid calculation, will bring me another stick pin. And so on. Egbert, you see, is like that. . . . . On Christmas morning when I break the Red Cross seal on my parcel and behold the cuff links in their irridescent and familiar splendor I am going to cast aside all violent and unlovely thoughts, pull myself together and exclaim in a loud voice, "Oh, goody goody! That's just what I wanted." My manners may profit by this procedure. My immortal soul must take its chances.[12]

Cards had significant advantages over the unimaginativeness and inappropriateness of gimcracks. Their message could hardly be considered inappropriate as they said nothing about the relationships they symbolized, save that the senders regarded their addressees as friends. They did not define the content of a relationship. They were also "safe" because they were short-lived remembrances: those who gave them expected the recipients to throw them away at the end of the Christmas season. Because the recipients' exposure to the cards was limited, their assessment of them did not matter much. In contrast, those who gave gimcracks expected recipients not only to keep them but, often, to display them in their homes, no matter how ugly they might be.[13]

While the numbers of cards exchanged began to increase as early as 1906, the most dramatic increase occurred during World War I. The war in Germany and Austria disrupted those countries' production of Christmas cards, thereby protecting American manufacturers from their most formidable competition. The German and Austrian companies who were able to produce a few cards in spite of the war found it very difficult to get them past the Entente navy to the United States. Even then, the

German and Austrian producers had to overcome a widespread antipathy toward their countries because of the war.[14]

World War I further prompted the giving of cards by encouraging the government and the public to make careful use of the nation's resources and its manufacturing capacity. There was agreement that the demands of the war effort should take priority over more frivolous concerns, but American Christmas card manufacturers turned this economic climate to the benefit of cards by stressing that the production and exchange of cards did not divert any scarce raw materials from the war effort. Nor did they drain much of the nation's money, as cards were quite inexpensive compared to gimcracks. In any event, the seriousness of the war made gimcracks seem frivolous, wasteful, and inappropriate.[15]

The possibility existed that the strong public sentiment in favor of using resources carefully would soon lead some to suggest doing away with even card exchanges. In order to stave off this prospect, in 1918 manufacturers formed the Greeting Card Association, a trade organization that conducted a vigorous advertising campaign. Its message went beyond the earlier argument that Christmas card exchanges did not harm the war effort to a new emphasis on the positive contributions the cards made to the nation by raising morale both overseas and at home.[16]

To prevent a return to gimcrack giving after the war, the Greeting Card Association promoted cards as the ideal item for exchange between friends. However, in peacetime it was difficult to find a new advertising theme that was as effective as the wartime message that cards contributed to the war effort. The card companies thus adopted the innovative marketing technique of sending "dealer helps" to retailers, consisting of posters, store displays, and the like. The technique was apparently effective, as the American greeting card industry enjoyed a fivefold increase in sales between 1917 and 1927, from $10 million to $55 million.[17]

Sales of Christmas cards increased even further during the 1930s, largely as a result of the economic hardship of that decade. The Depression provided a somber backdrop for all holiday gift exchanges, including those between friends. As a writer noted in 1932, "Santa is at his old stand, but there's no nonsense about him as he whispers, '98 cents.' It's a realistic Christmas." Merchants noticed that holiday shoppers had become careful in making their gift selections: "people are looking longer, comparing values in one store against another, making careful decisions to insure the greatest return for their dollars." For the first time since

1900, large numbers of shoppers made a conscious effort to establish and abide by Christmas budgets: "Budgeting . . . is evident. . . . Less money is available for Christmas spending. It must be carefully allocated on paper to make sure that all relatives and friends are included." And frequently, shoppers looked only at items from price ranges they had determined beforehand: "Last year there was an evident tendency to stick to a certain price: 'What have you got for $5' was a common question. Pressure of continuing hard times has multiplied this type of shopper. The difference is insistence on even lower ranges." The economic constraints of the period encouraged those gift givers who had persisted in giving gimcracks to their friends finally to make the switch to cards.[18]

Christmas card sales stood at $60 million in 1931, but as a writer in 1937 observed: "Since 1932, when we experienced the low point of the depression, the number of cards sold and used has increased astonishingly." The large volume of Christmas card exchanges in the 1930s is evidence that, by the end of the decade, cards had almost totally replaced gimcracks as the standard type of remembrance exchanged between friends at Christmas. Thus the hope expressed during the first decade of the century by the critics of gimcrack giving had been realized.[19]

Besides friendships bound by mutual affection, there were other types of relationships to cultivate. One of the most important was between business associates, who frequently reaffirmed their bonds by the exchange of presents during the Christmas season. Business associates first began to exchange Christmas gifts around 1880, and they continued to do so with increasing frequency through the 1920s. Most agreed with the writer who said in 1924 that "around Christmas time, a little show of sentiment goes a long way toward strengthening the bonds between a manufacturer and his customers, be they jobbers or dealers." The economic value of the gift was frequently more than a "little show of sentiment," as an author in 1938 noted: "Time was, not many years ago, when the average purchasing agent of a large company was certain to receive several hundred dollars' worth of Christmas gifts from salesmen from whom he bought."[20]

But in the late 1920s, business associates became disenchanted with the exchange of substantial gift items and began to select cards instead. One reason for this change was the Depression. The economic collapse of the nation depleted the resources of many businessmen, who became reluctant to spend their remaining dollars on Christmas gifts for business associates. A writer observed in 1937 that "the bad business years from 1930 to 1934 delivered a crushing blow to the whole practice of giving expensive gifts" to business associates, and added that "as business has become better there have appeared few signs that the practice will be revived."[21]

Another reason for the decline in substantial gift items was a change in attitude by those who had received them. During the late 1920s, purchasing agents—who had received the lion's share of the holiday remembrances—began to object to getting gifts from manufacturers. Their opposition, even though it was against their individual economic self-interest, stemmed from broader business considerations. As a writer argued in 1937:

Every recipient of such gifts realized, either consciously or unconsciously, that those gifts were included in the cost of selling. . . . Therefore, some years ago local groups of purchasing agents began to agitate against this practice. Admitting, frankly, that they rather liked to receive valuable presents at Christmas time, they emphasized the fact that, as business men, they could not with equanimity observe the continuation of this practice.

One may be suspicious of statements such as this against the declarant's self-interest, but these same sentiments cropped up frequently enough to prompt the conclusion that many purchasing agents did indeed object to receiving Christmas gifts from their business associates, and that their opposition played a part in reducing the numbers received.[22]

Finally, gift-giving forms, while useful in expressing affectionate personal bonds, fit uneasily with the market basis of most business relationships. Business associates were forthright in acknowledging that making money was the true basis of these relationships and that they should therefore avoid using gift forms. In 1928 a trade-journal writer described this new attitude: "A really intelligent person resents being 'kidded.' I believe the days of the high-power salesman who considered every prospect his 'brother' are gone. . . . Only recently Amos Bradbury objected, in *Printer's Ink* . . . to back slapping by mail and some time ago a Chicago department store buyer put a sign outside his door bearing the words, 'No handshaking.' "[23]

By the late 1920s, businessmen were commenting in periodicals that they wanted the Christmas gifts they received to be expressions of true affection, not mere economic self-interest. Reflecting this sentiment, trade-journal writers set forth guidelines so that businessmen could judge whether the gifts they were thinking about presenting would be "true gifts" and therefore acceptable in the new climate of opinion. They recommended that exchanges take place only between individuals who knew one another; gifts sent from one company to another company, which lacked this personal element, were therefore inappropriate. In 1937 a trade-journal writer elaborated on one way in which companies conformed to this "rule": "Many companies believe that in sending out Christmas greetings these should come from the salesman rather than the company itself. The salesman is the company representative. He knows his customers personally. Therefore, these customers are likely to feel that there is a real sincerity in a greeting from the man they know."[24] In addition, they recommended that exchanges be more than mere guises to make money. They should be expressions of true affection between the parties involved. As a writer of the late 1920s stated, "the Christmas card of a business house should be based on friendship and not on business." In keeping with this guideline, they objected to presents that were really thinly veneered advertisements. Certainly the presents should not have order blanks attached to them, nor should the companies' names be written on them in large letters.[25] Finally, writers encouraged businessmen to make their gifts less substantial and send cards rather than more expensive items. Just as critics of gimcrack giving among personal friends had argued during the 1910s, critics of excessive gift giving among business associates argued during the 1930s that cards were more honest, and therefore more appropriate symbols of these relationships because deep affection was usually absent.

The inconsequential monetary value of cards had particular symbolic appeal for purchasing agents. Because their cost was trifling, it was clear that the cards were not being used to bribe the agents who received them. This elimination of any appearance of impropriety was important to agents, as a writer of 1937 pointed out. Agents, he wrote, "felt that the practice [of manufacturers giving them presents] savored too much of out-and-out commercial bribery. Whereas, in a number of cases they knew that the Christmas gift was a spontaneous token of appreciation, they also realized that in far too many instances it was a grudging and expensive effort on the part of companies or salesmen to curry favor."[26] In a sense, all gifts are bribes because they impose obligations on recipients to make return gifts. Such obligations had a special significance where substantial items were presented by business associates, because recipients were thereby being pressured to reciprocate by continuing their business dealings with the givers even if it was not maximally profitable for them to do so. Recipients were to make, as their return gifts, a partial suspension of the market criteria which they normally used in making business decisions. This pressure to suspend their usual market standards was a significant factor in prompting purchasing agents to object to receiving Christmas gifts and partly explains the new trend to send Christmas cards as symbols of their relationships.

Trade journals recommended three guidelines to help businessmen decide whether to present gifts: (1) only those business associates who personally knew one another should exchange remembrances; (2) exchanges should express true personal regard; and (3) remembrances should be the economically insubstantial cards rather than more substantial "bribing" gifts. In short, the market element in the relationships should be subordinate to the personal element before it was appropriate to symbolize them even with Christmas cards. During the 1930s, businessmen increasingly abided by these guidelines and thereby did much to reform a custom they believed had gotten out of control.

During the sixty years between 1880 and 1940, remarkable changes occurred in the exchange of Christmas gifts among friends. After 1880 friends and business associates had begun to exchange gifts in increasing numbers, so much so that many friends were moved to reform these exchanges after 1910, and business associates followed suit during the late 1920s. Reformers advocated the presentation of less substantial items to their friends and business associates because such relationships did not merit weighty symbols. They felt that substantial gift items should be reserved for presentation to one's immediate family and a few close friends.

During the thirty years between 1910 and 1940, the reformers' efforts achieved substantial success. Americans altered their gift-giving practices, consistent with the suggestions of the reformers. Instead of gimcracks and more substantial items, they sent either Christmas cards or nothing at all. The reforms were pursued and achieved through conscious effort and deliberate action. Gift exchanges among friends and business associates were made subject to human intellect and will, and therefore do not conform to the popular view that Christmas gift giving has moved steadily beyond the power of celebrants to control it.

CHAPTER 6

The Feminization of Christmas: The Expanded Role of Women in the Celebration

Before 1880, men and women contributed equally to America's Christmas festivals by sharing the tasks necessary to create an appropriate celebration. For example, men generally got the Christmas trees, turkeys, and raw materials to make presents, while women cooked the turkeys and prepared the Christmas feast. They cooperated in making presents, although men were more active in making wooden toys while women did the sewing. As the Yule season approached, adults of both sexes became busy.[1]

After 1880, with the emergence of the modern Christmas celebration, holiday duties began to be allocated unequally. Women became responsible for virtually all preparations for the celebration, while men only provided the money. For example, women not only continued to prepare the food for the Christmas dinner, but they shopped for most of it as well. In the new urban settings, they purchased the turkey and other holiday foodstuffs at local markets, thereby supplanting the older rural pattern in which men had acquired the foodstuffs through farming, hunting, or husbandry. Women also began to play a larger role in the acquisition of Christmas trees by accompanying their husbands to the places where trees were sold and participating in their selection. No longer did men trudge off into the woods alone in search of trees for their families.

Women's holiday responsibilities were greater than they had been and greater than the duties expected of men. Christmas became a female sphere of activity.[2]

Reflecting on the expanded Christmas duties of women in 1912, Margaret Deland observed:

It is women who sigh [at the approach of Christmas]; so far as men are concerned, Christmas is safe enough with them; they don't sigh because they dread the weeks before the 25th of December. Nor do the young people of our sex groan over the approach of the "merry" day; to them the seven weeks mean only the pleasant hurry of anticipation. It is feminine middle age that sighs when it sees November slip into December. . . . Does this seem an exaggeration? Ask a dozen women, whose ages range anywhere between thirty and sixty. . . . How many of them can truly say that they never lie awake at night and think about Christmas?[3]

One of the most important Christmas duties performed by women was the shopping. In most homes, women purchased the gift items presented by other family members, except for the items given them by their husbands. A writer in 1912 noted that "men are so few and far between at the crowded, ill-tempered, vulgar bargain-counters, that they don't count." In 1924 a male writer acknowledged that "I am a Christmas shopping slacker. I let my wife do it. . . . A Christmas shopping throng is no place for a male person. It belongs to the female of the species, which, as Kipling said, can take more punishment than the male. Man has no chance in the Great American Stampede of the Battering and Benevolent Order of Buffeting Bundle Balancers and Bargain-counter Beleaguers." Contemporary observers placed the ratio of women shoppers to men shoppers at about ten to one.[4]

In part, women began to dominate Christmas shopping after 1880 because they were also beginning to do most of the nation's regular, year-round shopping. They were expected to purchase most of the items that their families needed. To a writer of 1906, it stood "unchallenged that, while the man does the earning, the woman does the spending, be she wife, mother or sister." A number of surveys conducted in the early 1920s revealed that women were making about 80 percent of their families' purchases. This preponderance of women in American marketplaces was strikingly different from the preceding American practice in which men had loomed large in making purchases for their families.[5]

Two contradictory sets of values served to guide women in their shopping. The first encouraged them to shop expertly and efficiently, to

31. Lorain Oven Heat Regulators, *SEP*, 193 (18 Dec. 1920): 115.

Plate 23. In the modern Christmas, women became responsible for doing the vast majority of tasks required to produce an appropriate celebration. This ad played off women's heavy holiday burden by assuring readers that a Lorain Oven Heat Regulator would free them from their tasks long enough so that they, too, could enjoy Christmas.

regard shopping as a part of the profession of home management. Wives were to trim every excess or wasted penny from household expenses. Writers made meticulous calculations that showed how much money an efficient wife could save her family (these figures were also well used by those who thought that women's place was in the home). For many observers, efficient shopping and housekeeping not only benefited individual families, but were also essential to the future well-being of the nation. This goal became so important that the public school system undertook to teach girls how to shop well, making such instruction a cornerstone of the new home economics movement. Thus an influential segment of American culture encouraged females to become the primary instruments of thriftiness within their families, an ideal that was fundamentally different from the earlier notion that men should play that role.[6]

If the shopping of some women was guided by the goal of saving money through efficiency, the shopping of other women was guided by a second, diametrically opposed goal: conspicuous consumption. The most outlandishly expensive items were preferred, even where differences in function or form were trivial or nonexistent. The fundamental characteristic of this style of shopping was the wasting of money, at least according to rational standards. Although not economically rational, the wasting had a purpose: to demonstrate the wealth of the spender. After all, in order to spend money frivolously, one must first have ample money. It followed that the more irrational the purchase, the stronger the implied message of wealth, and the more certain it was to earn the admiration and envy of others.

In addition to spending lavishly, women had other ways of conveying conspicuous consumption values. For example, they shopped during working hours, a sure signal that they did not work and that their husbands' incomes were large enough to support them as ladies of leisure. Moreover, the type of activity in which the wives engaged—shopping—emphasized this point. Not only were they freed from working to earn money for their families, they could pass their time spending the money that had been accumulated by their husbands. Thus the implicit message was that their husbands' incomes were not only adequate, they were *more* than adequate.[7]

Whether women shopped efficiently or consumed conspicuously, their role as purchasers of Christmas presents revealed a conflict in the American value system. On the one hand, Americans believed that all gift givers should use their own money (that is, money they had earned) to purchase the items they gave as gifts in order to give the items symbolic weight. If givers had not earned the money to make those purchases, their gifts remained but hollow gestures.[8]

Earned gift items carried more symbolic weight mainly because of the labor that givers had expended to acquire money to purchase the items. Such exertions implicitly promised that the givers were willing to exert themselves to maintain the relationship, that the recipient could call upon the giver's energies in a time of need. Handmade gift items expressed this element of effort directly, but gifts purchased with hard-earned money also carried considerable weight as symbols of the giver's efforts, especially gifts that were fairly expensive.

Earned gift items symbolized more than the physical exertions of givers. They also symbolized time given out of givers' lives. As givers' money-making efforts required time, they had, in a sense, given parts of their lives to the task of earning money to purchase the gift items. Because of this sacrifice, such gifts readily became infused with the "spirit"—with the personal essence—of the givers.[9]

On the other hand, Americans thought that wives should be economically dependent on their spouses, that the money they spent ought to come from their husbands. If, in the modern Christmas, men had become relegated to being only money providers, it was a role they guarded zealously, and for good reason. Control over the family purse was a source of considerable power. Economically dependent women obviously had to rely on someone to give them their Christmas shopping money and, in almost all cases, those someones were their husbands. Otherwise, such women would not have money to purchase any presents they gave away, including presents to their husbands.

Husbands usually gave their wives Christmas shopping money early in the season. This transfer of cash influenced the meaning of all subsequent presents exchanged between them. Most importantly, because the husbands' transfer of cash included the money the housewives would later use to purchase the presents they gave to their husbands, housewives found it difficult to feel that they had presented their husbands "true gifts." They rightfully sensed that their husbands had really given their presents to themselves.

The wives' reservations about receiving shopping money from their husbands went beyond their feeling of not being able to give their hus-

bands gifts that carried weight. The act of asking for money was humiliating, even though many husbands were forthcoming with shopping
money when asked for it. Wives were not made to beg. As one woman
observed, "No more generous being exists than the average American
husband. But he does not seem to be able to get it through his well-
meaning but halting mind that nothing on God's earth humiliates a wife
more than to be compelled to ask her husband for money." [10] Women
objected for good reason. Asking for money ritually confirmed their
husbands' financial authority and their own dependent status and under-
lined the fact that they had no economic resources of their own. Because
Americans generally equated economic independence with social status,
it is no wonder that married women found the act of asking for Christmas
gift money humiliating.

Housewives had several possible paths of escape from the potential
humiliation rooted in their economic dependence on their husbands. The
most obvious was to take a job outside the home during the holiday
season and thereby earn their own Christmas money. This solution was
appealing because their wages would be the fruit of no one else's labor,
and the Christmas presents purchased with that money would carry the
weight of their personal efforts.

In spite of the important symbolic and material advantages to women
who assumed temporary employment, writers did not explicitly encourage them along that path. They seem to have approved of seasonal
employment, but any encouragement remained implicit, for example, by
not overtly criticizing women who wanted to earn their Christmas shopping money. From one perspective, this strategy made good sense. The
entry of women into the work force was still a highly controversial topic
during the early twentieth century. Any arguments in favor of the employment of women, even temporary employment, could have disrupted
family harmony, a serious consequence for Christmas articles which were
expected to foster harmony and happiness. Moreover, such arguments in
magazine articles might have alienated readers and had dire consequences
for advertising revenues. Thus writers chose to keep their articles on
Christmas gift giving as noncontroversial as possible, even though the
seasonal employment of women was a logical solution to their economic
dependence during the gift-giving season. [11]

As a second potential solution to the problem posed by the economic
dependence of women, some magazine writers suggested that wives ar-

range with their husbands to be paid a regular allowance over the course of the year for their housekeeping labors. This would allow them to accumulate a fund of earned money by the end of the year without leaving their regular duties of keeping the household. This solution seemed fair, as it compensated women for the work they did in caring for their homes and families. It also saved them from the humiliation of asking for Christmas shopping money. Still, it was up to the wives to make this proposition, which contained some risk to family harmony. Magazine writers were sensitive to this risk and, at least in their Christmas articles, did not encourage readers to make such requests at the risk of creating family disharmony during the holidays. They relegated the promotion of housekeeping allowances to articles that had no connection with the holidays.[12]

Writers' reluctance to discuss the economic dependence of women in their Christmas articles was obvious in articles where such discussions were absent but would have been directly relevant. For example, articles on Christmas Club bank accounts did not mention that these accounts could serve as a way to eliminate the wives' annual ritual of asking for shopping money. Couples would have had to agree only on the amount necessary to cover their holiday expenses and then make regular and appropriate deposits, which would later be available for the wives' use in holiday shopping. Similarly, when writers prompted wives to handmake their Christmas gifts, they did not say that spending time making items was one of the few ways that economically dependent women could give weight to the items they presented at Christmas.[13]

During the early twentieth century, Americans harbored contradictory attitudes toward women's economic status at Christmas. On the one hand they thought that women should be economically dependent on their husbands, while on the other hand they thought that women should be economically independent at Christmas so that they could purchase the gift items they presented. For their part, periodical writers failed to face up to this contradiction in their Christmas articles; they failed to promote several obvious solutions to women's condition of dependence, such as assuming seasonal jobs or receiving money for their housework. Such solutions were thought to raise too many controversial issues during a season that was supposed to foster family harmony.

CHAPTER 7

Within the Marital Bond: Gifts between Men and Women

Gift givers select items for particular recipients not only to meet the individual needs or desires of the recipients, but also because the items seem appropriate for the social roles which the recipients play. A husband thinking of giving a certain gift to his wife is reassured by knowing that husbands have presented others of the type to their wives, and that it is compatible with the image of women in the society. Thus the types of gifts selected for the members of a particular social group is closely related to the cultural image of that group.

During the first two decades of the twentieth century, women were usually portrayed in Christmas ads and articles as dignified matrons. They were almost always married, a message that was often conveyed by including their children in ad illustrations and by referring to their children in stories; moreover, these women were usually nurturing their children rather than paying attention to their husbands. Not only were there relatively few romantic scenes of wives and husbands, but husbands were rarely shown at all in ad illustrations with the matronly women. The women ostensibly lived in a state "purified" from romantic involvement and sexual desire.

Ad women looked to be between thirty-five and fifty years of age. Frequently, their children were shown as young adults, with the women being shown, appropriately, as a generation older. The demeanor of the women was calm and dignified, a demeanor that befitted the ideal of the

period that women should create a refuge from the world for their husbands.[1]

These dignified matronly women received small inexpensive gift items
at Christmas, such as minor articles of clothing. "Christmas furs" (priced
at less than four dollars a piece) were popular, as were handkerchiefs,
blouses, low-cost jewelry, little decorative knickknacks (figurines, for
example), and candy. Most of these presents were gimcracks, that is, they
were inexpensive and of limited utility. As such they were no different
than gift items others received at Christmas; for example, they resembled
the handkerchiefs and cufflinks that men got, and the knitted goods and
small toys given to children.[2]

Gimcracks recommended for women were often set apart from those
recommended for other recipients by a particular quality: daintiness. Ad
writers urged Americans to give women dainty handkerchiefs, dainty
shirtwaists, and dainty stationery. The daintiness of these matched the
ideal for women recipients: women's gifts were to be dainty, just like the
women who received them. "Dainty" is defined in the 1922 edition of
Webster's New International Dictionary thus: "Of a delicate or fragile beauty
or charm; tenderly fair . . . exquisitely tasteful. . . . Having or exhibiting
delicate taste, sensibility or discrimination; nice; fastidious. . . ." There,
succinctly, is the Gibson Girl.[3]

About 1910 the image of the ideal woman as mature, dignified, and
dainty began to change, and so did the types of items that women
received at Christmas. The ideal woman of the ads now became more
active than her predecessor. In the 1910s, during the early years of the
transformation of the ideal, the primary outlet for the ad women's energies was the home. Many were shown receiving household appliances
from their husbands at Christmas, implying active housekeeping. However, during the '20s, the ideal woman began to be active not only in the
domestic setting, but in a wide variety of pursuits outside the home. For
example, women were shown ready to play tennis, to bicycle, to picnic,
to shop, and to go to shows, in many cases having just finished their
housework. The gifts they received during the holidays began to reflect
this larger sphere of activity.

During the 1910s a more positive regard of housewives who did their
own housework was prompted by social forces, most importantly the
pronounced shortage of domestic workers, commonly called "the servant
problem." During the second half of the nineteenth century, middle-class

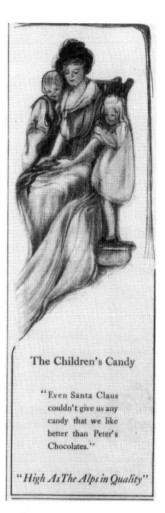

33. Peter's chocolates, *SEP*, 184
(23 Dec. 1911): 27. General Research Division. The New York
Public Library. Astor, Lenox
and Tilden Foundations.

32. Bellas Hess & Co. shirtwaists, etc.,
LHJ, 28 (Dec. 1911): 81.

Plate 24. Between 1900 and 1920, the ideal American woman was mature and matronly.
To emphasize her role as a mother, she was frequently pictured with her children, as in the
Peter's Chocolates ad.

families had employed large numbers of domestic workers and had become accustomed to their services. However, after 1900 these families found it more difficult to engage housekeepers because lower-class women, from whose ranks virtually all domestic workers were drawn, became reluctant to take such employment because they had better prospects in other sectors of the economy. As a result, middle-class wives had to do their housekeeping chores themselves.[4]

As they confronted these chores, women became a ready market for any appliances that promised to lighten their workload. Gift givers picked up on this development and made appliances the most popular type of gift item for presentation to women throughout the 1910s and '20s. While the demand for appliances does much to explain their popularity at this time, it is nevertheless significant that they did not appear earlier. After all, the technological breakthroughs for many of them (for example, vacuum cleaners and electric refrigerators) had been made during the mid-nineteenth century, several decades before manufacturers began to mass produce them. Why then the delay between the invention of appliances and their production? The reason is that when the technology for the appliances became available, the economy did not yet have enough capacity to allow Americans to satisfy their desires for increased efficiency in housecleaning. They still had to focus their energies on satisfying the more essential needs for food, shelter, and clothing. It was only after 1900, when there was ample industrial capacity to meet these basic needs, that producers could divert a substantial portion of the nation's productive capacity to satisfying the less essential desires such as the desire for increased efficiency in housekeeping.[5]

After 1920 women's activities expanded beyond housekeeping to include a wide variety of leisure-time pursuits. They became less focused on their domestic chores and more interested in activities following the completion of the chores. This shift prompted a new theme in ads for appliances. The main value of appliances was now not merely that they reduced the time and effort required to keep a house, but that, in so doing, they allowed women more time to pursue their leisure-time interests. For example, a 1920 ad for Torrington vacuum cleaners showed a woman ready to take off for a pleasurable afternoon after finishing vacuuming, whereas earlier she would have been shown using the cleaner.[6]

The ideal woman of the Christmas gift ads of the 1920s was significantly younger than her earlier counterpart—between fifteen and thirty-

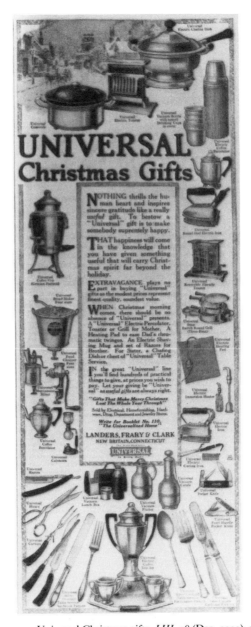

34. Universal Christmas gifts, *LHJ*, 38 (Dec. 1921): 79.

Plate 25. Around 1910, Americans became disaffected with the uselessness of gimcracks. At the same time, the "servant problem" made women receptive to devices that would lighten their household chores. These two developments made appliances the preferred type of Christmas gift for women until 1930.

35. Torrington vacuum cleaners, *LHJ*, 37 (Dec. 1920): 110.

Plate 26. During the 1910s, ads had shown women using the appliances they were given at Christmas, but by the '20s, as in this ad, they were shown ready for leisure activities after having completed their chores. The shift from usefulness to leisure in these ads reflected the general shift to consumption values during the 1920s.

36. Queen-Make dresses, *LHJ*, 38 (Dec. 1921): 168.

Plate 27. The ideal woman of the 1920s was younger than the mature, matronly woman of the early twentieth century had been. Her youthfulness in years was paralleled by her youthfulness in clothing. She adopted a flat-chested, short-skirted style, previously worn only by girls.

37. Nayvee Middiwear, *LHJ*, 37 (Dec. 1920): 167.

Plate 28. During the 1920s it became difficult to distinguish between girls and women in ads, as they were close in age and began to wear the same styles of clothing. For example, compare this ad for sailor suits for young women with the ad for sailor suits for late adolescent girls in illustration 76.

Give him a Twinplex Stropper for his safety razor. He'll be grateful every day, for years to come! Twinplex improves new blades 100 per cent. and gives 100 perfect shaves from each new blade. No trouble—no adjusting; a few turns strop keen,—both edges at once. It speeds the shave. It's a regular gift for a regular fellow. Sold everywhere. Twinplex Sales Company, St. Louis, New York, Montreal.

Twinplex Stropper
FOR SMOOTHER SHAVES

for single edge blades $3.00

for double edge blades $5.00

38. Twinplex stropper, *SEP*, 195 (9 Dec. 1922): 115.

Plate 29. The playfully romantic behavior of 1920s women—as here, kissing a beau under mistletoe—would have been unthinkable for the reserved Gibson Girls of the early twentieth century. Women became increasingly independent—sexually, economically, and intellectually—during the century.

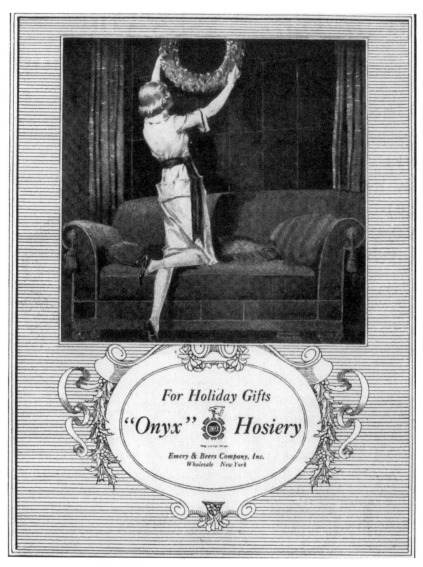

For Holiday Gifts

"Onyx" Hosiery

Emery & Beers Company, Inc.
Wholesale   New York

39. Onyx hosiery, *LHJ*, 38 (Dec. 1921): 152.

Plate 30. The woman in this 1921 ad appealed to readers with more than a pretty face. She exudes discrete sex appeal which, during the 1920s, became an acceptable advertising theme.

HERE is no gift more acceptable to the well dressed woman than dainty lingerie. It has a charm and freshness peculiarly suggestive of the Christmas season.

Whether the selection of lingerie is for a gift or for personal use, the fastidious shopper will find that WOLF-HEAD UNDERGARMENTS afford an unusual opportunity to combine durability with daintiness.

Skilfully tailored from the finest of silks and cottons, these garments are cut with an ample fullness which insures perfect fit and comfort. Trimmed with imported laces and the daintiest of ribbons and embroideries.

The needle-work is perfect —you will find no raw edges or careless finishing on WOLF-HEAD UNDERGARMENTS.

Dainty · Distinctive · Dependable

The
WOLF COMPANY
FIFTH AVENUE, NEW YORK

40. Wolf Company lingerie, *LHJ*, 37 (Dec. 1920): 179.

Plate 31. A lingerie-clad woman, such as the one in this 1920 ad, would have been out of place in ads of the early twentieth century. The advertiser could portray her in this scanty attire during the '20s only because the mature, matronly woman of the early twentieth century was no longer the ideal.

five years of age. In addition to her youthfulness, she was usually unmar-
ried, in marked contrast to the previous women who were not only
married but also mothers. These young, single women of postwar ads
were, unlike the prewar women, more commonly portrayed in romantic,
mildly sexual scenes. For example, coy young women were pictured with
young men underneath mistletoe, with a playful suggestiveness that would
have been unthinkable before the war. In other ads, advertisers portrayed
women in respectable "cheesecake" poses.[7]

Between 1880 and 1940 women showed increasing independence in
their relations with men. The Gibson Girl had remained economically
dependent and focused her attention on domestic tasks. As late as 1920,
women in ads showed their delight at being well provided for by their
husbands. Numerous ads showed grateful, dependent wives receiving
appliances from their confident, proud husbands. The giving of appliances indicated that men recognized their wives' housekeeping labors and
were making substantive, even generous, efforts to ease the women's
burdens.[8]

However, by the late 1920s the ideal for women—and for Christmas
gifts presented to them—was to be "smart." Ad writers encouraged
readers to present smart house slippers, smart blouses, and smart linens
to their smart wives. During these years the word retained some of its
traditional meaning of high intelligence, a fact suggesting that Americans
approved of women's thinking more for themselves and taking a somewhat more independent stance vis-à-vis men.[9]

More important than the traditional meaning of "smart" was a new
connotation of the word that was particularly in vogue during the late
1920s. Ad writers and others began to use "smart" to mean modern or up
to date. When used to describe women, this newer definition—like the
traditional definition—implied greater independence of women. Specifically, modernity involved questioning the Victorian ideal of female dependence as well as acknowledging an increased decision-making role for
females in sexual matters. No longer was it expected that women repel all
male advances until after marriage. One has only to compare the innocent, passive Gibson Girls of the early twentieth century with the party-
ing, petting flappers of the 1920s to see the changes that took place in the
image of the ideal woman between 1880 and 1930.

Around 1930, the image of women in Christmas gift ads changed once
again. They became older than women in the 1920s ads, about twenty-

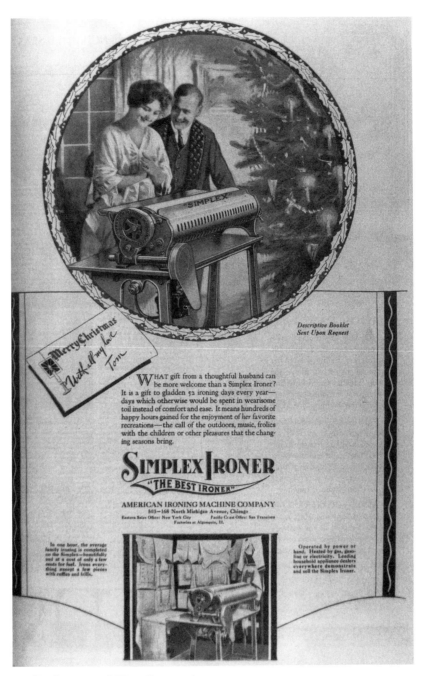

41. Simplex ironers, *LHJ*, 37 (Dec. 1920): 49.

Plate 32. Following their victory in World War I, men radiated confidence as heads of their families. Numerous postwar ads, such as this one of 1920, showed delighted women receiving appliances from their assured, providing husbands.

42. Sears retail stores, *LHJ*, 46 (Dec. 1929): 164. General Research Division. The New York Public Library. Astor, Lenox and Tilden Foundations.

Plate 33. The ideal woman of the 1920s was "smart," an adjective that meant she was up to date as well as mentally adept. Note, also, how even Sears, that bastion of rural, mail-order retailing, adopted urban, consumption values during the 1920s.

43. Martex linens, *LHJ*, 45 (Dec. 1928): 98.

Plate 34. Being in style and "modern" became the ideal for women during the 1920s. Appealing to this ideal, Martex created "the 9 most distinctive towel designs in America . . . for those clever women who achieve bright attractive homes with the new vogue for color." The emphasis on style and modernity was an important part of the consumption culture that dominated the postwar decade.

five to forty-five years old. In keeping with this maturity, they projected an air of seriousness. Apparently, writers now felt that the young, carefree, single women whom they had favored in their illustrations in the 1920s were out of place amid the economic distress of the 1930s. Also in keeping with the maturity of the 1930s women, advertisers commonly portrayed them as being married—for example, by placing them in obviously domestic surroundings. Even though they were home centered, they were not shown in the role of mother and nurturer nearly as frequently as they had been before World War I.[10]

Women in the 1930s ads were much wealthier than either the matronly women of the prewar ads or the stylish, smart women of the '20s ads, and they displayed their prosperity for all to see. They were sleekly ostentatious—ritzy—in appearance, wearing stylish evening gowns and expensive jewelry. They wore these formal clothes even though few, if any, ads indicated that they were actually going out to some formal occasion. Rather, the women were wearing their ritzy outfits as their normal at-home attire.[11]

These mature, ritzy women of the 1930s Christmas gift ads had a distinct air of aloofness about them, a demeanor that represents a further step in the increasingly independent stance of women vis-à-vis men between 1880 and 1940. Their aloofness frequently took the form of a solitary melancholy: numerous richly dressed women, seated on expensive couches, peered out wistfully toward the reader. Consistent with their remote demeanor, the women were commonly removed from other illustrations in the ads, for example, from illustrations of items being promoted for sale.[12]

What could one give these mature, ritzy, and aloof women at Christmas? Neither gimcracks, which had been given to Gibson Girls, nor the household appliances and recreational items that had made appropriate gifts for active young women during the 1920s seemed appropriate. Increasingly, men began to favor a new type of item—consumption items such as silverware, crystal, and fine watches—for presentation to women recipients. Several ads even went so far as to recommend automobiles as appropriate gift items. Cost seemed not to be a factor. The luxuriousness of these consumption items is remarkable when one considers the economic deprivation of the Depression. Gifts to men, in contrast, were more rational and declined in value.[13]

A new theme in American popular culture encouraged the giving of luxurious gifts to women in the midst of the Depression: wives were portrayed as the superior partners in American marriages and therefore deserving of luxurious gifts as tokens of that superiority. For example, in some ads gifts to women were characterized as "tribute" which husbands should humbly offer their wives. Other ads pointedly asked male readers whether the gifts they were planning to give their wives would fulfill their wives' expectations and meet their high standards of quality and aesthetics. Indeed, were husbands even capable of selecting and purchasing presents commensurate with their wives' newly elevated plane of existence?[14]

What did this concern with male adequacy mean? First, it suggested that men were uncertain that they could provide for their families. Their uncertainty had a basis in reality, stemming not only from the high rate of male unemployment during the Depression, but also from the significant competition for jobs they encountered from women. The story of women's relative economic gains during the 1930s is not very well known Even in the midst of the economic chaos of the Depression, many women found increased opportunities for employment. Some of their success was due to their willingness to work at lower wages than men, because they were less unionized. But because of their success in the job market, many laboring women were offered union membership for the first time. Unions feared that if women were not admitted, they would constitute a vast ununionized labor pool from which employers would hire, thereby placing great pressure on organized labor. In addition, for the first time, women assumed legal ownership of the vast majority of the nation's wealth. During the 1930s surveys showed that women had come to own roughly 70 percent of the financial resources of the nation, mainly because of their longer life expectancy. This was a matter of some concern to magazine writers, who were only slightly mollified by the fact that women did not usually exercise day-to-day control over their assets.[15]

There was also a sexual dimension to husbands' concern over the adequacy of their gifts to their wives. The most striking aspect of this dimension was the lack of confidence by males in the ads and articles of the Depression decade, and the concomitant rise in the self-assurance of women. One ad pointedly asked husbands, "Will your gift measure up?" An underlying phallic reference seems obvious. This theme of sexual inadequacy, combined with the ritziness and aloofness of women in the 1930s, suggests that men were becoming intimidated by women. The

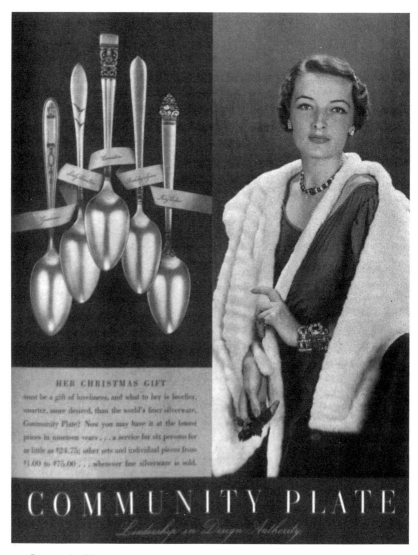

44. Community Plate silver plate, *LHJ*, 53 (Dec. 1936): 93.

Plate 35. No flappers here. The ideal woman of the 1930s was older and ritzier than her predecessor had been. She was also more passive than the active woman of the '20s.

45. Cadillac LaSalle automobiles, *SEP*, 210 (18 Dec. 1937): 35. Reprinted with the permission of Cadillac Motor Car Division, General Motor Corporation.

46. RCA Victrola records, *SEP*, 211 (10 Dec. 1938): 64.

Plate 36. The ideal woman of the 1930s was aloof from men and showed none of the playful sexiness of the flapper. How were men to woo this superior creature? At Christmas, men wondered whether their presents would measure up to their wives' high standards, revealing their underlying sense of inadequacy during the Great Depression.

47. 1847 Rogers Bros. silver plate, *LHJ*, 53 (Dec. 1936): 82.

48. Community Plate silver plate, *SEP*,   49. Coty perfume, *LHJ*, 55 (Dec. 1938): 79.
209 (5 Dec. 1936): 72.

Plate 37. During the 1930s, the ideal woman was so superior to men that the Christmas gifts she received were regarded as tribute. The lofty male egos of the first thirty years of the century had been brought low by the economic devastation of the Depression, while women enjoyed some relative economic gains.

doubts of husbands about whether they could provide for their families
in economic matters apparently generated doubts as well about their
ability to satisfy their wives sexually.[16]

One might think that changes in the image of men in advertisements
would correspond to changes in the image of women. However, what is
striking is the independence of those two images, with each having its
own history.

Between 1900 and 1920, Christmas gifts to husbands were selected
from a relatively narrow range of items, narrower than those from which
the wives' gifts were chosen. The range of appropriate men's gifts was
small because of the prevailing ideal for wifely behavior around the turn
of the century. The ideal wife was to focus her attention on the home,
isolating herself from the world outside and remaining ignorant of it; this
world included her husband's occupational activities. After all, the male-
dominated business world was assumed to be so complicated that it was
beyond the limited comprehension of housewives.[17]

As a result of wives' supposed ignorance of what went on in the outside
world, they were precluded from selecting Christmas gifts for their spouses
that could have aided them substantially in their jobs. It would have been
presumptuous and inappropriate for wives to give their husbands any of
a wide range of practical gift items designed to improve their job performance, such as ledgers, office chairs, adding machines, and cash registers.
If such practical gifts seem absurd, we need recall only that, after 1910,
many husbands thought they were qualified enough to judge what their
wives needed to perform *their* "occupational" tasks and gave them thoroughly practical appliances—stoves, electric refrigerators, vacuum cleaners,
and toasters. Ideal wives were not only discouraged from getting their
husbands items to aid them in their jobs, but they were also advised to be
circumspect in selecting tools for the home, lest they appear presumptuous about that area of male expertise. Home furnishings were also considered inappropriate as gifts for men, because it was assumed they cared
little about them.[18]

The problem for gift-giving wives was that these constraints left them
with very few choices. One possibility was to buy something that would
improve the man's appearance, for example, cuff links and watch chains;
this created no problems, as wives were supposed to be experts in matters
relating to appearance. Another type of acceptable gift was one that

50. Shirley President suspenders, *LHJ*, 29 (Dec. 1912): 64.

Plate 38. Women's domain was the home, and they made it a refuge from the harsh outside world. Because they focused on domestic matters, women were expected to have only limited knowledge of other matters. So at Christmastime they could select their gifts to men from only a narrow range of items. Gifts to men became so standardized that this woman could feel confident about giving suspenders to nine (perhaps all) of her male recipients—in obvious disregard of their individual preferences.

51. Paris garters, *SEP*, 194 (3 Dec. 1921): 90.

Plate 39. Gifts that women gave to men were selected from a few types of standard items that improved personal appearance, comfort, and grooming, about which women were recognized as authorities. Because of the standardization of men's gifts, the individual desires of various male recipients became irrelevant and could be disregarded. Therefore, each man could be given the same type of gift; here it is Paris garters.

52. Gillette razors, *LHJ*, 29 (Dec. 1912): 57.

53. Bondy hair brushes, *SEP*, 173 (8 Dec. 1900): 16.

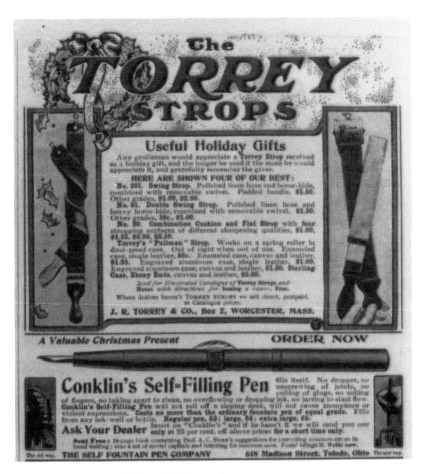

54. Torrey razor strops, *SEP*, 173 (7 Dec. 1901): 29.
55. Conklin's self-filling pens, *SEP*, 174 (7 Dec. 1901): 29.

Plate 40. Men received what seemed to them an unending stream of unimaginative, trite gifts at Christmas. And no wonder! Women were limited in their choices to a few types of items, such as these razors, hairbrushes, strops, and pens.

would contribute to a man's physical comfort, such as suspenders and garters. These items said very little about the content of a marital relationship, except that the wife preferred that her husband be comfortable rather than uncomfortable. Another acceptable gift, the watch, was markedly more expensive than the other two types. Watches symbolized a

Lord Elgin

HE gift that a man delights to receive and show. What a happy present to give husband, son or brother! With your picture inside the case!
    Men of affairs—of power and prestige—own this watch. And their reliance on its faithfulness is well founded. For a lifetime it runs true. A marvel of preciseness and beauty. The thinnest watch made in America. 15 and 17 jewels. Solid gold and 25-year filled cases. Prices range from $25 to $75. Examine it at your jeweler's.
    ELGIN NATIONAL WATCH CO., Elgin, Illinois.

THE WATCHWORD IS "ELGIN"

56. Elgin watches, *LHJ*, 28 (Dec. 1911): 76.

Plate 41. While most of the Christmas gifts that women presented to men were inexpensive, one expensive type of item, the watch, was sometimes chosen. Good watches discretely symbolized their owners' success in business (as well as their concern with punctuality), and were important male status symbols before 1920.

certain level of economic success attained by men in their careers and were an important, albeit discrete, vehicle for displaying that success. They also indicated their owners' concern with punctuality, precision, and the wise use of time, all of which were important to businessmen.[19]
    All told, the types of items deemed appropriate for men were fewer

than those for women. Husbands, not surprisingly, complained that the gifts they received were boring, trite, and predictable. In 1911 a male writer, apparently no longer patient with his annual gift of cheap cigars, had the "Maw" of his article ask her daughter, "Well, Ellie, what'll we get fer Paw?" as she looks "up from a pile o' packages." The matter is decided in an instant: " 'Why, se-gars, o'course, maw,' says Ellie." They got Paw "a nice fancy box full o' dried-out, shiny, vaneered, short-filler, 'samantha'-wrapped perfectos. . . . On Christmas mornin' when Paw takes one an' bites int' it th' dust flies just like steppin' on a dried puff-ball in th' woods, an' when he lights it it smells jist like a G string burnin' up. . . . An' Paw falls back in his chair while th' se-gar burns up like a load o' hay." Cigars were certainly not the only targets of men's dissatis-faction. A writer in 1924 noted:

Jokes about slippers and neckties as Christmas gifts fill the newspapers every year, yet they probably continue to be among the ten best sellers during the holiday season. I seldom fail to get at least three pairs of slippers, although two years ago I got only two pairs and a half. One of the bundles contained but one slipper. I was inclined to think that the giver had done it purposely, and that she would send the other slipper the following Christmas. It never came, so probably it was an error on the part of the store clerk. It made no difference. I had more than enough slippers that year and have had ever since I can remember.[20]

Men's boredom over their gifts conveyed an important message to their families. It told them that the husbands regarded themselves as being more sophisticated than other family members. Their blasé attitude toward the items they received told their wives that their selections were uncrea-tive, even if kind. The boredom implied that wives were too far removed from the world to delight or enlighten their husbands with novel or sophisticated material goods. In addition, the husbands' apathy served to preserve the hegemony they obtained from being breadwinners during the year. The debts that other family members owed husbands and fathers for their year-long support were at stake when husbands were given Christmas gifts. To the extent that men acknowledged a gift to be exciting or gratifying, they cancelled some of the accumulated debt. On the other hand, if they showed indifference, it indicated that the debts were not substantially reduced.

But how could Christmas gifts to men possibly reduce the debts owed them by other family members when the shopping money came from the men? It was as if men gave the presents to themselves, a quality that stripped them of economic weight. The economic weightlessness of gifts to men was further reinforced by the prevailing guidelines for their selection: first, they should have only small value; and second, they should cost less than the gifts men gave to others. In sum, far from canceling the year's debts, gifts between men and their families actually served to increase them.

During the 1920s, Christmas gifts to men changed in two important respects: they became more expensive, and they were of higher quality. Both of these changes are evident in presents of men's clothing. The small clothing items that had been popular before World War I—handkerchiefs, ties, garters, and suspenders—continued to be given in upgraded form after the war, but they were supplemented by more expensive articles such as dress shirts and overcoats. Ad writers offered no apologies for higher prices; indeed, they did not even discuss them. They simply stressed the luxuriousness of products, and that their high quality would attract attention to the wearer.[21]

The purpose of giving these items was to improve men's appearance, which became of heightened concern to them. Husbands received toiletry items such as men's cologne and grooming aids such as the safety razor in any of its constantly "improved" versions. Men wanted better-quality apparel, and began to use clothing as a means of display. Since 1800 Americans had believed that men should avoid showing their wealth by the clothes they wore and exhibit a reserved, financially conservative appearance. With regard to apparel, men were able to display their wealth only through the clothes they bought for their wives. However, during the 1920s, it once again became appropriate for men to use their own clothes for display. The ideal of male appearance was no longer the inconspicuously attired businessman, but rather the snappy Arrow Collar Man.[22]

Ad writers encouraged men to adopt current fashions, to become sensitive to style. Men should discard dated garments whether or not they had some useful life left, thereby placing stylishness over thriftiness. All told, the men's gift items that became popular during the 1920s reflected the new set of dominant values in American culture: consumption values. These values encouraged Americans to purchase goods that displayed their wealth.[23]

Men's fondness for the 1920s consumption items declined with the onset of the Depression, when they lost their interest in displaying what-

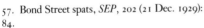

57. Bond Street spats, *SEP*, 202 (21 Dec. 1929):   58. Emery silk shirts, *SEP*, 193 (11 Dec.
84.   1920): 129.

Plate 42. In the 1920s, men showed increased concern with their appearance, and preferred
high-quality clothes, such as spats and silk shirts, over the unremarkable garments they had
previously worn. High-quality clothes were intended to show off the prosperity of the
wearer, a goal that was consistent with the consumption values of the postwar decade.

ever of their wealth had survived the economic collapse. Ads showed less
concern with personal appearance than they had during the 1920s and
returned to the early twentieth-century emphasis on practicality. However, all was not déjà vu. A new twist in Depression ads was the emphasis

59. Kuppenheimer overcoats, *SEP*, 195 (2 Dec. 1922): inside front cover.

Plate 43. During the 1920s, confident, young, style-conscious men, as portrayed here in Arrow Collar ads, were the masculine ideal. Men's heightened concern with style and good appearance not only reflected the new consumption values of the decade, but also helped men achieve the older goal of business success.

on the durability of suggested gift items. Givers apparently wanted assurances that items they presented would give pleasure to their recipients for years to come. This need for the assurance that a gift item, a form of property, would survive into the distant future was doubtless comforting to those who had lost much of their property—sometimes in bewildering ways—during the 1930s.[24]

The emphasis on practicality and durability of property during the 1930s reflects a temporary weakening of consumption values in American culture. Expensive types of gift items, such as overcoats, fell out of favor leaving the less expensive old standbys such as ties, garters, suspenders, razors, pipe tobacco, and socks to dominate the men's gift field. Consistent with the new climate of opinion, ads began to stress that the items they promoted were sensibly priced, and that their purchase reflected good economic judgment. This argument must have been doubly appealing in the wake of the demonstrable unsoundness of other purchases such as stocks. It played on the very strong public sentiment for order and control in economic matters as a response to the Depression.[25]

Christmas gifts to men were strikingly different from gifts to women. For example, the joyful scenes in ads immediately following World War I— ads in which women were shown delighting in gifts from their providing husbands—had no parallel in ads for gifts to men. Of course, during the 1920s, both men and women became fond of consumption items. But in the 1930s, the ritzy and aloof women of the ads were not the logical companions to the level-headed, cost-conscious males of the Depression decade. Indeed, who could have foreseen the ritzy, aloof woman as an ideal during the economic hardship of the 1930s? Instances such as this should caution us against over-generalizing about Christmas gifts exchanged by spouses, as well as those exchanged by others. Each type of exchange must be analyzed separately.

CHAPTER 8

"Something for the Kid": Gifts from Parents to Children

For centuries, Christmas has been a special time of the year for children, a time when the young received special consideration from their elders. Between 1800 and 1880, when the celebration first became significant in America, parents in most homes lessened their usual restraints on children's behavior, allowing them to enjoy special freedoms. For example, children could stay up past their customary bedtimes and eat sweets in larger-than-normal quantities. Furthermore, those children who transgressed were subjected only to lessened sanctions.[1]

As an additional way to make the holidays more pleasant for children, parents gave them presents from themselves and on behalf of that wondrous figure, Santa Claus. Between 1800 and 1880, parents usually gave handmade toys, small articles of clothing, books, edible treats, and inexpensive trinkets. These early gifts were smaller in size and monetary value compared to the gifts that came to dominate parent-to-child exchanges after 1880. They were usually handmade by parents, and their technology was uncomplicated. Because the gift items were relatively simple, children readily understood how they worked, unlike the case of the mechanically complex presents that have dominated these exchanges since 1880.[2] Although I have characterized children's gifts during the first eighty years of the nineteenth century as simple and inexpensive, the excited young recipients of those presents doubtless regarded them as impressive and exciting compared to earlier gifts.

Christmas presents given to young people, along with the loosened restraints on their behavior, had intrinsic value to their recipients. Toys promised hours of entertainment, edible treats delighted their tastebuds, and increased freedom meant that they did not have to exert their normal efforts at self-control. In addition, they indicated to children that their parents' usual authority over family property and over their behavior would be minimized during the holidays. The seasonal lessening of parental authority provided relief from the tensions parental authority inevitably produced and enshrouded the parent-child relationship in a benevolent seasonal glow.[3]

If the authority of parents was minimized during the holidays, it was not totally absent. Parents used one mechanism in particular, the Santa Claus myth, to maintain some control over their offspring at Christmas. The myth restrained children because it taught that Santa Claus would give them presents only if they were good; if they were bad, Santa would leave them only switches and ashes. Today's parents still tell their children this, but between 1800 and 1880 the threat was carried out more frequently than it would be thereafter. The Santa Claus of the first eighty years of the nineteenth century both rewarded and punished children. A writer of 1906 noted that in recent years Santa had grown

more gentle and forbearing with the children. We may say: "Now, Kenneth, unless you are a very much better little boy than you have been, Old Santy will not being you anything. No drum, no express-wagon, not a single thing." Yet I take notice that naughty, perverse Kenneth, who kicks and screams with temper, gets just as many pretty toys on Christmas eve from the fat saint as Dorothy, who never answers saucily and always does what she is told. Not so very many years ago bad children used to find lumps of coal in their stockings on Christmas morning. A century or so ago, if we may trust old German prints, he used to whip the naughty boys; and still more anciently, he scourged the first-born son, be he well or ill behaved.[4]

The punishing side of the early Santa is evident in an 1837 painting of the jolly saint by West Point artist Robert Walter Weir, in which Santa carries a pack that contains both toys and switches. For one of Weir's offspring, the symbolism of the switches was specific and ominous: a stocking hanging from the mantle carried the initials of Weir's eldest son and contained a switch—a stark comment on that child's behavior. Santa had an elfish physiognomy and a mischievous demeanor to complement his switches.[5]

60. The Weir painting of Santa Claus. Courtesy of the New-York Historical Society, N.Y.C.

Plate 44. This was the Santa of the early nineteenth century: small, elfish, and mischievous. Also, he had a prominent punishing side, symbolized here in the switches he placed in one of the stockings. This side was not significant in the later, tall, genial, modern Santa.

The punishing side of the nineteenth-century American Santa Claus had its roots in the European past, where we find it portrayed even more sharply than in antebellum America. The Old World had two separate holiday figures—one who rewarded children while the other one punished them. St. Nicholas, the rewarder, first questioned the child; then, if he decided that the child's behavior for the year had been good, gave him a small present. However, accompanying the saint was an intimidating figure known as Ruprecht or Pelznickel. Ostensibly, Ruprecht's job was to drive Santa's wagon, but his more important task was to punish the children judged by the saint to have been bad. According to firsthand accounts, unruly children were actually switched or given coals by villagers who played the role of Ruprecht.[6]

About 1880, gift-giving patterns that had prevailed earlier in the nineteenth century began to change. Parents now presented manufactured gift items to children at Christmas, as part of the general shift toward presenting them to all recipients. As already discussed in chapter 3, the shift was caused by the rapid expansion of America's manufacturing capacity during the last third of the century, and by the need of urban wage laborers to purchase gift items quickly because of their lack of free time. This shift in gift giving was most striking in presentations to children because they had received the bulk of the earlier handmade gifts.[7]

Not only were the new toys produced by machines, but they were complex machines in their own right. For example, small, spring-driven trains were introduced into the toy market in the late nineteenth century and, after the turn of the century, they were joined by similarly powered model cars. The mechanical complexity of new items such as these were of concern to social observers. For example, Edward Bok, the influential editor of the *Ladies' Home Journal*, argued in 1902 that

the modern mechanical toy is, to my mind, nothing short of a modern abomination. . . . [The child] is to play with these toys and, pray, as an honest question, where does the spirit of play come in? The child is at first curious to learn the secret of how the toy is made to go, and he is interested until he masters it. Then, after he has learned to wind it up, what is his part in the game? Purely to look on, to see the contrivance go—a pretty wearisome process. . . . Watch the average healthy, normal child with a mechanical toy, and you will quickly see for yourself that the temptation is to drop the toy as soon as its mechanism is mastered. The child has no further use for it. There is no foothold for the child's imagination, and instinctively he turns to something else. And to what? To something simple—generally to something constructive. Look at the game of blocks and see how it has outlived all other forms of amusement. Why? Because the child can do something with blocks: he can build with them: he can make things.

Some particularly inquisitive children went beyond merely looking on, beyond seeing the contrivance go, but this course of action invariably came to a bad end, as Bok noted in a 1905 editorial:

Occasionally a child investigates the mechanism of his plaything, but always with bad results to the toy. The machinery, cheap or delicate, as the case may be, is not equal to the demands put upon it by the small investigator. And the plaything becomes useless, for a child will not play with a broken toy, especially a mechanical one, if he can possibly help it.[8]

Whereas Bok objected to the fact that mechanical toys fostered passivity and boredom in young recipients, the naturalist John Burroughs objected to the new toys on different grounds. In a 1906 article he argued that the new custom of showering children with these playthings at Christmas

corrupts their simplicity; it stimulates their destructiveness; it sates and blunts their curiosity and hastens the time of their general discontent with life. We try at the onset to destroy their interest in the plain and wholesome things of life by the multitude of strange and startling devices we shower upon them. We would have them believe that the world is one great toy shop made simply for their amusement. We create a false taste, a craving for ceaseless novelty, everything new everyday, every hour. The last surprise only sharpens their appetite for a greater, till they go from blonde dolls to brunette dolls, or to Japanese or negro dolls, and from jumping-jack to jumping-jack with utter weariness and disquiet. . . . Why sophisticate them? Why foster a craving for novelty and variety that life cannot satisfy. By and by they will cry for the moon or the stars. What are we going to do then? . . . We do not seek to excite or intoxicate them with the strange, the bizarre, the extraordinary. Let them alone. If their craving for novelty is stimulated there is danger that they will find life flat, stale and unprofitable.[9]

Thus Burroughs and Bok reached the same conclusion, but for different reasons. Burroughs believed that children's boredom followed from their having been unnaturally overexcited by the novel items, while Bok thought that it stemmed from their passive role in playing with such toys. The contention that mechanical toys bored children was the most common criticism of this new type of gift.

Other criticisms were close behind. Most agreed that they were overly

61. Ives toys, *SEP*, 184 (2 Dec. 1911): 56.

Plate 45. Throughout most of the nineteenth century, the American economy had been directed toward producing essential items: food, shelter, and clothing. However, after 1880, with the emergence of an economy of abundance, manufacturers turned some of their productive capacity to making nonessential items as mechanical toys for children. Although commentators expressed reservations about the effects of the new toys on children, consumers exhibited no such reservations and enthusiastically purchased the new playthings.

expensive and that parents gave their children too many of them. The writer of a satirical article in 1911 recalled

> how difficult I was to please when I was a boy. I remember how I threw myself flat on the floor and howled with rage because I had set my heart on a gingerbread cat with pink fur of frosting, and when I dug the cat out of my stocking it had blue sugar-sand fur. . . . My howls spoiled the day for the whole family. I must have been a little wretch. . . .
>
> How different it is with the children of today. No more crying over gingerbread cats! Little Mortimer, next door to us, had one of those severe disappointments last Christmas, but he did not drop on the floor and howl. Not at all. He walked around the automobile that his father had given him—they had the Christmas tree in the side yard, because an automobile is too large to take into the house—and kicked the tires to see if they were properly inflated. He examined the upholstery of the car, took a brief look at the magneto, the lamps, all the trimmings. All he said was, "Pretty punk!" No howling. No fit of rage. He merely walked around the car, with one hand in his pocket, and repeated in a low disgusted tone: "Pretty punk! Pretty punk!" Then he opened the hood and looked at the engine. A shade of deep annoyance passed across his face. "Doesn't little Morty like the pretty automobile Santa Claus has brought him?" his mother asked anxiously. "Well, all I've got to say," said Mortimer, "is that if I have to drive a four-cylinder machine when everyone is driving a six, the other kids will have the laugh on me." Then he turned to his father. "Dad," he asked, "what did they stick you for this junk?" His father blushed with shame. Who would not? . . .
>
> What is the matter with the modern child, anyway? Whence this sophistication? Why, my dear mister and madam, it comes from you and me. Don't blame little Mortimer or little Susie. The children are at heart as sweet and as easily satisfied as you and I were, but we pile gifts on them, and heap gifts on them, and smother good old Santa Claus, with his gingerbread cat, under heaps of silk and gold. Bless your heart, we have made of Christmas a mere occasion for showing off before our little ones, bragging with big gifts.[10]

Many other writers joined this one in the belief that the new pattern of Christmas gift giving to children was spoiling them. They warned that the result would be a materialistic and self-centered citizenry when the children reached adulthood.

So much for the commentary. If we look at what people were doing rather than at what they were saying, we get a very different picture. In marketplaces across the country, mechanical gift items enjoyed great popularity both with gift givers and recipients after 1880. The direction that gift giving was taking was clear, notwithstanding the nostalgic longings of magazine writers for the simpler presents of their childhoods.

The high cost and increased number of Christmas gifts that parents gave their children after 1880 paralleled changes in the personality and physiognomy of Santa Claus. Just as the new gift-giving system placed greater emphasis on rewarding children, the figure of Santa became more rewarding than the switching, ashes-leaving Santa of the early nineteenth century. The new Santa left toys and treats for virtually all children, regardless of their behavior during the year. Along with his new practice of rewarding almost every child was a greater joviality and kindness in his demeanor; his earlier punishing and mischievous side became suppressed. At the same time, Santa changed physically. He became significantly taller, but more importantly, his body became softer, a striking change from both the elfish figure of the early nineteenth century and the tall, thin St. Nicholas of Europe.[11]

The emergence of the modern, jolly, plump Santa began with Dr. Clement Moore's classic holiday poem, "A Visit from St. Nicholas," written in 1822. Although Moore's Santa retains some of the characteristics of the earlier form of the figure—for example, the name of St. Nicholas and his description as an elf—he is, for the first time, made to be jolly and plump:

> He had a broad face and a little round belly
> That shook, when he laughed, like a bowl full of jelly.
> He was chubby and plump—a right jolly old elf;
> And I laughed when I saw him, in spite of myself.

The poem had a powerful influence on the development of the Santa icon. A writer in 1925 noted that "it was Clement C. Moore who made him into the fat, genial soul he is now known to be throughout America." And, in 1919, another writer observed that "since Clement Moore wrote his 'Night Before Christmas' [sic] . . . an adjustable Santa Claus is no longer possible. . . . His nose—in spite of the anti-saloon league—must continue to be red. His whiskers must be of the correct hirsute length. His stomach must describe the proper Yuletide curve." Despite this comment, a few adjustments would later be made in Santa's appearance. Nevertheless, the importance of "A Visit from St. Nicholas" in setting forth the fundamental themes of the Santa Claus myth prompted an author in 1937 to observe that "when the Professor wrote about the stockings hung by the chimney and the jolly manners of the droll Saint, American Christmas belles lettres began (like Greek literature) with its epic."[12]

In spite of the vividness and popularity of Moore's verbal description
of St. Nicholas, some of Santa's features were not set until the 1860s. In
1863, Thomas Nast, the famous political cartoonist, produced a series of
drawings for *Harper's Weekly* that defined, finally, how the jolly saint must
look. Nast's Santas, as portrayed in American magazines and on Christmas cards over several decades, were of average adult height, and were
called Santa Claus rather than St. Nicholas. The use of this appellation,
though it did not originate with Nast, reflects the increasing seculariza-
tion of the figure. Also gone—along with the religious name of St.
Nicholas—were the mitre, staff, and bishop's robe that had adorned the
European St. Nicholas.[13]

The Nast Santa—plump, jolly, rewarding, secular, and of normal
adult height—has remained the modern standard, though there have
been some variations in the costumes used by persons who have masquer-
aded as Santa Claus. Moreover, there has been a fundamental change in
the type of person who played Santa at Christmas, and in the locales
where he is seen.

Between 1865 and 1900, the majority of Americans lived in rural and
small-town environments and could draw on only a limited pool of people
to play Santa. Most of those who assumed the role during the last thirty-
five years of the nineteenth century were either relatives or close friends
of the families for whom they played Santa. In some households, the
father reserved for himself the joys of donning the red costume. In any
event, the actors were persons whom children would almost certainly
have recognized had they been out of costume. In order to conceal their
familiar faces, the Santas wore masks of flesh-colored, wax-coated cloth
with holes for the eyes and mouth and attached white whiskers. Around
their bodies they wrapped simple togas of red muslin or felt, with regular
pants, not costume pants, underneath. Some Santas covered their shoes
with high black boots of felt or waxed cloth. Compared to disguises of
later Santas, those worn by Santas in the late nineteenth century were
crude and of poor quality, perhaps because they were purchased by
individual Christmas celebrants for limited, private use.[14]

The crudeness and poor quality of these costumes—especially the
stiffness of the masks—might have made them unconvincing to children.
However, children have vivid imaginations and considerable powers of
belief, especially when they stand to benefit. In addition, most of these
youngsters had lived all their lives in rural or small-town surroundings

Merry Christmas

62. The Nast Santa Claus.

Plate 46. Thomas Nast set the standard for how Santa should be represented visually in a series of drawings following the Civil War. His Santa was as tall as a normal-sized adult, and would have towered over the elfish Santa of the early nineteenth century. Children appreciated that his earlier punishing side was no longer in evidence.

and were probably not as sophisticated as urban children would have been. We don't know what they believed or didn't believe, as they left virtually no contemporaneous statements in the historical record.

Around 1900 the American Christmas celebration—along with most other facets of American culture—began to become urbanized and produced a new style of Santa Claus: the "street-corner" or "department-store" Santa. It was this new-style Santa whom the nation's children encountered most frequently during Christmas seasons after the turn of the century. The main difference between street-corner Santas and their domestic predecessors was that the former were hired and paid to assume the role, usually by retail establishments, charitable groups, or civic organizations. The red-suited employees were stationed on business-district street corners or inside stores for the entire holiday season. Because they spent a longer time in the role than had the domestic Santas, many of them became comfortable as St. Nicholas and developed polished techniques for dealing with the variety of children they encountered.[15]

Street-corner Santas were well received by the public and the demand for their services rose steadily during the early twentieth century. By 1937 the demand for Santas prompted the founding of the first Santa training school, located in Albion, New York, which was soon followed by similar schools across the nation. By 1954 there were at least three such schools in New York City alone. Santa schools instructed their students in Santa lore, proper appearance and demeanor, and techniques for handling common, difficult situations.[16]

Street-corner Santas wore full uniforms consisting of red pants, a red jacket, and black boots. The costumes were of better quality than those of domestic Santas, primarily because of economic considerations: since the suits received heavy use, purchasing well-made outfits made good economic sense, and the large organizations that usually hired Santas could well afford them. In addition, street-corner Santas changed the way they disguised their faces. They attached the obligatory whiskers directly to their faces, a technique that gave flexibility and "life" to their faces, but did not disguise them as well as masks would have. Perhaps street-corner Santas dared to use these whiskers as their only facial disguise because they generally did not know the children for whom they performed. In the cities, there was little danger that children would recognize them. Although the disguises of street-corner Santas were more realistic than the earlier disguises, they did not necessarily produce a higher level of belief among the children who saw them. The credence accorded the two styles of costumes remains an open question.[17]

In spite of the popularity of street-corner Santas, they were not free from criticism. In 1928 managers of a large New York department store announced that they would no longer employ a Santa because they felt that only a small group—namely, very young children—still believed in the myth, and because a "Santa Claus Headquarters" would take up valuable floor space. Others began to complain, beginning in the 1920s, that there were too many Santas in business districts at Christmas time. By 1937 the Salvation Army discontinued its use of Santa Clauses because it thought that their proliferation had aroused the suspicions of children. Expressing this same concern, the City Council of Boston in 1948 requested that their mayor limit the number of Santas in the city to only one, and locate that one on the Boston Common.[18]

Such actions were indicative of a more general debate during the first four decades of the century over whether the Santa Claus myth should be perpetuated at all. What, Americans began to ask, were the long-range consequences of the myth for the nation's children? One group of citizens thought that its perpetuation should be discouraged. Within that group, some opposed the myth because they believed it encouraged children to think about presents they would receive rather than about the "true religious meaning" of the festival. Others did not like the fact that parents had to lie to their children to perpetuate the Santa myth. The children's inevitable discovery of that deception, they thought, surely disillusioned them and irreparably damaged their trust in their parents. In 1900 Jacob Riis gave a vivid description of the reaction of his childhood fellows to their discovery that they had been deceived:

We sulked like young larks beneath a cloudy sky. We became wicked, like an orphan nation suddenly bereft of its gods and institutions. Our faith shrunk as when a morning glory looks upon the sun. Our doubts enlarged upon us, and we soured into miniatures of despair. We gave up our reindeer with a sigh. We looked at the North Pole upon our tearstained map (an area that we had heretofore regarded as sacred), and sneered wisely. If there was no Santa Claus there could be no North Pole!—when we set our heads to it we could be as logical as any other materialists. . . .

This doubt of Santa Claus marked the beginning of our downfall from the high estate of childhood. We were never the same afterward. Our good fairies stared at us reproachfully from remote distances. The funnel of our chimney became commonplace; and we became merely secular; losing sight of our divinities one by one as we traveled further from the fireside where Santa Claus performed our first miracles.[19]

While some Americans wanted to do away with the Santa Claus myth altogether, others wanted to perpetuate it, but within defined parameters. For example, writers noted with concern that Santa Claus and Jesus were sometimes mixed up in children's minds, and one was horrified to hear his young daughter praying to Santa. In order to clear up such confusion, they favored a strong emphasis on the differences between the two holiday figures and discouraged such practices as talking about Santa Claus in Sunday school.

Others favored the perpetuation of the myth if parents could be more truthful with their children. They suggested that parents explain to their children that Santa Claus was not a real person, that he was "make believe," after which they could, with some moral justification, still convey the story and pretend with their children that the myth was true. Parents could also tell their children that Santa Claus was an idea, the spirit of kindness and generosity. (One can only guess how attuned the excited youngsters would be to the tenets of philosophical idealism.) The best-known expression of this solution is the open letter written in 1897 by Francis Church, a writer for the *New York Sun*, in response to a query from a young reader. It begins with the famous line: "Yes, Virginia, there is a Santa Claus," and continues:

He exists as certainly as love and generosity and devotion exist, and you know that they abound and give to our life its highest beauty and joy. Alas! how dreary would be the world if there were no Santa Claus! It would be as dreary as if there were no Virginias. There would be no childlike faith then, no poetry, no romance, to make tolerable this existence. We should have no enjoyment except in sense and sight.[20]

If some Americans wanted to abolish the Santa Claus myth and others wanted to modify it, still others wanted to perpetuate the myth unchanged. They looked at the criticisms leveled by the others and concluded that the problems they cited were not serious enough to warrant changing a custom that was dear to their hearts. They thought that the children's belief in Santa did not usually diminish their appreciation of the religious significance of the holiday. The little ones could love both Jesus and St. Nick at the same time. They further argued that parents' deception of their children through the myth did little, if any, harm and that any disillusionment that occurred was more than offset by the happiness that belief in the myth engendered.[21]

This wish to perpetuate an unchanged Santa Claus myth was exemplified not only by the actions of the Salvation Army and the Boston City Council, but also by those of the Santa Claus Association. This association was formed in 1914 in New York City for the express purpose of preserving children's belief in St. Nick. Its main activity was to pick up letters from the post office which New York City children had mailed to Santa; the association's six thousand donors would then fulfill the Christmas wishes expressed in the letters. The idea spread rapidly across the country, and within two years of the founding of the New York association, citizens in nineteen other cities had established similar organizations. The original New York group remained active until 1928, when postal authorities refused to continue to turn over the Santa letters.[22]

The modern pattern of gift giving has been dominant since 1880, and within it, there have always been significant differences between the gifts received by boys and girls. Gifts to boys encouraged them to be physically active, to be morally upright, and to exhibit a "manly" demeanor. Writers in periodicals agreed that boys "worth their salt" were "gogetters." As an expression of this ideal, young males received bicycles, sleds, ice skates, rifles, and pocket knives at Christmas, and ads for boys' books and magazines promised that they would instill "true manly sportsmanship."[23]

Parents' encouragement of their sons to be vigorous and manly was partly a continuation of the self-made man ideal that had guided the nation's males since 1830. Even though Americans had already been encouraging boys to be vigorous and manly, between 1890 and 1920, they placed an especially strong emphasis on these two traits. Writers cajoled boys to conduct themselves, to the best of their ability, like the successful men around them. They should strive to become prosperous, responsible "men of affairs" and eschew any effort to prolong their childhoods. For example, an ad writer in 1913 suggested that a gift of a Howard watch to "the boy" would show his parents' high hopes for him and would express their "expectation for him and the work he is to do in the world" as it is "the watch of successful Americans."[24]

In large part, this heightened emphasis on vigor and manliness after 1890 stemmed from the widely held but erroneous belief that the Western

63. Winslow's skates, *SEP*, 185 (14 Dec. 1912): 29.

Plate 47. Between 1900 and 1930, cultural leaders strongly encouraged boys to be vigorous, a style of living that they thought was vital to well being and America's success following the closing of the frontier during the 1890s.

64. Iver Johnson bicycles, *SEP*, 185 (7 Dec. 1912): 60.

frontier had closed. Americans thought that, with its closing, males would no longer be able to struggle against a rugged natural environment to develop, test, and prove their virility. Because the struggle of boys and men with the West was the source of the most desireable and characteristic American traits, the closing of the frontier also augured ill for the future of the country.[25]

In an effort to avoid national decline, late nineteenth-century parents began to present their sons with such manly outdoor items as B-B guns and rifles at Christmas. A 1902 Stevens rifle ad told readers that "every boy should be taught how to handle a firearm and parents should encourage them in an out-of-doors life." A 1911 ad showed a young boy in the woods stalking nothing less than a large bobcat with his new .22 caliber Remington rifle. Just in case the small-bore rifle and large, deadly prey were not enough to project a sense of adventure, the ad also showed an Indian lurking in the background. The future well-being of the nation apparently hinged on a continuing line of wild-game hunters cultivated

The Howard Watch

One very good way to show your affection and your high hope for the boy is to give him a HOWARD Watch for Christmas.

The HOWARD means so much more than the giving. It pledges the young man to a fine tradition. It expresses so well your expectation for him and the work he is to do in the world.

To own a HOWARD Watch is to be in distinguished company. The HOWARD is identified with the life and history of prominent Americans ever since 1842. It is pre-eminently the watch of successful Americans today.

A HOWARD Watch is always worth what you pay for it.

The price of each watch is *fixed* at the factory and a printed ticket attached—from the 17-jewel (*double roller*) in a Crescent *Extra* or Boss *Extra* gold-filled case at $40, to the 23-jewel at $150—and the EDWARD HOWARD model at $350.

Not every jeweler can sell you a HOWARD Watch. Find the HOWARD jeweler in your town and talk to him. He is a good man to know. Admiral Sigsbee has written a little book, "The Log of the HOWARD Watch," giving the record of his own HOWARD in the U.S. Navy. You'll enjoy it. Drop us a post card, Dept. N, and we'll send you a copy.

E. HOWARD WATCH WORKS
BOSTON, MASS.

Canadian Wholesale Depot: Lumsden Bldg., Toronto

65. Howard watches, *SEP*, 186 (13 Dec. 1913): 34.

Plate 48. Between 1900 and 1930, boys were encouraged to adopt manly behaviors rather than cling to their youth. This boy, on the verge of manhood, is being given a firm maternal push toward growing up.

from the ranks of the young. In another ad of the same year, a young recipient of a Daisy air rifle boasted that his new gun "looks just like father's" and that "Mother likes it because she says it's safe and father because it is just the thing to keep me out of mischief and to teach me to be manly and self-reliant. I guess Father's right because I feel just like a regular hunter when I get into the woods with my Daisy." For boys too young for an air rifle, the ad suggested Daisy pop guns.[26]

Because Americans believed that the frontier was the source of men's virility, they were especially anxious that urban boys not become effete. A Maxim gun silencer ad of 1911 showed an urban boy firing a rifle at a target he had set up inside the city, with the urban skyline clearly visible in the background behind the target. According to the ad, a major benefit of a silencer is that "it enables him to set up a target in the yard and gain many short opportunities to shoot which he has not had because of the noise." The citizens of the city could therefore thank Maxim that their equanimity would be disturbed only by the flying bullets. And just in case the boy's firing of his rifle was not a strong enough statement of his virility, an oversized illustration of the silencer juts, phalliclike, out from his groin.[27]

Americans believed that urban environments did not produce a healthy virility in boys, and they were quite fearful that cities might stimulate an unhealthy sexual desire that would lead young men into nighttime carousing, debauchery, and other moral excesses. To counteract any pernicious influence, many ads stressed that urban boys should develop an upright, morally rigorous character. During the early twentieth century, *The American Boy Magazine* showed the depth of public concern with the character of the nation's youths. A 1912 ad for the periodical encouraged parents to

[L]ook your boy straight in the eyes! Read his mind! Know it is clean and pure! Safeguard your boy! Don't let yourself believe he is an exception. He isn't! *He's the rule*—because he's human! Your first duty is to ward off the basis of greatest evil—suggestive, diseased reading! Don't let that poison soak into his system! You must keep his mind healthy, manly! You are responsible! Temptations spring up everywhere. The boy problem increases every day, every hour! YOUR instant duty is to counteract it—not tomorrow or next week, but NOW while this burning question confronts you in its naked truth! Know your boy's mind by *knowing what he reads!* . . . You must not wait! Don't let this biggest of problems get away from you for an instant! Realize your boy's future may rest upon *your* decision today! Keep him pure-minded, clean as a whistle, by giving *him* The

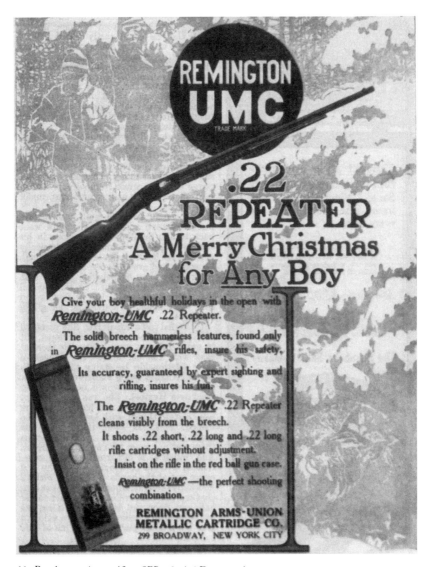

66. Remington Arms rifles, *SEP*, 184 (16 Dec. 1911): 45.

Plate 49. During the early twentieth century, boys—especially urban boys—were encouraged to develop their virility through vigorous, manly activities associated with the frontier. This ideal could be carried to extremes, as in this illustration of a young boy stalking a large bobcat with a small-bore rifle.

67. Daisy Manufacturing air rifles, *SEP*, 184 (9 Dec. 1911): 41.

68. Maxim Silent Firearms Co. silencers, *SEP*, 184 (2 Dec. 1911): 53.

Plate 50. Historically, American males had developed their virility through outdoor activities on the frontier. But after 1890, Americans tried to use the same outdoor activities to foster virility of boys in urban settings, with frequently incongruous results. For example, the Maxim ad promoted gun silencers as a way to let urban boys practice marksmanship in their yards without disturbing neighbors with noise. One would think that neighbors would be more disturbed by the bullets.

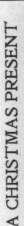

69. Brunswick-Balke-Collender Company billiard tables, *LHJ*, 18 (Dec. 1900): 43.

Plate 51. If frontier activities, such as hunting, could be relied upon to develop the virility of urban boys, urban activities, such as billiards, threatened to lead boys into dissolution. This ad offered mothers a way to keep their sons out of the cities' pool halls: "Provide them with the amusement they want" at home.

American Boy. Let the great work The American Boy is doing spread to *your* home, to *your* boy! A half million boys are reading it! Your boy *needs* it and *wants* it!

To push boys toward a stricter morality and away from carousing, the Brunswick-Balke-Collender Company made the following suggestion in a 1900 ad: "Mothers—keep your boys at home. Provide them with the amusement they want" by (lest one's imagination go too far) giving them a billiard table of their own. The company also made available, at no charge, their pamphlet entitled "Billiards—the Home Magnet."[28]

After 1920 the strong emphasis on vigor, manliness, and moral uprightness that had guided the rearing of boys since 1890 began to wane.

No new, clearly defined or strongly held values emerged to guide their parents, and the void was filled only by relatively weak and vague guidelines. The proper rearing of male youths—a subject that had only a few years earlier seemed vital to the future well-being of the nation—was now of minor concern to magazine writers.[29] Along with this lack of a new vision of how to raise boys after 1920 came a lack of concern about the types of gifts they should receive at Christmas.

After World War I, the only notable shift in gift items was that a higher percentage of them were manufactured in America. Before the war, Americans had imported toys primarily from Germany and Austria-Hungary, which also provided the nation's Christmas cards. In addition, inexpensive toys—frequently made from paper—were imported from Japan. However, with the outbreak of World War I, the importation of toys from abroad dropped sharply. The conflict on the continent disrupted production, the naval conflict in the Atlantic made shipping difficult, and the pro-Entente sympathies of most Americans made them reluctant to purchase the German or Austro-Hungarian toys that made it past the Entente blockade. Thus World War I protected American toy manufacturers from their major competitors, and they responded vigorously to this opportunity. Starting from a small prewar capacity, they increased their output fifteenfold between 1914 and 1925 and came to control 90 percent of the domestic toy market.[30]

The shift to American-made toys also involved a change in the purpose of toys. While European manufacturers intended their toys merely to delight children, American manufacturers thought it important that toys give practical instruction as well. In 1937 a writer recalled:

When the war-time embargo on German merchandise went into effect, the American toy industry capitalized on this opportunity for advancement by breaking with the novelty tradition in toy designs and emphasizing purposeful toys. The industry has continued year after year to improve the purposefulness of toys and to adapt them to the changing interests and needs of the child so that they have really become only second to the schools themselves as influences on child life. The dominant emphasis in American toys is the development of safe, workable miniatures of arts, industries and sciences.

Child play in 1937 features skyline building, the mysteries of radio, engineering, and electro-chemistry, as well as up-to-the-minute technique in transportation, architecture, housekeeping, scientific baby care, art and handicrafts. . . . Modern American toys have been transformed rapidly from the class of holiday novelties to the category of educational necessities.

70. Meccano Company model sets, *SEP*, 186 (20 Dec. 1913): 28.

71. American Mechanical Toy Co. model sets, *SEP*, 185 (7 Dec. 1912): 57.

72. Holgate Educational toys, *LHJ*, 55 (Dec. 1938): 97.

Plate 52. Before World War I, the American toy market had been dominated by European-made toys, which were designed to amuse the children who played with them. However, during World War I, American-made toys, such as these, began to dominate the domestic toy market. They were intended primarily to educate children, especially in practical and applied skills. It was assumed that children would also be amused in the process.

Toys that parents had presented to their offspring in previous periods had been didactic to some degree, but toys presented to children after World War I were, for the first time, consciously designed as educational toys. For example, those given to boys had the express purpose of training them in new industrial skills such as engineering, chemistry, and electronics.[31]

In spite of the importance that some writers of the 1920s and '30s attached to presenting educational toys to young males, these two decades saw a decline in the popular concern with holiday presentations to boys. For example, fewer periodical articles were devoted to the subject than previously. This decline in the concern about boys' Christmas gifts seems to coincide with the fact that, after 1920, the closing of the frontier receded into the past, and Americans no longer regarded the "manly" rearing of boys to be central to the future of the country. The socialization of boys did not raise as many cultural tensions in the 1920s and '30s as it had earlier in the century.[32]

Gifts to daughters ran a different course. During the late nineteenth and early twentieth centuries, parents raised their daughters to be home-centered housewives. This ideal dominated their selection of Christmas presents. Almost all items encouraged daughters to make-believe they were housewives, with playthings that included dolls, kitchen sets, and sewing kits. Ads reinforced the housewife ideal by portraying girls playing at domestic tasks, a symbolic expression of the popular belief that women's attention should be focused on the home. Girls were made to look helpless and dependent by virtue of their age—usually those depicted were from three to seven years old, which was younger than the boys in ad illustrations.[33]

For example, the central figure in a 1902 Stevens rifle ad is a boy of about twelve years of age who is proudly showing his new rifle to his younger brother, while their sister—younger than either of the boys—plays contentedly with her doll on the floor behind them. The boys perform the central action of the ad, that is, they admire the rifle, while their sister is relegated to a peripheral role. She functions as a foil for her brothers by symbolizing the helplessness of the family's female members. Her brothers, through the symbolism of the rifle, were cast into the role of protectors from the dangerous competitive world outside the home.[34]

Following World War I, a different ideal girl appeared. She became

73. J. Stevens Arms & Tool Company rifles, *LHJ*, 20 (Dec. 1902): 4.

Plate 53. On one level, this is just another ad of the early twentieth century for rifles for boys. However, note the little girl playing off to the side. She is much less active than her hunting brothers and serves as a passive symbol of domestic calm and helplessness. She is typical of the portrayal of girls between 1900 and 1920.

older, an adolescent rather than a small child, and exhibited, for the first time, an aura of sexiness, albeit of a playful and innocent type. This sexy, adolescent ideal had great attraction not only for girls, but also for mature women. During the 1920s, women rapidly adopted the flat-chested, short-skirted fashions associated with girls, clothes that came to be known as the flapper style. In their youthful sexiness, the ideals for girls and women were more similar following the war than they had been earlier in the century.[35]

The popular ideal for both girls and women now included physical activity. For example, girls in Christmas gift ads were more active than they had been before the war. They recommended gift items, demonstrated the use of gift items, and in numerous other ways participated in the central action of ads. Gone were the very young girls who had quietly played house in the backgrounds of prewar illustrations. Consistent with this emphasis on activity, girls in the '20s began to receive items associated with physical activity. For example, bicycles, sleds, Kangru-Spring-shus (springs which could be fastened to the shoes), Kiddie Kar foot-propelled cars, and various other active toys became perfectly acceptable gifts for girls.[36]

The characteristics of ideal girls in the 1920s—namely, their physical activity, playful sexiness, and late adolescence—were most in evidence immediately following the First World War, but these characteristics have remained important elements in that ideal ever since. The Depression had little effect on this ideal, except that her age became younger and the age of the ideal woman older, as opposed to the merger at late adolescence which had characterized the 1920s ads.[37]

The complexity of the history of Christmas is evident. Some developments affected virtually all gifts that parents gave to their children. For example, the elfish St. Nicholas, who had punished bad children during the early nineteenth century, was by the end of the century a jolly plump Santa Claus who never punished children, no matter how bad they had been. Similarly, gifts to both boys and girls were affected by the industrialization of America during the last third of the century, as simple handmade gifts were replaced by complex machine-made items.

Other developments affected gifts for girls differently than gifts for boys. The ideal girl changed from being a very young and dependent child early in the century, to being an active, playfully sexy adolescent

74. Buick automobiles, *SEP*, 203 (13 Dec. 1930): 41.

Plate 54. If it were not for the text, it would be difficult to tell whether this young female was the daughter or the wife of the man. This is typical of ads of the 1920s in which women were in their early twenties and girls were in their late teens, thus blurring distinctions between girls and women.

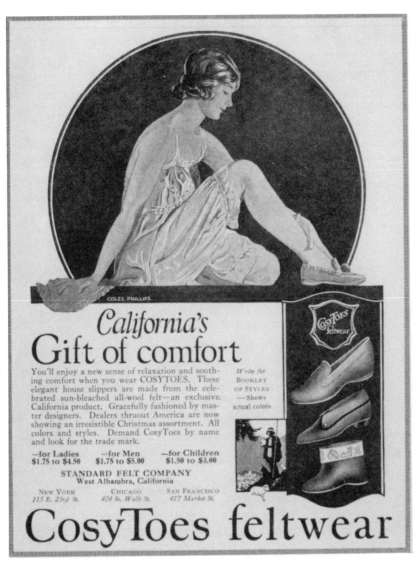

75. CosyToes Feltwear slippers, *LHJ*, 38 (Dec. 1921): 165.

Plate 55. During the 1920s, it became acceptable to portray late adolescent girls in alluring poses such as this. This was a striking—almost shocking—change from the younger, more passive girls of the ads of the first twenty years of the century.

PAUL JONES MIDDIES

make Happy Christmas Kiddies

Shows fine judgment on the part of the giver and good taste on the part of the wearer. *No one can have too many.*

A Paul Jones Middy is the highest quality middy made. Compare it with any other and its distinctive tailoring, cut, workmanship and material are readily apparent — indicative of the long wear it will give.

Paul Jones is the original girls' middy — the first ever made. For more than 15 years Paul Jones Middies have held first place.

Various styles, materials and colors for all tastes. Sold by good dealers. *Every garment guaranteed.* You can always identify a Paul Jones by the label (shown below).

Paul Jones Garments: Middy Blouses, Middy Dresses, Skirts, Bloomers, Boys' Middies, Boys' Middy Suits.

MORRIS & CO., INC., BALTIMORE

76. Paul Jones middies, *LHJ*, 37 (Dec. 1920): 185.

Plate 56. During the 1920s, the ideal girl was in her late adolescence and the ideal woman was in her early twenties, thus blurring the line between girlhood and womanhood. The blurring applied not only to their ages but also to their clothing styles. For example, this girl is wearing a style that was originally worn only by girls but during the 1920s became popular with young women as well. Compare this ad with illustration 37, a contemporaneous advertisement for women's sailor suits.

77. Daniel Green Comfy slippers, *LHJ*, 54 (Dec. 1937): 63.

Plate 57. During the 1930s, the ideal woman became older and the ideal girl became younger than they had been during the '20s. Once again girls and women were portrayed at two distinct ages, as they had been during the early twentieth century.

by the 1920s, then to being a child again during the '30s, with corresponding changes in the gifts she received. In contrast, the image of the ideal boy remained stable. Boys were supposed to be vigorous, manly, and morally upright, and they received guns and bicycles at Christmas to help them fulfill these expectations. This ideal began to decline after 1920, but was not replaced by a different vision of young malehood. The modern Christmas can be understood only by appreciating its internal diversity as well as its common themes.

CHAPTER 9

The Ever Wider Horizon: Reaffirmations of Community Ties

The last two decades of the nineteenth century were, even for Americans, a time of extraordinary movements of people from one place to another. The nation was in demographic turmoil, largely because of the dramatic mechanization of production and the expansion of the transportation system during the last third of the century. These developments pushed people from Europe to America, from the countryside to cities, and from neighborhood to neighborhood within cities. The forced geographic mobility made many Americans new arrivals in their neighborhoods and denied them that special identification with their communities which only the passage of time can bring.[1]

Most late nineteenth-century migrants ended up in cities, whether they began their journey on European farms, in East European stetls, on farms in the American hinterland, or in other neighborhoods of the same city. After they arrived, they found it difficult to identify with their new urban locales because the highly dynamic and expanding nature of the cities made it difficult to make friends with more than a small percentage of residents. Similarly, it was hard to get to know most of the streets, neighborhoods, stores, and parks. Because many of the elements of their cities remained unfamiliar to them, residents lacked the strong sense of belonging which comes from intimate and thorough knowledge of one's community. Some were indeed able to form attachments to their neighborhoods, but even these attachments were weakened by the high rate of movement of people from neighborhood to neighborhood. No wonder, then, that many urban Americans at the turn of the century did not feel they were true, full members of their cities.

This alienation troubled social commentators during the first twenty years of the new century. The weak sense of community membership which they saw in metropolises paled in comparison with the strong sense of belonging that characterized small towns. In the hope of solving this problem, metropolitan social leaders embarked on ambitious projects to cultivate the intimate community atmosphere of small towns. One of the most successful of these projects reached its heyday during the 1910s and '20s: community Christmas celebrations.[2]

The first such celebrations were organized in 1912 by social leaders in New York, Boston, and Hartford, with the New York celebration proving to be the most significant. New Yorkers not only originated the idea of community Christmas celebrations, but they also became the most vigorous and effective advocates of establishing the festivals in cities nationwide. They established a permanent organization to advise potential organizers in other cities about the festivals. As a 1915 article noted,

Working incognito, the same group of people who planned and carried out the first public Christmas tree in New York is directing the national movement. What to do and how to do it—the best carols to sing, the most desirable sort of music, the use of phonographs, how to organize, how to enlist helpers—in fact, any information desired by anyone interested in planning a community festival may be obtained by addressing the "Tree of Light," P.O. Station G, New York City.[3]

The person who initiated the first New York City community festival was a woman, but her identity remains a mystery, largely because of her own doing. She wanted celebrants to focus their attention on the community, on the group. This goal, she reasoned, militated against recognizing her as the organizer of the festival, and led her to prefer the more community-oriented explanation that the festival came spontaneously from "the people" of the city. Not only did she choose to remain anonymous herself, but she convinced other organizers to do the same. A writer in 1919 remarked that "so impersonally was the planning done that even now few persons—except newsmen who, from the first, favored and fostered and spread abroad the story of the Tree of Light—know the names of the founders of this rarely spiritual interpretation of Christmas thought."[4]

In spite of their cloak of anonymity, it is clear that the organizers were prominent citizens of the city. Consider, for example, the method they selected for obtaining money, materials, and services for the festival: a discrete word-of-mouth campaign among leading businessmen, politicians, and publicists. This method surely would not have been chosen unless the organizers enjoyed easy access to these leading citizens, probably based on prior personal relationships or common circles of friends. Furthermore, the word-of-mouth campaign proved to be very successful in getting the resources they needed. The Lake Placid Club donated the tree, the Edison Company gave lights to illuminate it, and the city government provided the location for the festival in Madison Square and installed and later disposed of the tree. In addition, newspapermen gave the celebration generous coverage in their publications, thus eliminating the expense of advertising the festival.[5]

The warm support of New York's leading citizens for the festival was echoed in the response of the general public, as ten thousand people attended the first night of festivities on Christmas Eve, 1912. The size of the crowd was all the more remarkable because the organizers had not publicized the celebration beforehand—though newspapermen were willing— since they wanted the gathering to be a surprise and appear spontaneous. The people of the city continued to attend the festival throughout the week, in numbers one journalist estimated as being "in the tens of thousands" per night. The largest gathering, about eighty thousand people, was on the final night of the celebration, New Year's Eve.[6]

The 1912 community Christmas celebration in New York City, together with those in Boston and Hartford, caught the imagination of city dwellers across the nation. Only one year later, community leaders in over one hundred cities had organized similar celebrations. Among the cities were Baltimore, Chicago, Cincinnati, Cleveland, Dayton, Detroit, Philadelphia, Pittsburgh, San Francisco, and Washington, D.C. In later years, sentiment for community Christmas celebrations continued to spread: in 1914, over three hundred cities had festivals, and by the 1920s they were commonplace across the nation in cities of all sizes.[7]

The appeal of the celebrations for all social classes in all types of cities indicates that they met widely felt needs. For their part, organizers and other elites supported community Christmas celebrations because they wanted to make the atmosphere of metropolises more like the atmosphere in America's small towns. They sought to introduce small-town characteristics to cities in three ways.

First, they tried to create more friendship ties, which they thought would help residents to solve urban problems through a personal understanding of the needs of other residents. They thought that the gathering of people at Christmas celebrations would generate friendships. Though this attempt was praiseworthy, it had practical shortcomings as a solution to the nation's urban problems. It could never have significantly ameliorated the impersonal tone that characterized American cities in the early twentieth century. Even if each urban resident dramatically widened his or her circle of friends, it would still amount to only a small percentage of all the residents of the city. Because the vast majority of residents were bound to remain unknown, the predominant tone of the city was bound to remain impersonal.[8]

The second way that organizers tried to make their cities more like small towns was by strengthening the identification of residents with those cities, and by convincing people that their cities, whatever their size, were true communities. The organizers sought to accomplish this by repeatedly asserting that their cities were true communities, and by providing special events—the festivals—through which residents could symbolically express their community membership. Organizers always referred to the celebrations as *community* festivals; they held the celebrations in public parks rather than on private property; and they encouraged all city residents to attend. Not only were residents to develop affection for their cities, they were told that their cities were capable of returning that affection—that their communities cared about them. Organizers stressed the outpouring of warmth at celebrations, the spontaneous participation of masses of people in the festivals, and the residual feelings of friendship that remained after the festivals were over.

There is much that is praiseworthy about the organizers' efforts to strengthen community identification, but like the efforts to strengthen friendships, this effort was, in significant respects, unrealistic. Creating an intimate and familiar sense of identification between large cities and their mobile citizens was very difficult. So the type of citizen-community relationship that was destined to prevail was impersonal and abstract. In addition, heightening community identification was an unrealistic way to attack the full range of problems experienced by urban residents in a mature industrial society. In order for the "concern" of communities to have had a significant impact on urban problems, it had to have been expressed through substantive legislation dealing with defined groups of citizens, a matter of little interest to community Christmas organizers.

The third way organizers tried to make cities more like small towns was to encourage a citywide consensus on the basic Christian beliefs which they believed typified the nation's small towns; in other words, they wanted to promote religious homogeneity in cities. Although organizers refrained from stating this goal explicitly, it was an important motivation for their promotion of the festivals. It prompted them to select Christmas as the occasion for community festivals, and to make Christian symbols, such as manger scenes and stars atop the Christmas trees, prominent at the celebrations. Entertainment always included the singing of Christmas carols and hymns. Organizers hoped that such Christian symbols would create a common ground for the diverse groups that had teemed into turn-of-the-century cities.

From a narrow functional perspective, there is much to be said for the organizers' use of Christian symbols. The symbols had deep emotional significance for the Christian majority of urban residents and could bridge the language and ethnic differences among them; there were no existing secular symbols of comparable emotional weight or breadth of appeal. The most popular secular symbols were those associated with the Fourth of July, but this holiday did not have the depth of meaning that Christmas did for recent immigrant groups. Though the usefulness of Christian symbols did not justify the great prominence given to them at the community festivals, it does help us to explain why the community Christmas organizers found them appealing.

The liberal use of Christian symbols at community celebrations was an affront to the non-Christian residents, who felt they could not participate equally and felt less favored. In generating these negative feelings, the use of Christian symbols contradicted an important festival goal: strengthening the identification of all urban residents with their cities, regardless of religious or other preferences.

Still, festival organizers were more tolerant of ethnic diversity than most early twentieth-century Americans. They made no pejorative comments about non-Christian citizens in their discussions of celebrations, nor did they ever suggest that non-Christians should not participate in the festivities. Indeed, they often praised the richness and color that various groups brought to the celebrations, as shown in the following description of the 1912 New York City celebration:

There were people with costly furs and glossy hats, standing elbow to elbow with others shabbily dressed and thinly clad, with shawls drawn over their heads or quaint caps on them. There were pink and white faces and swarthy and tanned ones, rosy faces with fair, flaxen hair, and dark brown ones with black curly hair —so many different kinds.

At the New York festival of 1913, "a choir of Welsh male singers added their moving, characteristic rendering of Welsh songs . . . and later a Negro chorus of a hundred voices [sang] the old-time plantation songs." The tone of ethnic tolerance also characterized community Christmas festivals other than New York's. For example, at the 1913 Chicago celebration, a band played "A Salute to All Nations . . . a medley of national anthems," and the next year in St. Louis, "foreign-born citizens gave folk dances."[9]

The goal of significantly increasing religious homogeneity in the cities was, like the first two goals of the festivals, unrealistic. Although mass relgious conversions have occurred periodically in America's past, it was unlikely that such a conversion would occur at this time, given the significant cultural and economic differences among the residents of modern American cities. The disparity made it extremely difficult to create a sense of sameness on which common religious beliefs could have been founded.

If the organizers' enthusiasm for festivals lay in their desire for a small-town atmosphere, what explains the strong public support for the festivals? The most obvious reason was that they provided pleasant entertainment at no charge. Even in smaller cities, attractions included handsomely lighted trees and good music by either professionals or talented amateurs. Organizers in larger cities commonly added other entertainments, such as the special children's play that New York City organizers added to their celebration in 1915.[10]

Festivals were popular because they were also a comfort to celebrants during a period of heightened anxiety. As historian Robert Weibe argues, between 1877 and 1920 Americans were "searching for order" because so much was changing around them, challenging their values and making it difficult to maintain their former identities. Some aspects of community Christmas celebrations tended to reduce those tensions and provided welcome relief. Participation in festivals also symbolically asserted membership in the community. No matter how abstract or vaguely defined the communities might be, this feeling of belonging was doubtless appealing to the many recent arrivals and helped relieve their sense of uprootedness. In addition, the familiar holiday symbols reminded them of their previous Christmases and provided a comforting symbolic continuity with earlier periods in their lives. This continuity alleviated some of their sense of drastic change resulting from their move to the cities. A writer in 1913 noted celebrants' "little sighs of memories of the past, of happy childhood days, of Christmas celebrations on the old farm or in the old home in a foreign land." [11]

During the 1910s the metropolis was the community of most concern to Americans. But at other times during the twentieth century, different types of communities became centers of public attention. For example, during World War I the nation as a whole became the dominant community and inspired several ways to express one's membership therein. Some Americans purchased Liberty Bonds, which clearly symbolized citizens' awareness of the nation's military effort and their support of it. But this was a market exchange, not a gift exchange. When citizens bought bonds, they created contractual agreements that obligated their government to return their principal, plus interest. The only "gift element" in the exchanges was that citizens' surrendered the use of their money for a time, and interest compensated them for that. The contractual nature of bond purchases suggests that citizens saw their relationship with the government as being impersonal and of the market: they hired their government to provide them security, and did not feel any personal or friendship obligation to present the government true gifts in its time of need. [12]

Americans asserted their membership in the national community during World War I also by rationalizing their holiday gift purchases. They sent cards instead of items made from raw materials needed for the war effort, selected useful rather than useless items, and refrained from giving presents to adults. In rationalizing their purchases in this manner, celebrants followed the advice of national leaders who enjoined citizens to avoid holiday purchases that might hinder the war effort. Citizens' "gifts" to the national community thus were the resources saved by their rational purchases. As with Liberty Bonds, this gift to the nation was not of the usual type. [13]

Yet Americans could express their membership in the nation during World War I in a way that involved true Christmas gift exchanges. Many citizens sent presents to soldiers and European civilians that we will divide into two types, cash and all other types of presents, because the messages conveyed were substantially different. They needed the assistance of intermediary organizations such as the Salvation Army, Red Cross, and Y.M.C.A. to get either type of present overseas, however. When Americans contributed cash through an organization, it selected the gift items and ultimately delivered them to the recipients in Europe. The original givers, the American citizens who had given the cash, did not describe their relationships with their recipients like those who had personally selected and sent something. Gifts of money lacked the power to describe the quality of relationships; they could express only the quantity of givers' concern.

Besides cash, Americans often gave other types of gift items through intermediary organizations. But because they had either made or personally selected them, their choices conveyed messages to recipients about the quality of the relationships. For example, givers supported the soldiers' war efforts by sending them such useful items as suspenders, shoe laces, and knitted goods; or they expressed concern over soldiers' loneliness by sending them writing paper, envelopes and pencils. With such items, the function of the intermediary organizations was merely to deliver them.[14]

In spite of these differences between sending cash and sending personally selected items, all gifts still had certain similarities. For example, both types of gifts were sent to persons unknown to the givers. In a sense, therefore, givers sent their presents to abstract concepts, for example, to "the soldiers," or to "suffering fellow humans." Consistent with the anonymity of recipients, givers saw themselves as anonymous representatives of the national community rather than as independent individuals. They sent their gifts on behalf of "America," not themselves.[15]

The lack of personal acquaintanceship gave the exchanges a pronouncedly abstract quality. When givers sent their presents abroad, they knew their recipients did not know them, and had no practical way of getting to know them. Thus, gifts were sent without the expectation of acknowledgments, much less return gifts, from recipients. The obscurity surrounding givers' identities precluded reciprocation to individual givers, but reciprocation could be made to American givers as a group. European civilians sent American givers collective expressions of gratitude, but were able to send little else. Soldiers, however, returned the

more substantive reciprocal gift of participation in the war. Indeed, because the soldiers had already been serving in the armed forces before the
presents came, the American givers' Christmas presents were, in a sense,
return gifts rather than initial gifts. At the least, the gifts were expressions
of already existing feelings of gratitude to soldiers.[16]

The meaning that recipients attached to their gifts varied depending
on the group to which the recipient belonged. For example, to needy
European civilians gifts from America provided some relief and indicated
to them that at least some Americans were interested in alleviating their
suffering. To English and French soldiers fighting before America's entry
into the war, gifts from the United States were welcome symbols of the
support of Americans for the Entente cause although they made little
substantive difference in the prosecution of the war. They implicitly
suggested the possibility of more substantive aid from the United States
in the future. Similarly, gifts sent to American soldiers bolstered their
morale because they were symbolic of their nation's support of the war.
According to reports from the front, it was in heartening soldiers' spirits
rather than in meeting their material needs that Christmas gifts made
their most important contribution to the nation's war effort.

There were fundamental differences between the ways Americans
expressed their membership in the nation during World War I and the
ways they expressed their membership in their cities through community
Christmas celebrations. First, the tone of reaffirmation was entirely different: community Christmas festivals were celebratory, pleasant, and
joyous, while reaffirmations of national community during the war were
serious, a tone befitting the nation's military undertaking. Reaffirmation
of the nation during the war was a duty, not an entertainment. National
leaders had to push citizens to participate; they did not lure them as the
community Christmas organizers had. Second, participation in community Christmas festivals was public; celebrants saw, and were seen by,
the other participants. Indeed, the gathering of city residents was one of
the most important ritual elements of the community Christmas festivals.
In contrast, Americans usually expressed their membership in the national community during World War I privately, with no associated
public rituals. Finally, community Christmas celebrations generally did
not involve property exchanges, whereas such exchanges were central to
wartime reaffirmations of the national community. In sum, community

Christmas celebrations were cheerful, public rituals with very few property exchanges, while the wartime reaffirmations of the national community were serious, private property exchanges with no ritual element.

Following World War I, Americans continued their efforts to reaffirm their sense of belonging to their cities and the national community in much the same way as during the prewar and war years. For example, during the 1920s and 1930s metropolitan residents continued to organize and attend community Christmas festivals to express their sense of belonging to their cities. By the late 1920s these festivals had become so commonplace, so unexceptional, that they failed to evoke much comment in periodicals.

During the 1920s and 1930s, Americans continued to reaffirm their membership in the national community. For example, in 1923, the national Christmas tree ceremony was instituted in Washington, D.C. The Society for Electrical Development, an electric power trade organization, provided the financing and the publicity in an effort to encourage the new trend toward decorative outdoor lighting at Christmas. The celebration used a symbol—the Christmas tree—that was already associated in the public mind with household and community Christmas celebrations. Now the public was asked to regard the tree as an appropriate symbol for the national community as well.[17]

During the 1920s Americans continued to express their membership in the national community by giving to various charitable organizations, as they had done during World War I. Building on wartime experience, postwar leaders sought to continue and strengthen the habit of charitable giving. They pointed to the large sums Americans had donated to soldiers and Europeans during the war years, noting that this level of giving was achieved while donations to domestic recipients were also increasing from their prewar levels. If givers were able to continue this level of contribution in the postwar period, they would create a significantly more generous America.[18]

During World War I, Americans had also expressed their membership in the national community by being thrifty, by being rational in how they shopped, and this way of expressing identity with the nation continued to be very popular during the years immediately following the armistice. Postwar advocates of thrift were particularly fearful that America's battlefield victory might be lost through peacetime improvidence. For example, in 1920 a writer in a scholarly journal warned that "America may yet be the loser if she does not learn from the titanic conflict lessons that will make all she has suffered worthwhile. . . . We see the sign-posts pointing to established victory, to national and individual freedom, and these sign-posts are marked THRIFT."[19] The nation had benefited from the rational approach to spending during the war, according to thrift advocates, and they wanted Americans to continue the habit in order to perpetuate these benefits. Christmas shopping received special attention as an area in which continued rationality was necessary. Advocates of thrift encouraged Americans to express their national membership by controlling their property exchanges, a goal that contrasted sharply with the goal of charity advocates, who wanted national identity to be expressed through liberal generosity.

During the 1920s, Americans found a new way to express their membership in the national community. Citizens, whether at Christmas or during the rest of the year, began to identify with American culture by owning items regarded as typically American. You knew you were American if you owned things that advertisers said Americans should own. As this mechanism became more popular, items with an image of Americanness enjoyed enhanced value as Christmas gifts. This means of expressing membership in the national community through the acquisition of consumer goods was only one aspect of a fundamental shift in the nation's values during the 1920s from production-orientation to consumption-orientation. In that decade, Americans began to define themselves and their countrymen by what they consumed—by what they spent or owned—rather than by their productive achievements.[20]

The final way Americans expressed community membership in the postwar period involved a much larger community: the community of mankind. The new concern with this much larger community resulted in part from the war. The international scope of the conflict, and the widespread human suffering it caused, drew the attention of Americans beyond local and national horizons toward a consideration of the conditions common to all people. Beginning in the 1920s and continuing through the '30s, leaders encouraged their countrymen to use the occasion of Christmas to express their brotherhood with all peoples. In 1920 a writer knew that "the world just now is in sore need of Christmas. The human race is in a surly and disgruntled mood. . . . There is no way out of our present distress but by a fresh baptism of the spirit of good will. The world needs to breathe in the soul of Christmas."[21] During the 1930s, the Great

Depression, and the worldwide suffering it caused, served to further promote public concern with the community of mankind.

War and depression were joined by another factor that contributed to the new concern with the worldwide community: the increased exposure of Americans to life around the world. Beginning in the 1920s, Americans enjoyed the benefits of greatly improved communication and transportation technology—for example, telephones, automobiles, and radios were marketed on a mass scale for the first time. As a result, Americans traveled more widely than before, talked to others far away over telephone lines, and listened to news from around the world. They began to regard their own environs as but a small part of the immense world community.[22]

But it was complicated to express membership in the worldwide community at Christmas. For example, it was impossible to gather any significant percentage of community members for ritual purposes. In spite of this difficulty, celebrants tried to express their sense of belonging through other means, such as gift exchanges. Most commentators agreed that celebrants could give meaningful gifts to mankind if they first summoned up the appropriate mental attitude. In order for the presentations to be valid symbolically, it was necessary for givers to think of all people as members of one all-encompassing group, and to deemphasize all subgroups. If celebrants could conjure up this mental image, it followed that a gift to any one person was symbolically a gift to the entire world. Therefore it made no difference at all to whom a gift was presented—someone near or far, poor or even rich. As a consequence, when writers recommended gifts to the community of mankind, they logically could not, and in actuality did not, express strong preferences for some groups of recipients over others. No distinctive mechanisms were developed for making such presentations.

During the first forty years of the twentieth century, Americans became concerned with successively larger types of communities at Christmas time. The public focused its attention on large cities during the 1910s and '20s, on the nation between the outbreak of World War I and 1930, and finally on all mankind during the 1920s and 1930s. This widening of the horizon of public concern was a product of various factors: urbanization, war, the Depression, and improved technology. The transformation of the nation's cities into immense, tumultuous metropolises caused many

Americans to yearn for a small-town sense of community. Later, America's participation in World War I made the preservation of the nation a primary concern for most citizens. The global experiences of the war and the Great Depression, together with the widespread use of the telephone, automobile, and radio, finally fostered a new sensibility toward the community of mankind.

But with these ever-larger communities, Americans had considerable difficulty finding rituals, such as Christmas gift exchanges or mass holiday gatherings, through which they could express their community membership. Gift exchanges proved to be unwieldy as expressions of membership in large cities, abstract and impersonal as expressions of membership in the nation, and unclear and imprecise as expressions of membership in the community of mankind. Ritual gatherings of a sizable percentage of a community's members proved to be difficult in the larger communities. Indeed, it was possible only in the cities.

This inability to find appropriate ritual forms was symptomatic of an even deeper problem. The populations of all these communities were so large, mobile, and diverse that the sense of community based on personal familiarity, residential stability, and homogeneity characterized by small towns was impossible to achieve. While powerful economic, humane, and technological factors encouraged Americans to become concerned with successively larger types of communities, they were increasingly frustrated in their efforts to express their sense of belonging to them.

CHAPTER 10

The Rationalization of Charity: Gifts from the Prosperous to the Poor

Charity has been a part of celebrating Christmas for centuries, making it one of the oldest types of holiday gifts. Even before 1800, when the celebration was very small and included only few exchanges of gifts, prosperous citizens presented some remembrances to the less prosperous at Christmas. This was in keeping with the basic holiday theme that Christmas should be a special time, a mythical "golden age," in which disparities between major social groups do not exist, in this case, disparities of wealth between the rich and the poor. By giving charitable Christmas gifts, prosperous citizens reduced the economic distance between themselves and the poor and helped to create this contention-free golden age.[1]

Although charity has historically been a part of Christmas celebrations for centuries, its importance in the American celebration increased markedly in the mid-nineteenth century, inspired by the work of Charles Dickens. *A Christmas Carol*, published in 1843, was the first major literary piece in several centuries to advocate Christmas charity and it caught the public fancy. The book became popular in America soon after its publication and has remained popular to the present, making it the most widely read literary statement on Christmas charity.[2]

The heightened interest of Americans in Christmas charity, which began with Dickens, reached a peak in the early twentieth century, with most concern focused on the plight of poor families and poor children. Families, whether poor or not, had become a matter of concern, since many of its traditional functions had been taken over by public and private institutions. For example, public-school teachers rather than parents became the primary educators of children, and the weaving that had been done at home by women was now done in textile factories. By 1900 social analysts such as Charlotte Perkins Gilman asked whether there were any tasks that were intrinsic only to families, tasks which could give them an undeniable reason to be. Even posing the question acknowledged the possibility that families might no longer serve a function in a mature industrial society. This deep concern underlay the attention people gave to Christmas charity for poor families.[3]

Food baskets, it was agreed, were the most appropriate gifts for needy families. And they could contain one of two types of aliments, or both: special holiday foods such as turkeys, or staple foods such as flour and canned goods. The distinction between the two was not mere labeling, as each conveyed distinct messages. Holiday foods, for example, were special foods, those specific dishes which, according to custom, families ate in a ritual meal on Christmas Day. When family members partook of the holiday dinner, they symbolically reaffirmed the bonds between them. By allowing poor families to reaffirm their ties this way, gifts of special holiday foods were conservative in their intent as they reflected the givers' wish that family ties be maintained.[4]

Gifts of special holiday foods not only supported family ties, they also supported social ties. Prosperous Americans who gave this kind of gift knew their generosity enabled their less prosperous recipients to participate in feasts similar to their own. They also knew that other affluent people had acted similarly so even more Americans could enjoy the traditional meal. The ultimate goal was to help all families attain a sense of belonging to the society through partaking of the special foods. Those who gave Christmas baskets wanted poor families to feel that they were full members of their communities.

Staple foods differed from holiday foods in that they were totally ordinary, that is, they had no ritual significance. It was this ordinariness that conveyed their central message, namely, prosperous givers' awareness of, and concern for, the hunger of the poor. Moreover, the fact that staples were profane foods implied that givers' concern extended into the profane time of the year, beyond the holidays. As the purpose of staple foods was to relieve hunger, their inclusion in Christmas baskets conveyed the givers' beliefs that recipients were frequently hungry. These gifts were usually limited to gifts to poor recipients, but after 1920 the trade association for the grocery industry undertook a sizable advertising campaign through which they promoted gifts of high-quality food stuffs to others as well. The items were intended to give the pleasure of fine eating, not merely to quell hunger. They became acceptable as gifts between prosperous celebrants only because of this higher culinary purpose.[5]

Poor children were also of concern to Americans. Showing compassion for needy children at Christmas was not new with the twentieth century, but its intensity was.[6] These heightened feelings were the result of general social factors rather than Christmas itself. First, middle-class parents had begun to soften their treatment of their children in the antebellum period and continued to do so through the remainder of the nineteenth century. By the end of the century, they treated their children in a warm and kind manner, in sharp contrast with the stern discipline of the early nineteenth century. They thought that childhood should be a pleasant, carefree time during which many of their children's desires were gratified. However, parents of poor children were frequently unable to nurture their offspring in the new manner, and therein lay the problem. As a result, around 1900, poor children became objects of reformist zeal that bore fruit in the more lenient, special juvenile courts, in child labor laws, in Dewey's progressive educational philosophy, as well in efforts to include poor children in the celebration of Christmas.[7]

Second, by focusing on children, adults were able to ignore their own more serious problems. During the last third of the nineteenth century, social analysts such as Henry George and Edward Bellamy were asking why many people were still impoverished in an age of burgeoning production. Their inquiries led them to a class analysis of America's political economy that challenged the tenets of laissez-faire capitalism as well as the legitimacy of the existing social order. During the early twentieth century, many informed Americans—including most writers on Christmas charity—could not bring themselves to accept the ultimate conclusions reached by these analysts, that is, that economic relationships between the classes in American society should be fundamentally altered. But neither could they ignore the evidence concerning the extent of

THE RATIONALIZATION OF CHARITY

poverty in the nation. They would have been hard-shelled, indeed, had they not shown at least some concern for the poor. Encouraging prosperous Americans to give Christmas gifts to poor children was a palatable solution: it allowed such givers to express concern for some of the impoverished while avoiding the much more serious—even threatening—issue of adult poverty.

Those who wrote about Christmas charity did not want the concern for poor children to end with mere expressions of caring. They promoted specific programs that would get presents into the hands of needy young people. In 1904 a writer praised the achievement of a Philadelphia schoolteacher, Elizabeth Phillips, in organizing the Santa Claus Association, whose sole purpose was to get a Christmas present to each poor child. Her inspiration for establishing the Association had come from her experience at school:

"Some of the children in my school had never received a Christmas gift," she said. "Many of these unfortunate ones with poor parents were more dutiful and obedient than other boys and girls who would come to school and tell of the many toys Santa had brought them. I taught all the children that Santa Claus favors good little boys and girls, and the injustice and irony of it all struck me like a blow."

The Association "was designed to bring good cheer into the homes of the poor where the mythical Santa Claus had never ventured; to equalize matters so that no child shall be altogether bereft of the joy that is prevalent at Christmastime." To this end, the association collected donations, purchased toys, and then distributed the toys to children.[8]

The activities of the Santa Claus Association and similar associations may have allowed Americans to do something for the poor, but it did not require them to address the fundamental problem of adult poverty throughout the year. Many prosperous Americans were haunted by a growing realization that laissez-faire capitalism distributed its rewards inequitably. Their unsettling awareness of the selectivity of economic rewards explains, at least in part, the importance that leaders placed on getting a gift to each child at Christmas. This goal not only revealed their understanding of inequities in the economic system, but also their belief that the inequities should be ameliorated. Their response was to encourage an ideal economic subsystem during the Christmas season that rewarded all children, not merely the prosperous. This ideal system also sent the socially conservative message to poor children that they would receive shares of the nation's wealth as adults, that the system would ultimately reward them. The effort to make sure that all children received Christmas presents was intended, at least on one level, to prevent poor children from becoming skeptical and disillusioned about the economic system.

Those who promoted Christmas charity to poor children frequently expressed another conservative goal: to bolster and maintain parental authority within families. Prosperous gift givers respected the gift-giving role—that is, the economic authority—of parents in poor families; therefore they delivered the items in secret to poor parents, who could then present them later according to the family's customs.[9]

Not all of the goals of the movement to get Christmas gifts to poor children were conservative. Advocates were convinced that the adoption of such a custom could change society for the better. The groundwork for a more generous nation could be laid if prosperous parents trained their children to assume an active role in gift giving to poor children. When these advantaged children, having been trained in generosity, reached adulthood, the nation would receive a needed infusion of the spirit of charity. An author in 1909 encouraged his readers to "think of the immeasurable good which could not help resulting if every child were taught to spend its Christmas money . . . in doing good, in genuine charity."[10]

There is much to be said in behalf of the proposal that prosperous parents should teach their children generosity at Christmas time. Such training probably broadened the social consciousness of affluent children, and counterbalanced their urge to acquire. However, all this was, at best, a very limited plan to lessen the serious tensions between economic classes in a mature industrial society. After all, advantaged children were trained only for private, individual beneficence on one day of the year rather than being encouraged to take organized, year-round action. Nor were children educated about socioeconomic sources of poverty.

During the first decade of the twentieth century, how gifts were presented to the poor was a matter of some significance. Most writers wanted the public to present at least some of their gifts to the poor in person, rather than indirectly through intermediary charitable organizations. For example, in 1905 a writer heartily approved of a Christmas charity campaign by a Midwestern newspaper "to try to influence people to do a little individual giving, to go themselves among those less fortunate than they, rather than to make a wholesale donation for some chari-table organization to distribute."[11]

In addition to encouraging in-person presentations of gifts to the poor, writers thought it imperative that givers know personally those to whom they gave gifts. Recipients could either be people whom givers had known for some time, or those whose names givers had acquired for the specific purpose of presenting them with Christmas gifts. In all cases, recipients should not be strangers. As a writer advised in 1908:

> If you wish to be happier than ever, make your giving to the poor more personal. Give to the great organized charities if you choose, but on no account let your giving to others for distribution interfere with your more intimate charities to those whose needs and desires you have studied at close range. . . . Hasten, before another sun goes down, to find yourself a family, either among your own servitors or back-door callers, or through some charity office, and begin getting acquainted as a first step toward Christmas.[12]

Not only should givers present some charitable gifts in person and to individuals they knew, but the givers' choice of particular items should also reflect their personal concern for the recipients' wishes or needs. In order to make choices of gift items as personal as possible, writers encour-aged would-be givers to determine what would be the most appropriate gift for their prospective recipients, a goal that required some effort on the givers' part. Writers suggested various methods, including eavesdrop-ping on children in front of store windows, learning the wishes of poor children from letters obtained by charitable organizations, inquiring about personal needs and wants of the impoverished from officials who were in contact with them such as schoolteachers and social workers, and simply remaining attentive when around potential recipients.[13]

While writers emphasized meeting the wishes and needs of recipients, they were also not reticent about what constituted the most appropriate gifts for the poor. Virtually all observers divided suitable gift items into two major categories: useful items that met the material needs of the poor, such as staple groceries or warm clothing; and items that were basically pleasure-giving and would make the needy happy, for example, jewelry, toys or perfume.

There were advocates of each type of gift, but most shied away from making a choice. They wanted givers to meet the most pressing material needs of the poor but they also thought it best to include some items that just gave happiness, that provided the poor with at least a momentary respite from their year-round attentiveness to life's necessities. A writer in 1909 encouraged givers thus: "Let the poor have a taste of what they regard as luxuries. They appreciate the necessaries, oh, yes! But they may be enraptured if they find a few things for which they have often longed but have never enjoyed before."[14]

The advocates of Christmas charity were anxious to free up the givers' resources for presentation to the poor. To this end they suggested that the prosperous divert to the needy "wasted" or "surplus" items from existing gift-giving customs. One custom that was singled out as wasteful was gift exchanges between prosperous adult friends who by rational standards already had everything they needed. As an author noted in 1909, "Ten dollars is the minimum that the woman of moderate means allows herself for little gifts outside the family, 'in exchange.' What a spirit! and what a barren waste!" It was clear to writers that this money could be used to purchase gifts for the needy instead. Surely gift giving customs would be "much better if every one of these erstwhile wasted dollars were invested in toys for hapless children, who long with a piteous longing for something to play with, so that for once they can say, 'Santa Claus came to my house, too.' "[15]

Another way to free goods for presentation to the poor was through the donation of excess possessions. To encourage this practice, writers praised those who had organized the collection, wrapping, and delivery of used items for the needy at Christmas. Givers were encouraged not only to use such organizations, but to become personally involved in the distribution of the items as well.[16]

Advocates of this mechanism for redistribution were optimistic about its possibilities. They thought that affluent citizens could give enough items to meet many holiday needs and wishes of the poor. One organizer opined that for every person who stood to receive no Christmas present, there was another person who wanted to give one, and her job was merely to get them together. In addition, advocates thought that organizations that had arisen spontaneously to distribute goods would have enough continuity to make distributions year after year. However, events would prove that neither of these grounds for optimism was warranted.[17]

Although givers embraced presenting charitable Christmas gifts to the poor, they did not exhibit much enthusiasm for more ambitious programs to address national poverty at Christmas. Ad hoc organizations that had been formed to redistribute goods during the holidays were deemed sufficient substitutes for permanent governmental programs to ameliorate poverty. In addition, writers advocated making charitable giving more personal, and this goal was incompatible with the bureaucratic approach that would surely have been adopted by a governmental assistance plan. Writers preferred direct giving by individuals rather than giving through organizations; they wanted the recipients to be known personally by givers; and they wanted choices of items to reflect givers' understanding of recipients' individual needs and desires. Whatever benefits in symbolism the personal approach may have had, efficiency was not one of them. It was not suited to a centralized collection of funds, whether by private groups or by the government, and it did not allow for quick distribution of aid to the poor on the basis of objective and impersonally applied criteria.

By advocating the personal approach for presenting aid to the poor, writers sought to perpetuate a style of charitable giving which, by the early twentieth century, lagged behind the rational style that had been adopted by foward-looking leaders of non-Christmas charities beginning in 1880. At that time, they had begun to keep files on recipients, encourage professional training for charity workers, eliminate waste, and promote cooperation with other charities. Although the adoption of rational, bureaucratic methods had become an important goal of many leaders of non-Christmas charities by the turn of the century, it failed to attract leaders of Christmas charities or those writing about Christmas charity.[18]

However, around 1910 leaders and commentators on Christmas charity changed their view. They began to criticize personal giving to the poor as being an "old style" of charity that was wasteful and inefficient and proposed a variety of "reforms" that entailed increased use of bureaucratic methods for collection and disbursement of funds. In the "old style" the sources of inefficiency in the collection and disbursement of funds were different, so writers suggested different types of reforms for each.

A haphazard, uncoordinated system for the collection of Christmas charity had evolved during the second half of the nineteenth century. Almost always, funds were not gathered into pools for distribution but were spent by independent givers on specific presents for individual poor recipients. Not all funds took this highly individualized path. Most charitable organizations conducted drives to raise charitable contributions. However, significantly, each organization conducted its own drive rather than working in conjunction with others. The result was that organizations competed for funds, requiring each to expend resources to publicize itself in order to preserve its position vis-à-vis other charities. After 1910 some commentators on Christmas charity questioned whether such an uncoordinated system could be relied upon to produce sufficient funds for the poor. The old personal forms seemed perilously unreliable.[19]

In order to achieve their goal of making the collection of Christmas charity more efficient and reliable, writers advocated consolidating Christmas fund-raising drives in each metropolis into a single drive, with the money raised being divided according to predetermined percentages. To encourage the adoption of consolidated appeals, writers produced glowing accounts of early efforts to rationalize the collection of charitable funds. For example, in 1914 charity leaders in Cleveland were praised for creating a unified collection campaign to which citizens contributed by buying "stock" in the city.[20]

After 1910 distribution of gifts also became a target for reform. Inefficiency in the existing system was due to each individual giver's and charitable organization's having its own list of recipients. Not surprisingly, some impoverished citizens were on several lists and received several gifts, while others, equally in need, received nothing. To eliminate this maldistribution, charities in some cities established one central citywide file containing the names of all prospective recipients. Givers were supposed to note in the file each gift they presented beside the name of the person who got it. Subsequent givers, by referring to the file, could easily discover whether prospective recipients had already been "claimed" by other givers and redirect their gifts to "unclaimed" recipients. One of the earliest such files was established in Orange, New Jersey, about 1914 by the Bureau of Associated Charities.[21]

Uneven distribution of assistance was not the only problem in dispensing Christmas charity. Gifts given on Christmas Day, even if they were well meaning, did not meet the needs of the impoverished during the rest of the year. After 1910, rather than continuing to praise the generosity of individuals who helped the poor at Christmas, writers pointed out the serious shortcomings of prevailing charity customs that left the poor in need the rest of the year. As an author in 1915 chided her readers: "We have too much patience, I believe, with the sort of mind that contents itself in donating a Christmas Dinner to some poor family, carefully ignoring the question of that same family's dinners for the remaining 364 days of the year, and the far more serious question of why some folks should have dinners to give away and others not even have them to eat."[22] In the spirit of critiques such as this, Americans became less interested in charity that was limited to the Yule season. By the 1920s many had concluded that assistance to the poor had to be dispensed throughout the year in order to have a substantive impact, and it had to be dispensed by large charitable organizations, not individuals. During the postwar decade, very few writers encouraged Americans to make special presentations to the poor at Christmas. Gone from periodicals were the numerous articles that had appeared at the turn of the century, counseling the well-to-do about charitable giving. There were virtually no tips on how to find poor recipients, how to discover what they wanted, or what goods one might present to them.[23]

Americans were asked to address the shortcomings of one-day-a-year charity by giving assistance to the poor throughout the year. For example, leaders in some cities selected their recipients during the Christmas season and presented them a special gift immediately, as had been the custom, but now in addition arranged to provide them aid throughout the year. The most common plan was to give recipients monthly sums of money or monthly food baskets. This recognized that the poor needed assistance beyond Christmas Day while preserving the previous custom of giving special remembrances to the needy during the holidays. Although this new plan was certainly an improvement over one-day-a-year charity, it usually entailed a reduction in the number of recipients who received assistance, as each recipient now was given twelve gifts per year rather than just one. Furthermore, it still left this smaller number of recipients unaided for twenty-nine days of each month. In sum, while the collection and distribution of Christmas charity was rationalized, it stopped short of a full confrontation with the problems of the nation's poor.[24]

If the Progressive spirit pushed Christmas charity toward rational giving, the First World War influenced it in other ways. Americans gave generously to charities that aided victims overseas, but this raised the question, shouldn't Americans attend to their own needy first? Wouldn't overseas contributions reduce contributions for the domestic poor? In spite of these concerns, leaders of domestic charities supported charity to distressed Europeans though they made sure to encourage their countrymen to make a contribution to the domestic poor as well. No leaders suggested that Americans give to the domestic poor exclusively.[25]

This strategy seemed to work. In addition to giving large amounts to recipients overseas, Americans actually increased the sums they directed to the domestic needy. Obviously, during the war, the total amount that Americans gave to charity—to recipients both at home and abroad—was dramatically larger than the prewar total. The striking increase in charitable donations gave leaders and periodical writers hope that citizens had learned how to give at a new high level, that their wartime experience had given them a new understanding that they were able to be much more generous than they had previously thought possible.[26]

During the 1920s contributions to the poor remained at a high level, in part as a continuation of the wartime habit of giving, but more importantly because of the increased skill of charity leaders in coaxing funds from contributors. The coordination of efforts to raise funds expanded during the postwar decade, as did the more rational disbursement of funds. The popularity of one-day-a-year charity waned, and virtually no one continued to advocate the presentation of gifts to the needy on Christmas Day only.[27]

The Great Depression of the 1930s sharply increased the number of Americans who needed assistance and thus became the next major influence on the evolution of Christmas charity. Early in the Depression, the astute recognized that funds of major private charitable organizations were insufficient to aid the larger number of needy citizens. Indeed, the resources of private charities had been depleted during the 1920s by efforts to assist workers who had lost their jobs because of the rapid technological advances of the decade. There was simply no way that private charities could meet the greatly expanded demands for assistance.[28]

In response to this serious situation, charity leaders prodded the government to become more active in collecting and dispensing aid to the poor. To their credit, they took this position knowing that they were forfeiting some of the power they had held over the formulation and implementation of charity policy. The leaders' support for expanded government action in providing welfare paralleled the increased support for general governmental regulation among influential policy makers in the Roosevelt administration, such as Rexford G. Tugwell, as well as among the American public. The extent of the distress of the 1930s, together with the inability of private organizations to ameliorate it, re-

THE RATIONALIZATION OF CHARITY

solved the question for most people about whether government should assume an important role in social welfare.[29]

The way the government went about caring for the poor during the 1930s added an entirely new dimension to the rationalization of Christmas charity. The government collected its revenues, including the money it used for welfare, through the tax laws. Unlike private charities which had no choice but to allow individuals to donate whatever they wished, the government mandated the amount that people had to pay. Because the relinquishing of the funds was compulsory, the government had the luxury of making its collections whenever it wished, and did not have to tie its appeal to a holiday. In sum, the government raised its funds through mandatory rational techniques at a profane time of the year rather than through voluntary contributions at a sacred time.

The government also used impersonally applied criteria, not ad hoc decision-making, to determine who would receive aid. Because prospective recipients became entitled to receive assistance by meeting certain criteria, the aid they received was not a gift dispensed at the behest of the giver, as, for example, earlier Christmas baskets had been. The personal element, which had been so important in earlier Christmas charity, became irrelevant. The government made no effort to know recipients personally, nor to acquaint taxpayers with their recipients. The assistance tendered by the government was made more rational in that it was offered year-round, not just on one day out of the year. In fact, Christmas Day was a holiday for bureaucrats.[30]

When it entered the welfare field during the Depression, the government used rational, bureaucratic forms to collect and dispense aid to the needy. In using these forms, it built upon the rationalization of non-Christmas charities begun during the late nineteenth century and on the rationalization of Christmas charity that had begun during the 1910s. As the government assumed an increasingly larger role in caring for the nation's poor, the older, more personal forms of charity were pushed to the background. By the 1930s, personal individualized Christmas charity was rationalized almost out of existence.

But not entirely. In addition to encouraging the rational distribution of aid, the writers of the Depression years once again encouraged Americans to perform small acts of kindness or to give small remembrances to the poor at Christmas. These personal kindnesses were not mere revivals of the "Lady Bountiful" gifts of the early twentieth century, since they were less substantial than the earlier gifts. They were mere tokens of thoughtfulness of little monetary worth. In many cases, they were not even tangible items, only thoughtful acts.[31]

But why did writers not encourage the giving of more substantial items during this distressful decade? They preferred token gifts because they were overwhelmed by the distress they saw around them and right-fully concluded that the nation's economic chaos must be addressed on a broader, collective, governmental level. Surely it was unlikely that the poverty of the Great Depression could be ameliorated through private action. Significant portions of the nation's wealth had to be redirected by the government from the prosperous segment of the society to its needy segment. By emphasizing that personal gifts should be of inconsequential monetary value, social leaders implied that substantive relief for the unemployed had to come from the government, not through an expanded private benevolence. Still, the small gifts were important symbols of the concern and good faith of the prosperous toward the needy. In the depths of the worst depression in the nation's history, this message was not to be scoffed at.

The small gifts of thoughtfulness of the 1930s conveyed a different conception of the poor than had earlier charitable gifts. In the early twentieth century, givers' had thought that they were different from their poor recipients. Reflecting this conception, writers had described in detail the poverty of the needy in their articles on Christmas charity, since prosperous readers usually lacked personal knowledge of the conditions of the poor. Writers had further emphasized class differences by their continual advice to readers about such matters as finding recipients and what to give them. In short, they assumed that their readers did not know much about the poor, and that the experiences of the two classes were so different that the prosperous could not extrapolate from their own lives to understand the poor.

In contrast, in the 1930s both the prosperous and the needy were seen as belonging to the same large economic class, the middle class. Thus the poor were not basically different from the well-off; they were only tem-porarily needy because of the special situation of the Depression. Reflect-ing this view, writers in the 1930s omitted the detailed descriptions of the impoverished conditions in which the poor lived.

Indeed, writers of the 1930s stressed the similarities in the everyday experiences of the two groups. For example, those who gave Christmas gifts to the temporarily needy of the 1930s articles lived closer to their recipients than had the givers in early twentieth-century articles. Recipients were "neighbors" who lived "close by" rather than across town, on "the other side of the tracks." In 1934 Mrs. Thomas A. Edison, for example, wanted to strengthen the "spirit of neighborliness" through the giving of small gifts at Christmas, and a writer two years later favored giving to those with whom one had frequent contact, those "at our very doors." Because of the emphasis on the fundamental sameness of givers and recipients of Christmas charity, the tone of articles in the 1930s was distinctly less patronizing than those of the early twentieth century.[32]

The small gifts of thoughtfulness of the 1930s must be viewed against the fifty-year trend toward rationalization that had preceded them. Beginning in the late nineteenth century, leaders of non-Christmas charities, followed by leaders of Christmas charities, succeeded in making their methods of collecting and dispensing funds more rational. The Depression furthered this trend by forcing the government, with its bureaucratic methods, to address the welfare problem, rather than leaving it to private organizations. Yet in the midst of this powerful trend, Americans still gave small tokens of thoughtfulness on a personal basis. The revival in the 1930s of small personal gifts that offered no substantive relief to recipients during the dire economic distress of that decade clearly suggests, as Marcel Mauss has argued, that gift exchanges are more than mere responses to economic necessities, more than mere rationalized redistributions of property: they reaffirm bonds between the exchanging parties. Such reaffirmations were highly appealing to Americans of the Depression decade who feared their society might fall apart.[33]

CHAPTER I I

*The Rationalization of
Christmas Bonuses: Gifts
from Employers to Employees*

During the nineteenth century, Americans had shown some interest in
the relationships between employers and employees at Christmas time.
However, it was only after 1900, when the form of the modern Christmas
celebration had taken shape, that significant attention was turned to this
subject.

One employer-employee relationship was particularly near at hand:
the relationship between prosperous Americans and the domestic servants
they hired to perform their household chores. The approach of Christmas
brought many face to face with a touchy question: How could the household's needs for services be balanced against the servants' wishes to
celebrate fully themselves? While writers concerned with this question
agreed that servants should not be worked long or hard, they did not
dwell on the hardships endured by domestics, though one would have
expected the muckraking journalists of the early twentieth century to do
so. But writers restricted themselves to suggesting how mistresses of the
house could make their servants' holidays as enjoyable as possible. This
soft style was probably chosen to avoid offending the magazines' readers,
many of whom employed domestics.[1]

To make domestics happy at Christmas, writers recommended that
family members present a range of gifts to each servant. Some items

178

should assure that the domestics could celebrate the holidays in the accepted manner, for example, a turkey for Christmas dinner. Other items, such as a coat or scarf, should meet material needs. Still other presents should simply make recipients happy, for example, perfume, lingerie, or candy. All gifts to domestics should reflect the personal concern of household members for their servants. In addition, presents should be wrapped, and the atmosphere surrounding their presentation should emphasize the brotherhood of all, rather than highlight the authority or higher status of the household members. The goal was to create a conflict-free golden age for the duration of the holidays in which the usual inequality and formality of employer-employee relationships did not exist.[2]

Writers encouraged household members to make the domestics' duties at Christmas as light as possible so that servants could enjoy the holidays themselves. The mistresses of the house were to be as thoughtful and understanding as possible. In 1906 a contributor to an article observed that "if there is ever a time when we ought to put ourselves in [our servant's] place it is at Christmas," while another contributor advised housewives "to give [your servant] as much time as possible so that she may have an opportunity to do some shopping, or attend to other little personal matters."[3] Reliance on the individual beneficence of the mistress of the house sprang from the same mind set as the patronizing "Lady Bountiful" charity of the late nineteenth and early twentieth centuries.

After 1914, as the nation became absorbed in World War I, periodicals dropped their discussions of how to treat domestic workers during the Christmas season. The energies that Progressive reformers had directed toward improving working conditions and other aspects of American society became redirected toward the goal of winning the war. In addition, writers discussed domestics less because there were fewer of them in the nation's work force. During the early twentieth century their numbers had declined sharply, a trend that caused considerable concern and became known as the "servant problem." Finally, the proper management of domestics became of less concern because housewives were doing much of the housework themselves with the new household appliances that were first mass produced and marketed during the 1910s.[4]

In addition to being concerned about their domestic workers in the early twentieth century, Americans also became attentive to the plight of those working in the Christmas trade, for example, retail store clerks and factory workers. During the nineteenth century, they had shown little concern over holiday demands placed on these workers. While some of this apathy may be attributed to a climate of opinion that was insensitive to labor issues, much of it stemmed from the fact that only a small percentage of Americans were employed in the Christmas trade during that time, consistent with the relatively small scale of the celebration before 1880. However, around the turn of the century, Americans became keenly aware that the scale of Christmas shopping and the burdens it imposed had increased dramatically during the previous twenty years. The hectic nature of the emerging modern form of celebrating made a deep impression on many social observers.[5]

In some part, the heightened consciousness was generated by periodical writers who used the muckraking style of journalism to publicize the exhausting grind that had become part and parcel of the modern holiday. Their graphic descriptions of holiday fatigue had two major purposes: first, to get the public to identify with the exhausted shoppers in their articles so that they could see the state of fatigue that they worked themselves into and, second, to make shoppers aware that their frenzied purchasing sorely taxed those who labored in the Christmas trade—the workers who manufactured, sold, and delivered Christmas gift items. Writers believed that, by raising public consciousness of the plight of these workers, substantive reforms of holiday customs would follow. This strategy of trying to achieve reform through the force of an enlightened public opinion was characteristic of the progressive movement.

Writers particularly disliked three basic characteristics of Christmas-trade working conditions: low pay, long hours, and poor physical and psychological environments. Certainly none of these criticisms was new —laborers in non-Christmas jobs had been voicing them for decades— but the criticisms were distinguished by the muckraking style in which they were presented, and by the writers' reliance on public opinion to solve social problems.

Pay earned by Christmas-trade workers was low compared to that received by others in the work force, with one clerk estimating that she had received only about eight cents an hour. The reasons for the low pay are no mystery: many Christmas-trade jobs were only seasonal, and many who worked at them were female or young or both, characteristics that have traditionally been associated with low wages. To dramatize the low compensation of Christmas-trade workers, writers produced moving accounts of clerks who, having lost small amounts of money in the midst of harried holiday transactions, became anguished as they contemplated the subtraction of the sum from their pay. A writer in 1907 observed that, as a consequence of fatigue, "change spilled on the floor was a common thing. One girl lost a quarter in this way, and her distress was a pathetic revelation of a poverty so dire that 25 cents one way or another was happiness or misery."[6]

Writers also criticized the excessive length of workdays that employers required of employees during the holidays. For example, a writer in 1906 rendered the following impassioned account:

In the East Side box-factories the children, in the Christmas season, begin their work at seven-thirty and keep it up till nine at night, Sundays included. From seven-thirty to nine at night! Reader, do you take into your heart how long these hours are for little fingers and little feet? But how are these tired workers kept at the wheels. You will not believe me when I tell you that the factory doors are locked to keep the little wage-slaves at their tasks till the factory pasha is satisfied with his day's profits. . . . Here is impressment of American citizens! Here is the outrage that in 1812 we thought it worthwhile to go to war about! What is 1907 going to do about it?[7]

Finally, writers criticized the poor physical and psychological environments provided for Christmas-trade workers. When they publicized the conditions in factories, they focused on the poor physical conditions. Many manufacturers, according to a 1906 article, "keep their workers in dark, ill-ventilated, and unclean rooms; many stand all day, many operate dangerous machines, and most work at high speed." Retail stores, on the other hand, provided a poor psychological atmosphere, with the work behind the counters being hectic beyond imagination and a strain on the nerves. A writer of 1906 informed his readers that "the holiday season is no holiday for [the clerks]. They hate it, and can you wonder that they do? The season means naught to them but confusion and noise, and loss of temper and vexation of spirit, and late hours. It multiplies their work, while it adds very little to their pay."[8]

Writers portrayed exhaustion, or even physical collapse, as the inevitable consequence of the long hours kept by Christmas-trade workers. A writer in 1910 observed:

Often these sales people, these cash-boys and girls, these change-makers and bundle-wrappers and parcel-deliverers, work in a sort of panic of haste, goaded by hurry, beset by floorwalkers and managers. These nerve-racked servants, young and old, harried by overwork, weakened by long hours and irregular food, exposed often to alternate overheating and chilling—these servants, many of them it has been found by investigation, will spend the next weeks in a sick bed, and some of them are doomed to end the holiday rush in the grave.

In their exhausted state, workers found it difficult, if not impossible, to enjoy the season during their few waking minutes at home after their workdays. These practical barriers to celebrating imposed on Christmas-trade workers violated a basic goal of the holidays that everyone should be able to celebrate Christmas in at least minimal fashion, and that everyone should have an especially pleasant succession of days.[9]

Writers infused their articles on Christmas-trade workers with the dramatic tone characteristic of muckraking journalism. They wanted to appeal to the emotions of readers and thereby win them to their reform cause. Writers selected symbols and themes that were sure to appeal to their readers, such as the work ethic, namely, the belief that hard work in itself produces important moral and economic benefits for workers and ultimately for their society. Writers effectively exploited the devotion of Americans to the work ethic by portraying Christmas-trade laborers as hard workers. Accounts in story after story followed the same pattern. Employees, whether in factories or retail stores, had "good attitudes" toward their jobs, they labored diligently at their tasks until they became tired, and then they continued to work until they became completely exhausted or collapsed. According to the articles, the workers' exhaustion or collapse was not the result of weakness but of trying to do more work than their bodies were capable of doing. Surely, these poor souls whose adherence to the work ethic carried them to such a dramatic end were entitled to the high moral esteem that devotion to the work ethic conferred.

The second symbols which writers used was women and children as employees. Exhausted workers were invariably either female or young, or both. Not only could their dependence and vulnerability be relied upon to inspire protective sentiments in readers, but the authors' use of women and children to represent Christmas-trade workers had a firm factual basis, as they composed the overwhelming majority of these workers. Men, on the other hand, were not portrayed as exhausted workers, even though writers could have used them effectively to make the point that Christmas-trade jobs required enormous physical effort. They could have described males in a state of total exhaustion, leaving readers to speculate about the devastating effects which Christmas work must have on "frail female constitutions." But early twentieth-century Americans were concerned about male adequacy and wondered whether American men were as virile and capable as their predecessors had been. Therefore, describing men on the verge of collapse might well have made readers anxious rather than have pursuaded them to reform Christmas-trade working conditions. In addition, most readers personally knew women who had worked at Christmas-trade jobs and had not collapsed, so one could not very well depict men as being weaker.[10]

The two symbols used by writers in their reform efforts—the work ethic and women and children as employees—were fundamentally conservative. The work ethic supported the production-oriented industrial order, while the belief that women and children were frail, vulnerable, and therefore in need of protection by adult males supported male domination within the family as well as within society.

While writers specifically criticized the low pay, long hours, and poor working environments of the Christmas-trade businesses, they also asserted that these conditions, and the hectic holiday shopping to which they were related, violated the "true Christmas spirit." But what was the true Christmas spirit? What ideal ways of celebrating did writers contrast to the emerging, market-oriented customs?

Writers used three images to symbolize the true Christmas spirit, the first of which was the nativity story. Writers contrasted the simplicity and purity of God's gift of Jesus to the world with the raw materialism of modern-day gifts. In 1909 an author observed that

Christmas represents the most important event in the history of Christianity, for on that day the greatest gift to man was made. . . . It is eminently appropriate that [man] should in his small way do what God did in his great way—that is, observe the heavenly gift by earthly gifts. How does it work out in actual practice . . . ? . . . We may find that the real Christmas spirit exists only in the minority, and that the majority of Christmas celebrators, instead of realizing and appreciating the significance of the season, use it for playing a game of grab and graft.

Similarly, a writer in 1907 had argued that existing shopping customs were

a sort of heathen revel. It was really a Christian festival, of course. That is what we intend Christmas to be, I know, and undoubtedly that is what it is. But it looks something terrifyingly different when you regard it from behind a counter.

I worked there only one week, but in that time what things I looked upon! I saw girls of seventeen and eighteen weeping with pain and weariness at eleven o'clock at night as with shaking fingers they made their counters attractive against the next day's brutal rush. I saw one girl drop in a dead faint while selling dolls to a fond mother of children. I saw little boys fall asleep in rubbish corners at the noon hour, their untasted luncheons in their tired hands.

To other writers, the intense buying and selling in stores at Christmas brought to mind the biblical description of moneychanging in the temple before Jesus drove out the offenders.[11]

Writers also thought that the true Christmas spirit had existed in Yule celebrations of the not-too-distant American past. They lovingly recalled the holiday celebrations of their youths, celebrations which, according to their memories, had emphasized simple pleasures, family ties, and a relaxed atmosphere. The hectic, materialistic modern celebration suffered in comparison. A writer in 1907 had

often been rendered inexpressibly sad by hearing young people in the metropoli-tan centers describe their Christmas gifts and complain that the gifts received from certain friends were less expensive than those given. . . . This view of Christmas, however, is that of a money-mad society suffering from a temporary spell of moral aberration. . . . To us Christmas suggests many things and the word has the magic power of opening the gate of memory and conjuring up scenes —dear, tender, hallowed scenes—of the long-vanished past. It suggests our childhood days and lo! before the mind there rises a picture, vivid as though the canvas of a master-artist stood before us. Here is a little country home in Illinois; a six-room house, with a long porch extending more than forty feet along the southern exposure, facing a broad valley studded with rural homes, each nestling in the midst of orchards and groves of noble forest trees.[12]

As their final image of the true Christmas spirit, writers suggested that an ideal celebration was any celebration that embodied brotherly love and peace as its central values. It differed from the other two images in that it was secular (with no references to the nativity story) and it accepted the modern world (it was free from nostalgic longings for a rural past). A 1910 article used it to criticize Christmas-trade working conditions by noting that "instead of its being a time of simple, gentle sharing of love and service, Christmas has become a time for exploiting the work-folk of store and factory and delivery."[13]

If working conditions in Christmas-trade businesses were harsh, how could that harshness best be ameliorated? Reform-minded citizens joined in several specialized organizations to address the problem of the overworked and underpaid laborers and received enthusiastic support from writers. One such reformist organization, formed in 1912, was the Society for the Prevention of Useless Giving, or SPUG, as it was commonly called. One of its goals was to eliminate all compulsory gift giving, that is, gift giving unsupported by true affection. It adopted as its prime target one particularly onerous type of gift exchange: presents which department supervisors in retail stores commonly received from the clerks working under them. The clerks' expenditures for these gifts were not only a financial burden, but the items often symbolized the clerks' subordinate position rather than any personal affection for their bosses. The primary object of SPUG became, in the words of a writer of 1913, "to destroy [this] system of collective giving, closely resembling petty graft, which prevails in many business establishments, large and small, for the purpose of giving Christmas presents to the heads of departments by the employees. This often results in unfair taxation of working men and women on small salaries, and is most unfair in that it is called Christmas *giving*, whereas in many instances it is practically compulsory." The method of abolishing the custom was straightforward: SPUG wanted clerks to refuse to present the gifts, a technique they believed would succeed if clerks had widespread public support. Writers did their part to generate this public support by educating their readers about the existence of the offensive exchanges, and about SPUG's activities to eliminate them. Their articles effectively set forth criticisms of gifts from clerks to their supervisors, as well as other compulsory gifts.[14]

Writers also supported another specialized organization, the Shop Early Campaign, in its effort to reform undesirable Christmas-trade working conditions. The campaign, which was begun around 1906 by the Consumer's League, sought to persuade givers to do their holiday shopping several weeks ahead of time. This would spread Christmas purchases out over a longer period, and make the final shopping days less hectic. The main beneficiaries of these reformed purchasing habits, they argued, would be retail clerks and shoppers; but factory workers, delivery boys, and postal employees also stood to benefit.[15] The organization had a second, equally important goal: getting stores to keep their regular business hours throughout the Yule season, rather than lengthening them for the holidays. The fear of store owners, of course, was that they would lose sales if they did not make themselves fully accessible to Christmas shoppers. As a way of protecting complying stores against this prospect, the Consumer's League stirred up public support for stores that retained regular hours. It also exerted pressure on noncomplying stores by compiling and publicizing a "White List" that contained the names of the businesses which met its guidelines regarding the length of the work day. The League encouraged shoppers to refer to the list and purchase their gifts only in the complying stores. The stores that were not on the list would thereby be pressured to eliminate their extra hours in order to attract White List shoppers.[16]

Support for the Shop Early Campaign was stronger in some parts of America than in others. For example, many New York City residents were persuaded to shop earlier in the Christmas season, and many stores eliminated their extra holiday business hours. Generally, the campaign won more converts in cities than in small towns and rural areas. Support for the Shop Early campaign also varied from one type of store to another. Of all retail stores, those which catered to the upper and upper-middle classes—the "better" stores and shops, as they were commonly called—complied most readily with the drive to abolish extra Christmas hours, while large department stores—which serviced the middle and lower classes—were most resistant. This pattern suggests that the upper and upper-middle classes supported the reform drive more strongly than the lower and middle classes. An additional—and probably more important—reason for the success of the campaign among the "better" stores was that keeping their regular business hours did not affect their holiday sales much, if at all. Their leisured patrons could shop anytime during the day, a flexibility not enjoyed by many of the lower- and middle-class customers of department stores, who generally shopped in the evenings, after they had finished their workday.[17]

Efforts of those in the Shop Early Campaign soon bore fruit. As early as 1915 a writer observed that "the custom of keeping retail stores open during the evening for a week or longer before Christmas is happily decreasing every year." By 1930 the Shop Early Campaign could point to significant changes in America's urban centers (especially New York City) and in "better" stores across the nation. While the campaign could boast about these achievements, its impact was limited because it accepted the pervasive buying and selling that characterized the emerging modern celebration and voiced no objections to advertising and promotion. It never encouraged Americans to make one reform that would surely have improved working conditions during the holidays: sending fewer Christmas gifts. Americans were told only to shop earlier, not less.[18]

The impact of the Shop Early Campaign was also limited by the technique it used to achieve its goals. It relied on public pressure—on the independent decisions of numerous unorganized shoppers to pressure merchants into keeping their normal hours throughout the holidays. Its leaders did not propose legislation to limit holiday working hours, even though such legislation would probably have been effective.[19]

Writers showed sensitivity in appealing to public opinion on behalf of the campaign. By consistently referring to callous employers who were responsible for bad Christmas conditions in factories and stores as "they," writers deftly avoided the suggestion that their readers might themselves be exploitative employers. The writers' refusal to broach the question of their readers' guilt was not only good tact but also good tactics, as they needed support from as many people as possible. After all, they could expect their readers to take only so much consciousness-raising where their own behavior was involved. They prompted readers to think of themselves as informed, civic-minded citizens who would strike out against "those" businessmen who abused their employees.

Christmas bonuses were another expression of employer-employee relations that played a significant part in the holidays. It was not until the last third of the nineteenth century that employers began to present gifts —Christmas bonuses—to their employees during the holidays. According to a writer in 1903, "it is safe to say that $1,000,000 is given to employees now where $1,000 was distributed a generation ago." In making these presentations, businessmen used traditional gift-giving forms, highlighting their personal relationship with each employee, or, if no relationship existed, pretending there was one. They frequently handed out bonuses themselves, a practice intended to express their personal regard for each worker. To further heighten the personal nature of the gifts, they created a special new environment for their presentations: the company Christmas party. This environment permitted the special presentation of bonuses, thus distinguishing the Christmas bonus symbolically from the regular labor-for-wages paychecks.[20]

Businessmen took pains to personalize the bonuses by giving each worker a different item or by varying the amounts of monetary gifts.

Employers usually made such distinctions on the basis of each worker's job performance during the year. But the question of making these distinctions begs the more fundamental question of why workers should be given bonuses at all, as they had been paid wages for their labor during the year. The unstated rationale behind bonuses was that the laborers had given the company greater value in labor than they had been paid in wages. The appropriate amount of the Christmas bonus therefore became the difference between the value of the labor the company had received and the amount of the wages the worker had been paid.

During the late nineteenth century employees had preferred the traditional gift-giving forms in presenting bonuses, but between 1900 and 1920 they switched to impersonal market forms. For example, in unionized industries, management and unions began to regard Christmas bonuses as an acceptable—even expected—subject in contract bargaining sessions. The cold, hard negotiation of the amount of bonuses represents a fundamental change from the voluntary presentations made by employers in the late nineteenth century. In addition to increased use of negotiation, companies began to distribute written tables or formulas that showed workers how much their bonuses would be, based on some objective factor such as years of service or salary. Consequently, the amounts of bonuses were not affected by the subjective assessments of managers and made them less personal. In addition, companies increasingly presented bonuses unceremoniously in paychecks rather than in the special setting of the company Christmas party.[21]

The use of rationalized forms for presenting Christmas bonuses reflected a new attitude not only by employers but also by labor. The strength of unions increased markedly in the twentieth century, and laborers now wanted to bargain with management as equals rather than accept their patronizing benevolence. They did not feel much gratitude over companies' seasonal offerings, as they regarded bonuses as pay to which they were entitled and not as true voluntary gifts. Because some companies had presented bonuses to their employees at Christmas for many years, workers began to expect them and included them when projecting their annual incomes. Bonuses became seasonal bulges in regular earned wages rather than "real Christmas gifts," and were used to purchase "real gifts" for relatives and friends. In 1951 the National Labor Relations Board gave the force of law to the view that bonuses had become, in effect, a part of workers' wages: it ruled that employers who had customarily presented Christmas bonuses to their workers could not stop doing so by claiming they were voluntary gifts from management.[22]

During the 1920s employers devised a new type of holiday item that was related to the Christmas bonus custom: assortments of the company's line of products packaged for gift presentation. But employers would *sell* these products to their employees, rather than present them as gifts. The employees' purchases took place in mundane environments, such as shipping offices, rather than in the festive atmosphere of company parties, environments which further emphasized the impersonality of the purchases.[23]

Assortments also differed from true bonuses in that the assortments were motivated purely and simply by the desire of businessmen to make money. Generosity toward workers was not a consideration. Businessmen expected to make some money from the assortments they sold to their employees, even though they were sometimes sold at a discount. In addition, employers exposed employees to their full line of products this way, which encouraged them to buy the products during the rest of the year. Finally, businessmen expected to profit from the assortments by encouraging employees to present them as Christmas gifts to their friends, thereby enlisting them as advertisers for the company.

This last motive—getting employees to advertise products by giving away assortments—was the most important reason for creating the assortments, and the most intriguing analytically. Businessmen packaged assortments well before Christmas and then offered them for sale to their employees. Workers then purchased and presented the assortments as "real gifts" to relatives and friends. This two-stage process, whereby businesses assisted employees with their shopping and workers used that assistance for the "real gifts" they presented, paralleled developments regarding monetary Christmas bonuses, which were not regarded as real gifts but as seasonal wage bulges enabling workers to purchase real gifts for those on their Christmas lists.

Items in Christmas gift assortments were made by the workers who presented them and, in that regard, were similar to the older types of handmade gifts, such as a baker's gift of breads or a leather worker's gift of belts or bags. But the earlier gifts had usually been made from start to finish by one person, whereas workers who sent their relatives and friends manufactured gift assortments had usually made only a small contribution to the transformation of the raw materials to finished products. They were made by a productive process having a full division of labor. When workers perform only a small task in the production process, they find it difficult to see the results of their work in finished products. Yet it may well be this division of labor that made the assortments so popular with both workers and employers. In giving the assortments as Christmas gifts, workers proudly displayed to their recipients an array of items they had helped to make, and employers were able to foster a sense of teamwork with their employees. The gift packages were concrete expressions of what they had produced through their joint efforts.

The predominant trend in employer-employee relationships at Christmastime has been toward reform and control—toward rationalization. During the nineteenth century, factory laborers and retail clerks had to rely on the individual generosity of their employers for raises in pay, for shortening their hours of work, and for improvements in working conditions. However, the reform spirit unleashed during the Progressive era pushed employers to improve the lot of their workers and shoppers to effect further improvements by rationalizing their shopping habits. Similarly, during the nineteenth century, employers had presented bonuses to their workers according to traditional gift-giving forms and in ways that emphasized their personal concern for each worker. However, after 1900 employers sent bonuses and gift assortments to their employees through impersonal, rationalized forms: by standardizing monetary bonuses included in paychecks, negotiating the amount of bonuses, and offering gift assortments for purchase by employees. This trend toward rationalization necessitates that we revise the popular view that Christmas has gotten more out of control since the nineteenth century.

CHAPTER 12

Riches and Uncertainty: Superabundance and Retailers' Anxieties since 1940

The preceding chapters have described the emergence of the modern Christmas celebration between 1880 and 1940. While the modern festival assumed its basic form during those years, it continued to develop thereafter, presenting new pleasures to be enjoyed and new issues to be resolved. The same general economic factors that had fostered the modern celebration during the late nineteenth and early twentieth centuries influenced its development after 1940. Both were periods of significant expansion in industrial production, a rising gross national product, and a substantially higher level of economic activity.

During World War II, Americans expanded the nation's industries to produce needed materiel, and, with peace, they turned the expanded capacity to the production of consumer goods in the largest quantities ever. Utilizing the expanded capacity for consumer goods was not mere self-indulgence but had become vital for the economic health of the nation. Political leaders as well as others believed that high government spending during the war had produced full employment, thereby ending the Great Depression. With the advent of peace, they became deeply apprehensive that consumption would drop precipitously, dragging the economy back into an economic morass. Consumption of production was, to them, a national priority. Government spending would do as well as private spending for this purpose, as the war experience had confirmed. In the postwar world, this insight underlay the government's funding of the largest peacetime military America had ever had—so large that, by 1961, Dwight Eisenhower was moved to caution his countrymen against the new "military-industrial complex" that had been created.[1]

A pent-up demand for housing and household goods also spurred the expansion of the postwar economy, since these items had been generally unavailable or unaffordable during the Depression and war. In their efforts to purchase homes of their own, Americans were aided by new federal programs offering low-interest mortgages. Demographic factors also fueled the economy. While the war had forced many young adults to delay starting families, with peace they produced so many children that the term "baby boom" was coined to describe the pronounced bulge in the nation's population. The large cohort of children increased the national demand for housing as well as for a wide range of goods.

Expansion of production during the postwar period also impacted the Christmas trade. The larger volume of goods being poured into the market increased consumers' discretion in making purchases. Because basic needs for food, shelter, and clothing were satisfied with a relatively small percentage of the productive capacity of the economy, the bulk of production could be devoted to more ephemeral wishes, such as engaging in conspicuous consumption or conforming with current styles. Nonfunctional characterisitics of products, such as color, which had not been very important before World War II, assumed a new importance in marketing. Because consumer purchasing decisions became increasingly divorced from basic consumer needs and functional design, the decisions became more difficult for businessmen to predict and more susceptible to wide fluctuations in demand. "Fads" for items could raise demand to red-hot intensity, followed by a precipitous—and financially catastrophic—cooling.

Thus, the years following World War II were a period of increased economic activity. Although retailers were generally delighted with this development, their pleasure was tempered by anxieties and uncertainties engendered by their new affluent circumstances. The greater discretionary element in consumer purchasing made it more difficult to predict purchasing patterns and, therefore, to make available to shoppers the correct quantities of goods. This general difficulty of prediction had several aspects.[2]

First, retailers had to judge which general price ranges would be most popular. Would consumers go for luxury, "big ticket," middle-range, or low-priced items? The variations from year to year were both significant and unpredictable. For example, in 1966 middle-range items sold unexpectedly well, unlike in the preceding years, when higher- and lower-priced gifts predominated. There also was the more specific question of what types of items within popular price ranges would sell well—furniture or clothes, appliances or jewelry? Finally, there remained the most specific question of all: what specific items within the popular types would buyers go for? Would they prefer a Westinghouse refrigerator to a General Electric? A green sweater to a red one?[3]

Judgments also had to be made about which types of stores customers would patronize: department stores, discount stores, specialty shops, luxury-goods establishments, or mail-order houses. This was a difficult prediction to make. For example, during the 1950s new discount houses began to cut into the sales of department stores. But in the '60s shoppers were returning to department stores, beginning a period of revival for them. Consumer preferences for various types of stores could change dramatically as a result of unforeseen developments. For example, in 1968 an outbreak of flu in much of the nation produced a banner year for mail-order houses.[4]

Another problem retailers had to face was that they never knew for sure in which part of the city consumers would prefer to shop. For example, during the 1950s stores located in downtown areas lost sales to stores in the suburbs. This consumer choice was not based on differences between merchandise in stores in the two areas because department stores with both downtown and suburban branches reported the same shopping pattern. However, retailers who counted on this trend continuing through the 1960s were surprised when downtown stores revived. In addition to the yearly variations in preferred shopping sites within cities, it was uncertain which parts of the country would have good or bad years. Such variations were often dependent on the basic economic activity of the area. Northeastern merchants usually prospered with the health of manufacturing, while southern sales commonly ebbed and flowed with the cotton crop. Yet variations in other years showed a remarkable independence of these economic factors and proved difficult to predict.[5]

Another conundrum that challenged Christmas retailers was predicting which days shoppers would do their shopping. In some years, shoppers waited until the very last days when they descended on the stores en masse, while in other years they shopped more evenly throughout the season. These variations complicated business decisions about the size of the seasonal work force and about keeping adequate stock levels at each point of the season. In the early twentieth century, retailers had guessed at the total season's volume and placed a single order for the goods they thought they would need. Later, as transportation and communication improved, manufacturers were able to send out goods on short notice, after retailers had gauged customer purchases during the early part of the season. Nevertheless, retailers were painfully aware that early-season sales might not be accurate indicators of the total Christmas volume.[6]

In addition to these problems, other factors, such as the weather, complicated the lives of retailers. Contrary to what one might think, the best weather for vigorous holiday business was cold and clear. In warm weather, shoppers did not seem to get into the holiday mood and certainly did not feel a strong need to purchase winter coats, gloves, and hats. Retailing decisions were also affected by strikes, whether by laborers directly involved in the Christmas trade or by others who, while on strike, did not have their usual paychecks to spend. Finally, Christmas sales were sometimes affected by the government's tax policies. For example, before the Christmas of 1964, the federal government announced that it would lower the excise tax beginning on January 1, 1965. Retailers were thus left to puzzle over whether shoppers would defer planned purchases of the affected luxury items until the new year.[7]

Because it was so difficult for retailers in the postwar era to predict with much accuracy what their Christmas sales would be, they became anxious with the approach of the shopping season—even though the vast majority of companies engaged in the Christmas trade made handsome profits. This apparent conundrum resulted from the differing competitive position of companies and the managers of those companies. In an uncertain marketing environment, managers competed against one another—with managers in their own companies as well as those in other companies—to maximize their sales. Their task was to win the largest share of holiday profits for their businesses. If we remember the highly competitive position of managers, we can appreciate their anxiety at the approach of the Christmas season. While businesses were likely to survive the

season, and even benefit from it, a manager who paled in comparison
with his peers might not.

As we survey the celebration of Christmas from 1940 to 1980, the anxieties harbored by retailers stand out. During World War II the celebration of Christmas in America was a remarkably hearty event when one
considers that wartime duties scattered family members, and that some
materials that had been used in the manufacture of gift items were now
requisitioned for the war effort. In spite of these difficulties, people
generally had greater economic means during the war than they had
during the economically distressed 1930s, and they were encouraged to
spend some of their money in celebrating Christmas. Periodical writers
agreed that everyone should continue to observe the holidays during the
conflict. Indeed, the Christmas celebration and "the American way of
life" became intermingled so that celebrating became an act of patriotism.[8]

During the first three Christmases following the war—1945, 1946,
and 1947—seasonal sales were strong, reflecting the continuation of wartime prosperity into peacetime. The volume of sales increased about 10
percent per year, to the delight of retailers who stood to gain a lot. In
addition, each season's profits pushed memories of the Great Depression
further into the background. But then came the unexpectedly slow
Christmas of 1948. Although some retailers had seen indications of wariness and price consciousness by shoppers during the previous holiday
season, they stocked goods as if 1948 were going to be yet another record
year. However, sales proved to be sluggish throughout the shopping
season, except for a modest buying spurt in the last two days. A writer
described a striking result of this situation:

On the edge of a Christmas buying season which had been expected to break all
records, U.S. retailers last week broke forth in a rash of unseasonal clearance
sales. Reason: for three weeks in a row, their dollar volume had fallen below the
level of a year ago. To step it up, they marked down prices and bulged the
newspapers with ads of eye-popping bargains. Retailers' worries were the customers' delights.[9]

In total, the Christmas sales volume for 1948 rarely equalled that of the
previous year, leaving retailers with surplus inventories.

Later, businessmen tried to understand why the unexpectedly slow sales of the 1948 season had occurred. A writer in a business journal noted that the

season . . . had given [retailers] their worst scare in who knows when. Most of them were relieved [at the final spurt in sales], but still shaken. They size up their situation about like this: Christmas sales were a big disappointment. But there was not a disaster. Volume for the season as a whole was at least equal to 1947. And that means that it was colossal by prewar standards. If retailers hadn't been counting on a year-to-year gain of 10% or more, 1948 Christmas sales would have looked wonderful to them. . . . Most stores are starting the new year feeling safe but cautious.

Retailers were concerned mainly about the discrepancy between how much they thought shoppers would buy and how much was actually sold. Their misjudgment in 1948 led some retailers to question their ability to predict consumer behavior accurately. Their primary indicator —the amount of disposable income—was apparently not reliable, since consumers had had plenty of money to spend.[10]

In subsequent Christmases, retailers demonstrated increased cautiousness in stocking for the holidays. Rather than placing a few large orders at the beginning of the season, they placed smaller but more frequent orders, spaced over the holiday selling period that were based on actual sales. This new strategy was effective: beginning in the late 1940s, stores had fewer January clearance sales than before. Although ordering smaller quantities of goods was generally safer than the earlier reliance on large orders, the strategy was not foolproof. Its shortcomings became most evident when particular items became "hot" and the small stocks on hand quickly sold out, resulting in lost sales.[11]

Since the Christmas of 1948, retailers never quite regained their earlier confidence. Even during years of good holiday sales, they remained uneasy. Their apprehension was understandable because they could see no discernible pattern in the occurrence of good and bad years. For example, the Christmas of 1952 was an unusually good one for retailers. Shoppers freely purchased the items they wanted because they feared that materials would be requisitioned for the Korean War effort as they had been during World War II. But this good Christmas of 1952 was followed in a year by a very poor Christmas, with little perceptible reason. Only in hindsight did analysts conclude that shoppers had curtailed their buying because they feared that a nationwide recession lurked in the near future. The problem for retailers was that consumer attitudes such as these were hard to discern in advance so that retailers could stock accordingly.[12]

The attitude of wariness and caution continued into the late 1950s, and proved to be well founded. In 1957 buyers were hesitant in making Christmas purchases, resulting in a disappointing sales volume, and the volume of 1958 barely equalled it. Two years later, sales were again fairly slow. Following these uneven but basically disappointing years, retailers enjoyed a string of good years in the early 1960s. The value-conscious, fussy attitude of Christmas shoppers between 1948 and 1960 gave way to a yen for luxuries, fashion, and fads. Retailers were generally happy about the freer spending, but the new importance of fad buying made their stocking decisions more difficult. Who could predict which items would be the darlings of that year's consumers? They only knew that when certain items caught on with the public, their sales soared and they scurried madly after dwindling supplies. For those merchants who were fortunate enough to get them, there always lurked the possibility that new stocks would arrive just as consumer fervor for the item waned, leaving retailers stuck with slow-moving, out-of-date merchandise.[13]

Following the steady strong sales of the early 1960s, the Christmas business again became sporadic. For example, in 1966 total volume was disappointing, although merchants were somewhat heartened by strong sales of middle-priced items, which contrasted with the previous strong sales of high- and low-priced items. Mediocre sales characterized the 1967 and 1969 seasons, followed by bad sales in 1970. During the 1970 season, shoppers proved to be unusually price conscious and chose their gifts from the lower-priced end of lines of goods, a pattern of selection retailers had not been able to foresee.[14]

During the early 1970s, the retailers' lack of confidence in their ability to predict consumer preferences increased. Their expressions of self-doubt became almost painfully explicit, and were more widespread throughout the business community. Previously, businessmen had expressed their surprise at Christmas shopping preferences, but now they acknowledged their inability to understand the mysteries behind stocking the right amounts and kinds of merchandise. In 1974 retailers openly admitted that they simply did not know why the holiday sales volume that year was bad. Americans had plenty of disposable income, but for some perplexing reason, they chose not to buy. The next Christmas proved to be particularly good, although economic conditions that season did not justify freer spending. Retailers again acknowledged their bewilderment at consumer behavior. They were not even able to glean any lessons from previous mistakes that might help them predict future buying patterns better.[15]

As a strategy for coping with the uncertainties of holiday shopping, retailers began to offer more services to their customers in the hope that those services would exert a more predictable pull on shoppers than their merchandise had. On the surface, advocates of this strategy hoped it would provide them some stability, yet they remained uneasily aware that the strategy might not work. For example, it became easier to get credit in some stores. Several large department stores offered to lend shoppers a few hundred dollars worth of special "Christmas money," ersatz currency that could be spent in their stores and need not be repaid for several months. Other retailers offered credit cards to attract and hold customers. The easy credit appealed to shoppers and allowed them to exercise greater discretion in making their Christmas purchases. The access to credit freed them from the constraints of their current cash situation and allowed them to exercise a wider choice, within the expanded limits of the credit. This greater latitude contributed to more impulse buying and made Christmas marketing more difficult.[16]

The Progressive and post–World War II eras faced similar problems regarding Christmas gift giving. In both periods, shoppers enjoyed greater discretion in Christmas purchasing because of the expanded productive capacity of the nation's industries. Americans no longer directed their energies toward satisfying their basic needs and could indulge their more subjective desires. But this greater choice made marketing at Christmas very difficult.

In spite of these underlying similarities in the two periods, the responses of public leaders to them differed significantly. Progressives pushed for reform of the celebration—an effort that achieved some notable results—while postwar business leaders, among others, remained passive and resigned themselves to being anxious over consumer behavior. By using the early twentieth century for contrast, we can identify, as a significant characteristic of the celebration in recent decades, the absence of any significant effort to reform Christmas gift giving. Therefore, one must view popular complaints about a runaway celebration in a different light. Those who were anxious about the difficulty of predicting holiday sales or who objected to the large scale of the recent celebration could have transformed their disgruntlement into organized efforts to bring about change, rather than remaining passive on the assumption that nothing could be done to rein in a celebration which they thought was hopelessly out of hand.

CHAPTER 13

Conclusion

A widespread popular interpretation of Christmas dominates our thinking about the festival. Since 1900, most Americans have believed that "in the good old days" Christmas was delightfully simple, and that its simplicity was derived from—and appropriate to—the nation's agricultural economy. The elements of this idealized, nostalgic Christmas were a visit by St. Nicholas, the exchange of small presents around a Christmas tree, the reverent celebration of the birth of Jesus in a nearby church, and the family Yule dinner. The goal of these efforts, stated time and time again, was to foster family togetherness. Celebrants produced by themselves almost all of the food, gifts, Christmas trees, and other items they needed, and therefore made few cash purchases in connection with the celebration. In virtually all respects, the scale of the celebration was smaller than it later became.

Unfortunately, so the popular interpretation goes, this simple rural Christmas of "the good old days" was overwhelmed by a new form of celebration that reflected urban and industrial values. Americans began to celebrate on a much larger scale. They gave not only more presents, but also more expensive ones, and they gave them to a constantly widening circle of recipients. The simplicity of the earlier celebration was lost in the bustle of expanded shopping and gift giving. In short, the festival became commercialized. For their part, businessmen contributed to the new commercial atmosphere as they became active and successful in exploiting the festival. Indeed, many believe that the modern form of celebration was the creation of businessmen, who foisted their commercialized festival on a public that did not truly want it.

Broadly sketched, this is what most Americans regard as the major transformation in the celebration of Christmas over the last century. In many respects, this interpretation is correct. Certainly, Christmas was a smaller festival in the nineteenth century than it became in the twentieth. And, just as surely, there were fewer economic ramifications of the earlier festival than of our own. However, even if the nostalgic view has some validity on a general level, it is misleading in other significant regards.

First, the popular interpretation is chronologically imprecise, as it never defines accurately when the nostalgic Christmas existed, and when it was transformed into the modern celebration. Those who have rhapsodized about Christmas celebrations in "the good old days" have used that phrase to denote widely varying times in the past, anytime from a single generation back to over a century. Others have simply left the time unspecified.

Second, the popular interpretation of Christmas tends to talk about the "festival as a whole," and in so doing, to overgeneralize about the celebration. It obscures the diversity of the many aspects of the celebration. In order to answer some of the important questions about the festival, it is necessary to distinguish and analyze its different elements, hence the separate discussions in this book on Christmas gifts to women, men, children, friends, community members, employees, and the poor. The patterns of gift giving and celebration from group to group varied significantly. For example, after 1900 many people concluded that gimcracks were too substantial a remembrance to present to friends and began to send cards. At the same time, however, the community Christmas movement tried to foster friendship ties in the nation's cities through public festivals. At some points, the kinds of gifts presented to one category of recipient changed in precisely the opposite way than did gifts to another category of recipient. We saw that, during the Great Depression gifts to men became more practical while gifts to women became more luxurious. At the same time, other categories of gifts, such as those to boys, did not change. One cannot do justice to details such as these while talking about the celebration "as a whole."

Third, those who adhere to the popular interpretation of Christmas believe that the shift from the old to modern form of celebration has been for the worse, and particularly that the changes have diminished the celebrants' enjoyment of the holiday. However, they overlook the enthusiasm with which Americans have embraced the modern form of celebration with its purchased manufactured gifts. The overwhelming majority of the nation's Christmas celebrants showed their approval of the new Christmas by their numerous shopping trips to metropolitan business districts—undertaken with a spirit far from grudging.

Finally, the popular interpretation of Christmas infers that the celebration is out of control at present and will probably be uncontrollable in the future. The desire for expensive gifts, fueled by manufacturers' and merchants' promotions of holiday sales, are seen as forces that Americans cannot bring into tow. However, this view ignores the significant reforms which Christmas celebrants achieved during the emergence of the modern festival. Although celebrants have embraced the modern festival, they have also exercised their critical faculties. At crucial points, they exercised control over the emerging celebration and shaped it to their liking. As a result, they got, by and large, the type of celebration they wanted. The modern Christmas was not forced on Americans against their will.

Efforts to reform the emerging celebration are found in diverse aspects of the festival. The early form of celebration began to change about 1880, as America became urbanized and industrialized. Celebrants began to exchange large numbers of manufactured gimcracks in lieu of handmade gifts. By 1900 reform-minded Americans had identified several undesirable elements of this modern Christmas.

It seemed clear to reformers that gift givers were presenting too many gimcracks to too many of their friends. Gift lists had grown steadily since 1880; by the turn of the century, getting some trifle for everyone on the list had become a major annual chore. In addition, the giving of small presents, which had been an integral part of rural culture, seemed too substantial for most urban friendships. Reformers began to make celebrants conscious of burdens they had imposed on themselves and encouraged them to forgo giving gimcracks to mere acquaintances. They created a special organization, the Society for the Prevention of Useless Giving (SPUG) to help them in this effort. About 1910 the gift-giving practices of celebrants shifted in exactly the way the reformers wanted. The number of gimcracks presented dropped substantially, and they were replaced by lower-priced, and more easily purchased, Christmas cards.

Reformers also took up the cause of workers who were harried from serving the crush of Christmas shoppers. The excessively long and grueling hours which women and children workers had to toil during the season became a favorite topic in holiday articles. The Consumers' League

"White List Campaign" during the 1910s sought to ameliorate abuses stemming from expanded shopping hours. The league made public the names of stores that kept their regular business hours throughout the holiday season, and made its list available to shoppers who, it hoped, would shop only in the stores listed, thereby putting economic pressure on those stores with lengthened holiday hours to reduce them in order to get themselves on the list. By the 1920s, the effort to shorten business hours had achieved substantial success in many urban centers.

Progressive era reformers saw that distribution of aid to the poor during the holidays was wasteful and inefficient. Some needy people received two Christmas baskets while others equally impoverished got nothing. To remedy this, reformers rationalized distribution of assistance by creating a single centralized file in each city which showed which recipients had already received assistance. At the same time, fund-raising efforts were made more rational by having all charities join in making a single unified appeal with the funds raised being later divided among participating charities on a percentage basis. Through these reforms, collection and distribution of aid to the poor at Christmas was made significantly more efficient than it had been under the "Lady Bountiful" system of the late nineteenth century.

When reformers of the Progressive period looked at relationships between inhabitants of the nation's cities, they saw too much influence exerted by the market. Impersonal buying and selling seemed to have pushed warm friendships from urban society. As a remedy, they established and promoted community Christmas celebrations, which were subsequently held in cities across America during the 1910s and 1920s. The hope was to promote individual ties of friendship within cities and create a warmer, more personal atmosphere throughout urban America.

Reform-minded Americans of the Progressive period aggressively addressed the problems in the society around them. They did not consider themselves to be helpless in the face of a custom that had gotten out of control. Rather, they confronted the shortcomings and abuses of the emerging custom and marshaled public opinion behind their efforts to reform the celebration. Not only did they make effective use of mass media, but they also established organizations to implement their goals, such as SPUG, the Consumers' League White List, the two Santa Claus Associations, the federated charities movement, and community Christmas organizations.

These efforts produced substantive reforms in the celebration by 1930. At least three of the Progressive period reforms have survived to the present: the curtailing of excessive gimcrack giving, the rationalization of Christmas charity, and the encouragement of stores to keep their regular hours during the holiday shopping period. Only the community Christmas movement, always the least realistic of the reforms, has largely passed from the American scene. All in all, the achievements of the reformers are impressive, and we celebrate today according to the basic forms they helped bring into being.

The reformers not only sought to improve the holiday, but also used Christmas symbols to correct problems that existed year round. For example, they wanted to improve working conditions of laborers not only at Christmas, but throughout the year. The Progressive era is the only period in which Christmas symbols were used to promote general social reform: they were not used to promote Franklin Roosevelt's New Deal, Harry Truman's Fair Deal, John Kennedy's New Frontier, or Lyndon Johnson's Great Society. Those reforms were achieved during regular, year-round time, with no regard for the holiday season.

Why was the Progressive period the only period to utilize Christmas symbols to bring about general social reform? If we look at the reforms promoted during that era—in the working conditions in the nation's stores and factories; of the provision of assistance to the poor; of excessive gift giving to friends; and of the sense of urban alienation—we see that they were matters about which governmental authorities had little to say at the time, regarding them as private matters. Therefore, reformers had to work outside the political system to mobilize public opinion and private organizations to support their goals. As a result of these efforts, governmental authorities began to include among their legitimate activities many of the goals of the reformers. Americans wanted their political authorities to see to it that working conditions were decent, that the poor were properly cared for, and that community activities and voluntary associations were supported in order to counteract urban alienation. At that point, Christmas symbols were no longer needed to focus public attention on these issues: they had become accepted as appropriate subjects for governmental action.

$\mathcal{N}otes$

The following abbreviations are used in the footnotes for the titles of periodicals:

A&S	*Advertising and Selling*
AgH	*Agricultural History*
Am	*America*
AHer	*American Heritage*
AHom	*American Home*
AJS	*American Journal of Sociology*
AMag	*American Magazine*
AMer	*American Mercury*
AQ	*American Quarterly*
ASR	*American Sociological Review*
AAA	*Annals of the American Academy*
Ar	*Arena*
At	*Atlantic*
BM	*Bankers Magazine*
Bl	*Bellman*
BH&G	*Better Homes and Gardens*
Bk	*Bookman*
BHR	*Business History Review*
BW	*Business Week*
CW	*Catholic World*
Cen	*Century*
Col	*Collier's*
C&F	*Commerce and Finance*
CB	*Consumer Bulletin*
Cos	*Cosmopolitan*
CR	*Contemporary Review*
CLif	*Country Life*

CH	*Current History*
CurL	*Current Literature*
ER	*Educational Review*
Et	*Etude*
Ev	*Everybody's*
Ftn	*Fortune*
Frm	*Forum*
GP	*Glimpses of the Past*
GB	*Golden Book*
GH	*Good Housekeeping*
HBaz	*Harper's Bazar*
HM	*Harper's Monthly*
HNMM	*Harper's New Monthly Magazine*
HW	*Harper's Weekly*
H&G	*House and Garden*
HB	*House Beautiful*
I	*Independent*
IW	*Independent Woman*
IAM	*Industrial Arts Monthly*
JHE	*Journal of Home Economics*
JSoch	*Journal of Social History*
JSouH	*Journal of Southern History*
LHJ	*Ladies' Home Journal*
Lf	*Life*
L	*Lippincott's*
LD	*Literary Digest*
LA	*Living Age*
MAH	*Magazine of American History*
MCl	*McClure's*
Men	*Mentor*
MH	*Minnesota History*
MR	*Missionary Review*
Mun	*Munsey's*
N	*Nation*
NH	*Natural History*
NEM	*New England Magazine*
NO	*New Outlook*
NR	*New Republic*
NW	*Newsweek*
NYHSQB	*New-York Historical Society Quarterly Bulletin*

NAR   *North American Review*

OH   *Ohio History*
Out   *Outlook*
Ov   *Overland*
OM   *Overland Monthly*

PM   *Parents' Magazine*
PI   *Printer's Ink*
PIM   *Printer's Ink Monthly*
P   *Psychiatry*

QJE   *Quarterly Journal of Economics*

RD   *Reader's Digest*
RR   *Review of Reviews*
R   *Rotarian*

SalM   *Sales Management*
SEP   *Saturday Evening Post*
SRL   *Saturday Review of Literature*
SA   *Scientific American*
ScrM   *Scribner's Magazine*
SS   *Social Studies*
Sdg   *Soundings*
SW   *Southern Workman*
SHQ   *Southwestern Historical Quarterly*
SJA   *Southwestern Journal of Anthropology*
Sun   *Sunset*
Sur   *Survey*
Sys   *System*

T   *Time*

USNWR   *U.S. News & World Report*

WC   *Woman Citizen*
WHC   *Woman's Home Companion*
WW   *World's Work*

1. Introduction

1. For a general introduction to the celebration of Christmas in America, see James H. Barnett, *The American Christmas* (New York, 1954). For a guide to works on Christmas, see Sue Samuelson, *Christmas: An Annotated Bibliography* (New York, 1982).

2. The comment by Margaret Deland is from her "Save Christmas!" *HBaz*, 46 (Dec. 1912): 593. For analyses of the Christmas celebration in a contemporary community, see Theodore Caplow, "Christmas Gifts and Kin Networks," *ASR*, 47 (June 1982): 383–92; Theodore Caplow, "Rule Enforcement without Visible Means: Christmas Gift Giving in

Middletown," *AJS*, 89 (May 1984): 1306–23; Theodore Caplow et al., *All Faithful People* (Minneapolis, 1983), 182–98; and Theodore Caplow et al., *Middletown Families* (Minneapolis, 1982), pp. 225–45.

2. Fundamental Themes

1. See Mircea Eliade, *Cosmos and History* (New York, 1959), 62–73.

2. For penetrating analyses of "golden ages," see the following four books by Mircea Eliade: *Myths, Dreams, and Mysteries* (New York, 1967), 39–72; *Myth and Reality* (New York, 1968), 21–53, 75–91; *Cosmos and History*, 49–92; and *Patterns in Comparative Religion* (Cleveland, 1963), 388–409.

3. For discussions of the connections between the celebration of Christmas and the New Year's and winter solstice celebrations, see C. Smith, "Christmas and Its Cycle," in *The New Catholic Encyclopedia*; Kirsopp Lake, "Christmas," in *Hastings Encyclopedia of Religion and Ethics*; E. Lehman, "Christmas Customs," in *Hastings Encylopedia of Religion and Ethics*; B. Botte, "Saturnalia," in *The New Catholic Encyclopedia*; C. Smith, "Epiphany," in *The New Catholic Encyclopedia*; Kirsopp Lake, "Epiphany," in *Hastings Encyclopedia of Religion and Ethics*; C. Smith, "Candlemas," in *The New Catholic Encyclopedia*; Frida Davidson, "How Our Christmas Customs Came," *NH*, 28 (11 Nov. 1928): 617–25; and G. C. McWhorter, "The Holidays," *HNMM*, 32 (Dec. 1865): 164–72.

4. For a discussion of creation rituals, see Eliade, *Cosmos and History*, 12–21, 30, 76–80.

5. The two ideal types of exchanges are for heuristic purposes. Most actual exchanges in societies have at least some characteristics of each of the ideal types. Consider, for example, the "gift exchanges" in which the predominant wish of the givers is to spend as little as possible in discharging their gift-giving obligations, in other words, to "get off" as cheaply as they can while saving social face. Consider, also, the "market exchanges" made at stores of small-town merchants, transactions in which merchants give special services to their customers and guarantee satisfaction whether they are contractually bound to do so or not. By conceiving of exchanges such as these as being somewhere on a continuum between two ideal poles, the analyst is able to gauge the admixture of gift values with market values.

6. Much of the interest in gifts on the part of social scientists stems from Marcel Mauss's *The Gift* (New York, 1967). Other helpful sociological and anthropological discussions of gift giving are Raymond Firth, *Symbols: Public and Private* (London, 1973), 368–402; Barry Schwartz, "The Social Psychology of the Gift," *AJS*, 73 (July 1967): 1–11; Bronislaw Malinowski, *Crime and Custom in Savage Society* (London, 1926), 39–45; Melville J. Herskovits, *Economic Anthropology* (New York, 1965), 155–79; Alvin Gouldner, "The Norm of Reciprocity," *ASR*, 25 (April 1960), 161–78; Alvin Gouldner, "Reciprocity and Autonomy in Functional Theory," in *Symposium on Sociological Theory*, ed. Llewellyn Gross (Evanston, Ill., 1959), 241–70; Claude Levi-Strauss, *The Elementary Structures of Kinship* (Boston, 1969), 52–68, 233–68; Paul Bohannan, *Social Anthropology* (New York, 1963), 229–65; Karl Polanyi, *The Great Transformation* (Boston, 1957), passim; Moses I. Finley, *The World of Odysseus* (New York, 1965), pp. 59–69, 100–105; Manning Nash, *Primitive and Peasant Economic Systems* (Scranton, Pa., 1966), pp. 26–33; Philip Drucker, *Indians of the Northwest Coast* (Garden City, N.Y., 1963), 131–43; Stuart Piddocke, "The Potlatch System of the Southern Kwakiutl," *SJA*, 21 (1965): 244–64, Lewis Hyde, *The Gift* (New York, 1983), 3–140; and Colin Camerer, "Gifts as Economic Signals and Social Symbols," *AJS*, 94 (supp.), S180–S214.

3. The Gifts Everyone Wanted

1. For discussions of the prevalence of handmade gifts during the nineteenth century, see John Burroughs, "Corrupting the Innocents," *I*, 61 (13 Dec. 1906): 1425; "Christmas in the Shops," *Out*, 96 (26 Nov. 1910): 662; Ellis Parker Butler, "Something for the Kid," *Cos*, 50 (Jan. 1911): 168–70; and Carl Werner, "Christmas When We Were Kids," *Out*, 102 (23 Nov. 1912), 678–83. See also the following recent discussions of handmade gifts in the nineteenth century: Harnett T. Kane, *The Southern Christmas Book* (New York, 1958), 17, 70fn, 172, 251fn; Bertha L. Heilbron, "Christmas and New Year's on the Frontier," *MH*, 16, no. 4 (Dec. 1935): 381–90; and Walter Prescott Webb, "Christmas and New Year in Texas," *SHQ*, 44 (July 1940): 361.

Handmade gifts retained some of their popularity into the twentieth century, as indicated by the following articles on making Christmas gifts: Lillian Baynes Griffin, "Home-Made Christmas Gifts," *HB*, 33 (3 Nov. 1900): 1723ff; Margaret Hamilton Welch, "Christmas Gifts," *HB*, 37 (Dec. 1903): 1180–84; Bessie Berrie Grabowski, "My Readers' Own Christmas Ideas," *LHJ*, 23 (Dec. 1905): 27; "Inexpensive Home-Made Christmas Gifts," *LHJ*, 23 (Nov. 1906): 41; A. L. Gorman, "Home-Made Christmas Gifts," *HB*, 42 (Dec. 1908): 1256–58; "Christmas Home Parties and a Novel Way to Bestow a Child's Gifts," *LHJ*, 28 (Dec. 1911): 87; and Mary E. Hopkins, "Handicraft Gift," LHJ, 31 (Dec. 1914): 41.

Some articles argued that the simple gifts that parents had presented to their children in the nineteenth century were superior to modern mechanical ones. See Edward Bok, "Are We Fair to Our Children at Christmas?" *LHJ*, 20 (Dec. 1902): 18; Burroughs, "Corrupting the Innocents," 1424–25; "Christmas in the Shops," 662; Emelyn Lincoln Coolidge, "Young Mother at Christmastime," *LHJ*, 29 (Dec. 1912): 54; and Werner, "Christmas When We Were Kids," 680–81.

The comment is from Werner, "Christmas When We Were Kids," 680. See, also, "Christmas Gift That Surprises Father and Mother," *LHJ*, 34 (Dec. 1917): 45. For examples of the types of gifts made by men, see "Home-Made Arts and Crafts," 27; and "Inexpensive Home-Made Christmas Gift," 41.

For discussions of the role of women as the manufacturers for the family, see Belle Squire, "Women and Money Spending," *HB*, 34 (Nov. 1905): 1054; and Andrew Sinclair, *The Emancipation of the American Woman* (New York, 1965), 4.

2. George Rogers Taylor, *The Transportation Revolution, 1815–1860* (New York, 1968), 207–24. See also Werner, "Christmas When We Were Kids," 678–83.

3. For discussions of the American economy during the last third of the nineteenth century, see Thomas C. Cochran and William Miller, *The Age of Enterprise*, rev. ed. (New York, 1961), 119–53; Edward Chase Kirkland, *Industry Comes of Age* (Chicago, 1967), passim; Allen Nevins, *The Emergence of Modern America* (Chicago, 1971), 31–74; Alfred D. Chandler, "The Beginnings of 'Big Business' in American Industry," *BHR*, 33 (Spring 1959): 1–31; and John A Garraty, *The New Commonwealth, 1877–1890* (New York, 1968), 78–127.

4. For recent analyses of the appearance of new manufactured items after 1880, see John W. Doss, *Everyday Life in Twentieth Century America* (New York, 1965), 129–54; David M. Potter, *People of Plenty* (Chicago, 1954), 172–78; and Siegfried Giedion, *Mechanization Takes Command* (New York, 1969), 512–627. For articles that discuss the acceptability of new types of manufactured items as Christmas gifts, see Werner, "Christmas When We Were Kids," 680–81; Theresa Hunt Walcott, "Gift You Have Never Given," *LHJ*, 34 (Dec.

1917): 43; Martin Hastings, Jr., "Odd Advertising Copy That Brought Christmas Business," *PI*, 121 (28 Dec. 1922): 33–34 +; and Frank L. Scott, "Sales Arguments That Help Get Christmas Trade," *PI*, 128 (7 Aug. 1924): 3–4 +.

5. For ads for halfway items that suggest giving them as Christmas gifts, see illustration 1: Potter pillow embroidery pattern, *LHJ*, 20 (Dec. 1902): 56; illustration 2: Herrick Christmas cards, *LHJ*, 28 (Dec. 1911): 82; and illustration 3: G. Reis and Bros. embroidery letters, *LHJ*, 28 (Dec. 1911): 72. See also Brainard and Armstrong embroidery book, *LHJ*, 19 (Dec. 1901): 36; Linn Murray furniture, *LHJ*, 20 (Dec. 1902): 21; Indian baskets, *LHJ*, 20 (Dec. 1902): 40; and William A. Smith Christmas cards, *LHJ*, 28 (Dec. 1911): 75.

6. The popularity of the halfway items with middle- and upper middle-class urban women in large part accounts for the appearance of ads for halfway items in the *Ladies' Home Journal* during the early twentieth century. The classic statement of the argument that conspicuously leisured activities are a means of demonstrating one's wealth is Thorstein Veblen, *The Theory of the Leisure Class* (New York, 1934), 35–67.

7. There were practically no ads for handmade or halfway items in the *Ladies' Home Journal* during the three three-year periods after World War I that I examined (1920–1922, 1928–1930, and 1936–1938). Also, after 1920, very few articles on handmaking holiday gift items appeared in periodicals, whereas such articles had been frequent before World War I.

8. For articles that emphasize the uniqueness of handmade items, see Edna Randolph Worrell, "Rimes to Go with Gifts," *LHJ*, 33 (Dec. 1916): 1; and Florence Lemmon, "Let's Have a Real Christmas Card This Year," *HB*, 58 (Dec. 1925): 628 +. The qualities of being unique or custom designed were the main bases for the often-stated claim that handmade gift items were more personal than manufactured ones. For articles that emphasize the personal nature of handmade gifts, see Griffin, "Home-Made Christmas Gifts," 1723; May Norton, "Christmas Gifts," *LHJ*, 22 (Dec. 1904): 44; "Home-Made Arts and Crafts," 27; "Christmas Editorial," *LHJ*, 27 (Dec. 1910): 5; Fannie Stearns Gifford, "The Spirit of Christmas," *HB*, 48 (Dec. 1920): 461; Lemmon, "Let's Have a Real Christmas Card This Year," 628 +; and Ralph M. Pearson, "Some Thoughts About Christmas Cards," *Frm*, 100 (Dec. 1938): 319.

9. The quotation is from Gorman, "Home-Made Christmas Gifts," 1256. For articles that discuss the gift of time in handmade presents, see Griffin, "Home-Made Christmas Gifts," 1723; Norton, "Christmas Gifts," 44; "Home-Made Arts and Crafts," 27; and "Christmas Editorial," 5. The possibility of giving time to recipients survived the shift to manufactured gift items, although in altered form. Those who gave manufactured items could give time if they spent long hours shopping for the most appropriate item for each recipient. For examples of this theme, see I. McDougall, "The Gift Successful, *HB*, 35 (Dec. 1913): 19; and Ronald Miller, "Our Billion-Dollar Christmas," *AMag*, 108 (Dec. 1929): 63 +.

10. An excellent discussion of contamination from an anthropological perspective is Mary Douglas, *Purity and Danger* (Baltimore, 1970), passim.

11. For examples of this decontaminating mechanism, see illustration 4: L. S. Berry furs, *LHJ*, 18 (Dec. 1900): 47; illustration 5: Newcomb-Endicott handkerchiefs, *LHJ*, 20 (Dec. 1902): 50. See also Linn Murray furniture, *LHJ*, 18 (Dec. 1900): 41; Self-closing tobacco pouch, *SEP*, 174 (14 Dec. 1901): 17; C. D. Peacock assorted Christmas gifts, *LHJ*, 20 (Dec. 1902): 46; Laughlin pens, *LHJ*, 20 (Dec. 1902): 48; Albrecht furs, *LHJ*, 20 (Dec. 1902): 56; Loftis Diamonds, *SEP*, 175 (6 Dec. 1902): 26; Book Supply Co., *LHJ*, 28 (Dec. 1911): 49; Lester lace goods, *LHJ*, 28 (Dec. 1911): 63; Reveillon furs, *LHJ*, 28 (Dec. 1911): 69; and Shackman assorted Christmas gifts, *LHJ*, 28 (Dec. 1911): 78.

12. The quotation is from John Allen Murphy, "How Manufacturers Are Getting Their

Goods into Santa Claus' Pack," *PI*, 121 (2 Nov. 1922): 17. See also Agnes Repplier, "The Oppression of Gifts," *L*, 68 (Dec. 1901): 734; McDougall, "The Gift Successful," 19; "Where Are the Christmas Stories of Yesteryear?" *LD*, 51 (18 Dec. 1915): 1427; "The Christmas Spirit," *At*, 128 (Dec. 1921): 860; and Margaret Dana, "Christmas Giving," *At*, 160 (Dec. 1937): 762–65.

13. The quotation is from C. B. Larrabee, "What About Your Christmas Selling Plans?" *PIM*, 10 (May 1925): 20. For articles that discuss this mechanism of arguing for the gift-giving appropriateness of some manufactured items, see Carroll D. Murphy, "American-made Christmas," *Sys*, 26 (Oct. 1914): 361–62; "Where Are the Christmas Stories of Yesteryear?" 1427; M. Hussobee, "Associated Campaign Puts Veils in Christmas Gift Class," *PI*, 113 (23 Dec. 1920): 50–52; Murphy, "How Manufacturers Are Getting Their Goods into Santa Claus' Pack," 17–19+; "Merry Christmas Awaits a Big Retail Outlet," *PI*, 128 (14 Aug. 1924): 33–34; G. A. Nichols, "Cold and Fishy Eye for Good Old Santa Claus," *PIM*, 13 (Nov. 1926): 73; "Now That It's Hot—Let's Think of Christmas," *PI*, 152 (17 July 1930): 10+; "Santa Will Carry Towels," *PI*, 161 (10 Nov. 1932): 82; "Commutation Tickets Enter the Gift Field," *PI*, 157 (14 Jan. 1932): 92; and "Check-Points for Christmas," *PI*, 176 (3 Sept. 1936): 83.

14. For articles that argue that there are few, or no, items that are inappropriate as gift items, see Scott, "Sales Arguments That Help Get Christmas Trade," 8; "Direct Mail Puts on Its Holiday Apparel," *PI*, 133 (26 Nov. 1925): 33; Larrabee, "What About Your Christmas Selling Plans?" 20; and "A Christmas Miscellany," *PIM*, 36 (June 1938): 21.

15. The articles to which I refer are, in order, Charles Noble, " 'Give Her a Zoofus Washboard for Christmas,' " *PI*, 144 (30 Aug. 1928): 10+; Walter Morton, "—if You Know What I Mean," *Out*, 150 (12 Dec. 1928): 1315; and John Burt Hardee, "'Twas the Month Before Christmas," *PI*, 149 (28 Nov. 1929): 68. See also B. F. Berfield, "Expedition Down the Christmas Copy Stream," *PIM*, 14 (Jan. 1927): 29; and Ed Wolff, "And Now We Point Toward Christmas," *PIM*, 19 (Oct. 1929): 40+.

16. See "Direct Mail Puts on Its Holiday Apparel," 33–34+; Larrabee, "What About Your Christmas Selling Plans?" 19–21+; and "For Puzzled Husbands," *PI*, 161 (8 Dec. 1932): 48–49.

17. For an ad that claims that its item is "the ideal Christmas gift," see illustration 6: Beehler umbrellas, *SEP*, 184 (2 Dec. 1911): 61.

For ads in which writers argue explicitly for the gift acceptability of items, see Angle oil lamps, *SEP*, 173 (8 Dec. 1900): 30; Putnam's books, *SEP*, 174 (7 Dec. 1901): 26; Merritt comforts, *SEP*, 174 (14 Dec. 1901): 15; Frohman Indian blankets, *LHJ*, 20 (Dec. 1902): 4; B B & B trucks, *LHJ*, 20 (Dec. 1902): 46; New England watches, *LHJ*, 20 (Dec. 1902): 51; Gillette razors, *LHJ*, 28 (Dec. 1911): 58; and Dromedary dates, *LHJ*, 28 (Dec. 1911): 80.

For ads in which writers try to decontaminate items by placing the illustrations of them near holiday symbols, see Waterman's fountain pens, *SEP*, 174 (7 Dec. 1901): 32; New Haven clocks, *SEP*, 184 (2 Dec. 1911): 45; Iron Clad socks, *SEP*, 174 (9 Dec. 1911): 50; Dromedary dates, *LHJ*, 28 (Dec. 1911): 80; Rubberset brushes, *SEP*, 185 (2 Dec. 1912): 81; Paris garters, *SEP*, 185 (14 Dec. 1912): 57; and Thermos bottles, *LHJ*, 29 (Dec. 1912): 61.

18. For ads in which store clerks assure shoppers of the acceptability of the items advertised, see Jewelry trade, *SEP*, 195 (2 Dec. 1922): 78–79; Westinghouse appliances, *SEP*, 195 (9 Dec. 1922): 64; Eureka vacuum cleaners, *LHJ*, 45 (Dec. 1928): 114; and Dan'l Green slippers, *LHJ*. 46 (Dec. 1929): 116. For ads in which movie stars recommend the items as gifts, see Whiting and Davis mesh bags, *LHJ*, 45 (Dec. 1928): 92; Spur ties, *SEP*, 201 (15 Dec. 1928): 90; Lane cedar chests, *SEP*, 203 (6 Dec. 1930): 171; Philco radios, *SEP*, 203 (20 Dec. 1930): 45; Richard Hudnut cosmetics, *LHJ*, 54 (Dec. 1937): 69; Coolerator

refrigerators, *SEP*, 210 (4 Dec. 1937): 95; and Liggett & Myers cigarettes, *SEP*, 210 (18 Dec. 1937): 49.

For an ad in which Santa serves as a gift consultant to the reader, see illustration 7: Interwoven socks, *SEP*, 201 (8 Dec. 1928): 162. See also Del Monte canned fruits, *SEP*, 195 (9 Dec. 1922): inside front cover; Biflex spring bumper, *SEP*, 195 (9 Dec. 1922): 138; Ladies' Home Journal subscription, *LHJ*, 46 (Dec. 1929): 184; Hamilton watches, *SEP*, 202 (7 Dec. 1929): 76–77; Hendryx bird cages, *SEP*, 202 (7 Dec. 1929): 248; Bicycle trade, *SEP*, 202 (14 Dec. 1929): 75; Rittenhouse chimes, *SEP*, 209 (5 Dec. 1936): 70; Whitman's chocolates, *SEP*, 209 (19 Dec. 1936): 4; R. J. Reynolds' tobacco, *SEP*, 209 (19 Dec. 1936): 34; Sunkist oranges, *SEP*, 209 (19 Dec. 1936): 94; Taylor instruments, *SEP*, 210 (11 Dec. 1937): 84; Gillette razors, *SEP*, 210 (18 Dec. 1937): 63; Telechron clocks, *SEP*, 211 (3 Dec. 1938): 57; Corona typewriters, *SEP*, 211 (3 Dec. 1937): 73; and Bendix washers, *SEP*, 211 (17 Dec. 1938): 62.

The quoted material is from Murphy, "How Manufacturers Are Getting Their Goods into Santa Claus' Pack," 19. See also Gamaliel Bradford, "Santa Claus: A Psychograph," *Bk*, 62 (Dec. 1925): 405.

The four three-year periods before the 1930s from which I examined ads were 1900–1902, 1911–1913, 1920–1922, and 1928–1930. The percentages of ads from those periods that contained illustrations of Santa Claus were, respectively, 3 percent, 3 percent, 5 percent, and 6 percent.

For articles which showed concern that ad writers were using Santa too much, see S. C. Lambert, "Advertising Comes Back to Santa Claus," *PI*, 113 (Dec. 2, 1920): 149–50+; A. L. Townsend, "What Has Christmastide Brought to Another Year of Advertising?" *PI*, 125 (Dec. 20, 1923): 103–4+; Nichols, "Cold and Fishy Eye for Good Old Santa Claus," 70+; "Santa Claus Laws," *T*, 28 (7 Dec. 1936): 52; "Check-Points for Christmas," 83; "Sporty Old Santa Claus!" *PI*, 174 (9 Jan. 1936): 43–44; and "A Christmas Miscellany," 21–22.

19. For ads of the early twentieth century that encourage readers to send for special Christmas catalogues, see C. D. Peacock assorted Christmas gifts, *LHJ*, 20 (Dec. 1902): 46; Dennison holiday goods, *LHJ*, 20 (Dec. 1902): 48; Newcomb-Endicott handkerchiefs, *LHJ*, 20 (Dec. 1902): 50; Bowen Merrill books, *LHJ*, 20 (Dec. 1902): 55; American Electric novelties, *LHJ*, 20 (Dec. 1902): 56; Albrecht furs, *LHJ*, 20 (Dec. 1902): 56; John Wanamaker, *LHJ*, 28 (Dec. 1911): 70; Bishop furniture, *LHJ*, 28 (Dec. 1911): 73; Westinghouse electric wares, *SEP*, 184 (2 Dec. 1911): 63; and Western Electric appliances, *SEP*, 184 (2 Dec. 1911): 68.

20. For articles that discuss the decontaminating power of gift wrappings, see Larrabee, "What About Your Christmas Selling Plans?" 70; Marjorie Lawrence, "Wrapping Your Christmas Packages," *AHom*, 1 (Dec. 1928): 220; Oscar DeCamp, "Gillette Blade Package Becomes $5 Gift Item," *PI*, 145 (27 Dec. 1928): 58; Hardee, "'Twas the Month Before Christmas," 68; "Staple in Gift Boxes Yields 80 Per Cent Sales Increase," *PI*, 23 (Nov. 1931): 48; "Santa Will Carry Towels," 82; and "Commutation Tickets Enter the Gift Field," 92.

21. For evidence that gifts were presented unwrapped during the nineteenth century, see "But Once a Year," *Mun*, 26 (Dec. 1901): 439; and Florence Hull Winterburn, "Money Well Spent," *GH*, 52 (March 1911): 374–75.

The quoted material is from Margaret Deland, "Save Christmas!" *HB*, 46 (Dec. 1912): 593. See also Lawrence, "Wrapping Your Packages," 220.

22. The account is from Murphy, "How Manufacturers Are Getting Their Goods into Santa Claus' Pack," 18.

23. Ibid. For additional articles that discuss the use of gift boxes by manufacturers, see

Murphy, "American-made Christmas," 361–62; Larrabee, "What About Your Christmas Selling Plans?" 21; "Santa Will Carry Towels," 82; "No Fancy Cover for This Gift Box," *PI*, 165 (2 Nov. 1933): 98; and "Check-Points for Christmas," 83.

For ads of items packaged in special holiday boxes, see Bedell clothes, *LHJ*, 19 (Dec. 1901): 36; Crane stationery, *LHJ*, 28 (Dec. 1911): 51; Brown Durrell stockings, *LHJ*, 28 (Dec. 1911): 56; Lester lace goods, *LHJ*, 28 (Dec. 1911): 63; Vegetable Silk hosiery, *LHJ*, 28 (Dec. 1911): 71; Larter shirt studs and cuff links, *LHJ*, 28 (Dec. 1911): 75; Caloric stoves, *LHJ*, 28 (Dec. 1911): 80; Shirley suspenders, *SEP*, 184 (2 Dec. 1911): 39; U.S. Leathergoods billfolds, *SEP*, 184 (2 Dec. 1911): 48; Maxim gun silencers, *SEP*, 184 (2 Dec. 1911): 53; Robeson pocket knives, *SEP*, 184 (2 Dec. 1911): 66; Lennox stationery, *SEP*, 184 (2 Dec. 1911): 71; Everwear hosiery, *SEP*, 184 (2 Dec. 1911): 73; Shawknit socks, *SEP*, 184 (9 Dec. 1911): 28; Swan pens, *SEP*, 184 (9 Dec. 1911): 39; Iron Clad socks, *SEP*, 184 (9 Dec. 1911): 39; Notaseme hosiery, *SEP*, 184 (9 Dec. 1911): 61; Ohio Knitting silk scarves, *SEP*, 184 (9 Dec. 1911): 62; Rubberset brushes, *SEP*, 184 (9 Dec. 1911): 73; Parker pens, *SEP*, 184 (16 Dec. 1911): 33; Eaton, Crane stationery, *LHJ*, 29 (Dec. 1912): 55; Shirley suspenders, *LHJ*, 29 (Dec. 1912): 64; Pad garters, *LHJ*, 29 (Dec. 1912): 65; Gordon hosiery, *LHJ*, 29 (Dec. 1912): 66; Crayola crayons, *LHJ*, 29 (Dec. 1912): 70; L. H. Field handkerchiefs, *LHJ*, 29 (Dec. 1912): 72; Cawson feather accessories, *LHJ*, 29 (Dec. 1912): 76; Royal Flower and Feather plumes, *LHJ*, 29 (Dec. 1912): 78; Bestyette raincoats, *LHJ*, 29 (Dec. 1912): 79; Book Supply Co., *LHJ*, 29 (Dec. 1912): 81; Conklin fountain pens, *SEP*, 185 (7 Dec. 1912): 37; Carborundum knife sharpeners, *SEP*, 185 (7 Dec. 1912): 50; O-Cedar mops, *SEP*, 185 (7 Dec. 1912): 52; Black Cat hosiery, *SEP*, 186 (6 Dec. 1913): 34; Hardright pipes, *SEP*, 186 (6 Dec. 1913): 57; Pioneer garters, *SEP*, 186 (13 Dec. 1913): 50; Huyler's chocolates, *SEP*, 186 (20 Dec. 1913): 34; and Calarab figs, *SEP*, 186 (20 Dec. 1913): 37.

24. For articles that discuss the use of removable sleeves by manufacturers, see Murphy, "How Manufacturers Are Getting Their Goods into Santa Claus' Pack," 19; "Direct Mail Puts On Its Holiday Apparel," 33–34; DeCamp, "Gillette Blade Package Becomes $5 Gift Item," 60; "Check-Points for Christmas," 83; and "A Christmas Miscellany," 24.

25. Larrabee, "What About Your Christmas Selling Plans?" 21.

26. For the early history of the Christmas Club accounts, see Mildred John, "The Christmas Club Idea in Boston," *BM*, 113 (Dec. 1926): 839; and "Christmas Club," *LD*, 122 (21 Nov. 1936): 42.

27. For statistics on the number of banks that offered Christmas clubs, see "A Saner Merry Christmas," 1–2; "The Cheerful Side of Saving," 449; Rawll, "Three Hundred Million Dollar Idea," 883–84; "$400,000,000 in This Year's Christmas-Club Fund," 50; John, "The Christmas Club Idea in Boston," 839–44; Lloyd M. Cosgrave, "Christmas Clubs," *QJE*, 41 (Aug. 1927): 733; C. W. Steffler, "Where Christmas Comes Every Day in the Year," *C&F*, 16 (21 Dec. 1927): 2614; Lawrence Dale, "This Christmas Business," *C&F*, 17 (19 Dec. 1928): 2687; William O. Scroggs, "Christmas and the Payroll," *Out*, 153 (18 Dec. 1929): 621; "Christmas Clubs Distribute $600,000,000," *BM*, 123 (Dec. 1931): 831; "Yuletide Spending Prospects," 36; "Christmas Clubs," *BW*, 23 Nov. 1932, 4; Lawrence Dale, "Santa Claus Comes Down to Earth," *C&F*, 21 (21 Dec. 1932): 1453; "Christmas Clubs," *BW*, 2 Dec. 1933, 9; "Christmas Clubs," *BW*, 17 Nov. 1934, 14; "Yule: $312 Millions," *BW*, 16 Nov. 1935, 42; "Christmas Club," *LD*, 42; and "Big Holiday Buying," *BW*, 5 Dec. 1936, 23. These articles also give figures on the total amount in the clubs and on the number of club members in various parts of the nation.

28. The population figure is from *The Statistical History of the United States from Colonial Times to the Present* (Stamford, Conn., 1965), 7.

29. For articles that discuss the various policies used by banks to regulate their Christ-

mas Club accounts, see "A Saner Merry Christmas," *Out*, 103 (4 Jan. 1913): 1–2; Herbert F. Rawll, "Three Hundred Million Dollar Idea," *BM*, 111 (Dec. 1925): 883–87; John, "The Christmas Idea in Boston," 839–44; "$400,000 in This Year's Christmas-Club Fund," *LD*, 91 (25 Dec. 1926): 50; Lloyd M. Cosgrave, "Christmas Clubs," *QJE*, 41 (Aug. 1927): 732–39; and "Christmas Club," *LD*, 42.

30. For articles that discuss the issue of paying interest on the Christmas Club accounts, see "A Saner Merry Christmas," 1; Rawll, "Three Hundred Million Dollar Idea," 886–87; John, "The Christmas Club Idea in Boston," 839; Cosgrave, "Christmas Clubs," 132–39; H. Fred Oltman, "Why the Christmas Club Pays," *BM*, 125 (Sept. 1932): 227–28; "Christmas Club," *BW*, 8 June 1935, 10; "Christmas Club," *LD*, 42; Leroy W. Herron, "Christmas Funds," *PI*, 174 (9 Jan. 1936): 92; W. H. Steiner and E. Shapiro, "Christmas Club Savings," *BM*, 135 (Dec. 1937): 493; and Winthrop P. Stevens, "Should Banks Pay Interest on Club Accounts?" *BM*, 140 (Jan. 1940): 71–72.

31. The percentage of Christmas Club deposits that members transferred to regular savings accounts was 28 percent in 1924, 28 percent in 1925, 28 percent in 1926, 28 percent in 1932, 26 percent in 1933, and 25 percent in 1934. For articles that break down the total club deposits into the major uses to which members put the funds, see "The Cheerful Side of Saving," *WW*, 49 (Feb. 1925): 448; Rawll, "Three Hundred Million Dollar Idea," 883; "$400,000,000 in This Year's Christmas-Club Fund," 50; "Yuletide Spending Prospects," *LD*, 114 (10 Dec. 1932): 36; "Christmas Clubs," *BW*, 23 Nov. 1932, 4; "Christmas Clubs," *BW*, 2 Dec. 1933, 9; and "Christmas Clubs," *BW*, 17 Dec. 1934, 14.

32. Winthrop P. Stevens analyzes how many Christmas Club depositors dropped their accounts when their bank adopted a no-interest policy in his article, "Should Banks Pay No Interest on Club Accounts?" 71–72.

33. For discussions of the shift from scarcity to abundance, see David M. Potter, *People of Plenty*, pp. 171–75; Warren I. Susman, "Introduction: Toward a History of the Culture of Abundance," in *Culture as History* (New York, 1984), xix–xxx; Patrick Johns-Heine and Hans H. Gerth, "Values in Mass Periodical Fiction, 1921–1940," in *Mass Culture*, ed. Bernard Rosenberg and David Manning White (Glencoe, Ill., 1957), 226–34; John Kenneth Galbraith, *The Affluent Society* (Boston, 1958), passim; Daniel J. Boorstin, *The Americans: The Democratic Experience* (New York, 1973), 89–164; Richard Wightman Fox and T. J. Jackson Lears, "Introduction," in *The Culture of Consumption* (New York, 1983), ix–xvii; and William R. Leach, "Transformations in a Culture of Consumption," *JAH*, 71 (Sept. 1984): 319–42.

34. The ranking of American industries by size is from Gilbert C. Fite and Jim E. Reese, *An Economic History of the United States* (Boston, 1959), 198–99.

35. For discussions of the American economy before the Civil War, see Curtis P. Nettels, *The Emergence of a National Economy, 1775–1815* (New York, 1969); Douglas C. North, *The Economic Growth of the United States, 1790–1860* (New York, 1966); George Rogers Taylor, *The Transportation Revolution, 1815–1860* (New York, 1968); and Paul W. Gates, *The Farmer's Age: Agriculture, 1815–1860* (New York, 1968).

For discussions of the American economy following the Civil War, see the works cited in note 3, above. See also Fred A. Shannon, *The Farmer's Last Frontier: Agriculture 1860–1897* (New York, 1968).

36. For a discussion of the appearance of household appliances, see Giedion, *Mechanization Takes Command*, 512–627; Ruth Schwartz Cowan, *More Work for Mother* (New York, c. 1983), 151–91; and Susan Strasser, *Never Done: A History of American Housework* (New York, 1982). For a discussion of the improvements in clothing, see Boorstin, *The Americans: The Democratic Experience*, 91–100. See also the secondary works cited in note 4, above.

37. The comment is from Margaret Deland, "Christmas Giving," *HBaz*, 38 (Dec. 1904):

1160. For other articles which are skeptical about whether gift givers can meet the individual subjective desires of their recipients, see George Fitch, "Christmas Giving That Is Sure to Please," *LHJ*, 27 (1 Dec. 1910): 28; Mrs. Woodrow Wilson, "Humors of Christmas," *GH*, 53 (Dec. 1911): 749–52; Carolyn Wells, "Givers and Receivers," *HBaz*, 47 (Jan. 1913): 13; and "The Annual Growl," *Ov*, n.s., 86 (Dec. 1928): 415. For an ad that expresses the anxiety which givers felt, see illustration 8: Hamilton watches, *SEP*, 211 (10 Dec. 1938): 85.

For articles that encourage givers to try to satisfy the personal desires of their recipients, see "The Christmas Problem," *HBaz*, 39 (Dec. 1905): 1164–65; Anna S. Richardson, "Your First Holiday Earnings," *WHC*, 32 (Dec. 1905): 27; Alice Preston, "When Christmas Finds Us with Little," *LHJ*, 24 (Dec. 1906): 35; B. O. Flower, "Christmas Spirit," *Ar*, 38 (Dec. 1907): 705–6; Gorman, "Home-Made Christmas Gifts," 1256; Catherine D. Groth, "Giving of Christmas Presents," *HW*, 53 (25 Dec. 1909): 29; "Worse Than Useless Giving," *Out*, 102 (21 Dec. 1912): 833; Sydney de Brie, "The Christmas Gift that Pleases," *CLif*, 39 (Dec. 1920): 114; "The Wisdom of 'Foolish' Christmas Giving," *LD*, 87 (19 Dec. 1925): 32–33; M. Harrington, "Assistant to Santa Claus," *GH*, 97 (Dec. 1933): 39+; Hope Hammond, "Gifts That Will Make You Popular," *WHC*, 61 (Dec. 1934): 58; "Bamberger's Plays Santa Claus," *A&S*, 24 (3 Jan. 1935): 34; Dana, "Christmas Giving," 762–65; Errol Flynn, "Not That I'm Ungrateful," *WHC*, 65 (Jan. 1938): 64; and "What Folks Want for Christmas: Cues for Holiday Sales Drives," *SalM*, 45 (1 Oct. 1939): 22–23+.

38. The following articles mention the fact that many Christmas gifts were new types of items: Werner, "Christmas When We Were Kids," 680–81; Theresa Hunt Walcott, "Gift You Have Never Given," *LHJ*, 34 (Dec. 1917): 43; Hastings, "Odd Advertising Copy That Brought Christmas Business," 33–34+; and "Christmas Sales Show That 1930 Has Bred a New Type of Buyer," *BW*, 17 Dec. 1930, 9.

39. For discussions of the adoption of urban values by rural Americans, see Paul Johnstone, "Farmers in a Changing World," *Yearbook of Agriculture, 1940* (Washington, 1940), 111–70; Richard Hofstadter, "The Myth of the Happy Yeoman," *AHer*, 7 (April 1956), 42–53; Boorstin, *The Americans: The Democratic Experience*, 118–36; and Dodds, *Everyday Life in Twentieth Century America*, 39–44.

40. Americans have a long tradition of liking their cities and liking urban life. From the centrality of the community in early America to the cosmopolitan civic responsibility of eighteenth-century merchants, to the city-building and transportation-building efforts of the western boosters and industrialists in the nineteenth century, Americans have given a highly positive assessment of cities. In addition, for decades cities had been where young rural Americans had moved to start their adult careers. They were pushed off the farms by the declining number of jobs remaining after the mechanization of agriculture in the mid-nineteenth century. Furthermore, they were pulled into the cities by their desire for adventure, and by their preference for industrial and white-collar jobs. These push-pull factors have produced a rural-to-urban migration pattern throughout American history. Fred Shannon is right when he says that cities have served as safety valves for rural populations rather than that western farms have provided safety valves for eastern, urban malcontents (Fred A. Shannon, "A Post-Mortem on the Labor-Safety Valve Theory," *AgH*, 19 [Jan. 1945]: 31–37). Because of this historic movement of populations, Americans came to think of cities as places where individuals went to make a new start. The cities were where aggressive, upwardly mobile Americans moved to work out their own destinies, as the Horatio Alger novels suggest.

For works discussing the importance of cities in the American past, see Susman, "The City in American Culture," in *Culture as History*, 237–51; Michael Zuckerman, *Peaceable Kingdoms* (New York, 1970), passim; John C. Rainbolt, "The Absence of Towns in Seventeenth Century Virginia," *JSouH*, 35 (Aug. 1969): 343–60; Carl Bridenbaugh, *Cities in the Wilderness* (New York, 1971), passim; Sam Bass Warner, *The Private City* (Philadelphia, 1971), 3–21; Richard C. Wade, *The Urban Frontier* (Cambridge, Mass., 1959), 322–36; Daniel J. Boorstin, *The Americans: The National Experience* (New York, 1965), 115–23; Harry N. Scheiber, "Urban Rivalry and Internal Improvements in the Old Northwest," *OH*, 71 (Oct. 1962): 227–39, 290–92; Hofstadter, "The Myth of the Happy Yeoman," 42–53; and Johnstone, "Farmers in a Changing World," 111–70.

41. For articles that encourage hinting, see Fitch, "Christmas Giving That is Sure to Please," 28; Corey Ford, "Breaking Even on Christmas," *Col*, 80 (17 Dec. 1927): 23 +; "For Puzzled Husbands," *PI*, 161 (8 Dec. 1932): 49; and Eloise Davison, "Christmas Presence," *AHom*, 15 (Dec. 1935): 77–79.

For ads that encourage hinting, see Daisy air rifles, *SEP*, 184 (9 Dec. 1911): 41; Wear-Ever aluminum cookware, *LHJ*, 29 (Dec. 1912): 65; Gordon & Ferguson furs, *LHJ*, 30 (Dec. 1913): 61; Caloric fireless cookstoves, *LHJ*, 30 (Dec. 1913): 64; Universal household appliances, *LHJ*, 37 (Dec. 1920): 114; Djer-Kiss cologne, *LHJ*, 38 (Dec. 1921): 41; Mirro Aluminum cookware, *LHJ*, 38 (Dec. 1921): 155; Hoosier kitchen cabinets, *LHJ*, 39 (Dec. 1922): 144; Robertshaw automatic oven thermostats, *LHJ*, 45 (Dec. 1928): 159; Rolls razors, *SEP*, 202 (21 Dec. 1929): 68; General Electric refrigerators, *LHJ*, 47 (Dec. 1930): 54; Arvin car heaters, *LHJ*, 53 (Dec. 1936): 127; Toastmaster toasters, *SEP*, 209 (12 Dec. 1936): 53; and Congoleum rugs, *LHJ*, 55 (Dec. 1938): 58.

The three ads to which I refer that suggest specific mechanisms for hinting are Caloric fireless cookstoves, *LHJ*, 27 (Dec. 1911): 80 (reproduced as illustration 9); Gilbert mixers, *SEP*, 209 (5 Dec. 1936): 93 (reproduced as illustration 10); and Hamilton watches, *SEP*, 209 (12 Dec. 1936): 117 (reproduced as illustration 11). For additional ads that suggest specific hinting mechanisms, see Wallace silver, *SEP*, 193 (11 Dec. 1920): 123; Rogers silver plate, *LHJ*, 45 (Dec. 1928): 93; and Horsman dolls, *LHJ*, 45 (Dec. 1928): 160.

For articles that suggest hinting mechanisms, see "Gifts Which Embarrass," *GH*, 51 (Dec. 1910): 653–58; Fitch, "Christmas Giving That Is Sure to Please," 28; "Waterman Holiday Drive," *PI*, 169 (22 Nov. 1934): 48; and "Check-Points for Christmas," 84.

42. "This Store Acts as a Good Fairy to Perplexed Shoppers," *PI*, 166 (4 Jan. 1934): 74. See also "Bamberger's Plays Santa," 34.

43. "Bamberger's Plays Santa," 34.

44. For articles that discuss giving money as Christmas gifts, see L. E. Colby, "When You Send Christmas Money," *LHJ*, 27 (Dec. 1909): 37; "New Ways to Give Christmas Money," *LHJ*, 29 (Dec. 1912): 70; and "The Ethics of Receiving," *LA*, 279 (4 Oct. 1913): 57–60.

45. "Selling Christmas," *BW*, 15 Dec. 1934, 5–6. For an ad that makes gift certificates its central theme, see illustration 12: Stetson hats, *SEP*, 202 (14 Dec. 1929): 199.

46. The two ads to which I refer are Ingersoll watches, *SEP*, 174 (7 Dec. 1901): 32 (reproduced as illustration 13); and Onyx hosiery, *LHJ*, 37 (Dec. 1920): 150 (reproduced as illustration 14).

For ads that show characters expressing a desire for the items advertised, see Barler document files, *SEP*, 173 (8 Dec. 1900): 19; Mexican Art and Leather goods, *LHJ*, 19 (Dec. 1901): 34; Ives model railroads, *SEP*, 184 (16 Dec. 1911): 27; Bissell carpet sweepers, *LHJ*, 30 (Dec. 1913): 50; Gordon & Ferguson furs, *LHJ*, 30 (Dec. 1913): 61; Wrigley's gum, *SEP*, 186 (13 Dec. 1913): 26–27; Hamilton rifles, *SEP*, 186 (13 Dec. 1913): 43; Djer-Kiss cologne, *LHJ*, 38 (Dec. 1921): 41; Rogers silver, *LHJ*, 34 (Dec. 1922): 116; La Tausca pearly necklaces, *SEP*, 195 (9 Dec. 1922): 150; Johnson's floor polishers, *SEP*, 201 (8 Dec. 1928): 122; Hoover vacuum cleaners, *SEP*, 201 (15 Dec. 1928): 82–83; Royal vacuum cleaners,

SEP, 209 (5 Dec. 1936): 70; General Electric refrigerators, *LHJ*, 54 (Dec. 1937): 61; Hotpoint ranges, *SEP*, 210 (4 Dec. 1937): 43; K-M waffle irons, *SEP*, 210 (11 Dec. 1937): 99; and R. J. Reynolds tobacco, *SEP*, 210 (18 Dec. 1937): 39.

For ads depicting characters hinting for the items, see Emery shirts, *SEP*, 195 (16 Dec. 1922): 50; Robertshaw Automatic oven thermostats, *LHJ*, 45 (Dec. 1928): 159; Johnson's floor polishers, *SEP*, 205 (8 Dec. 1928): 122; General Electric refrigerators, *SEP*, 209 (19 Dec. 1936): 54; Belden electric plugs, *SEP*, 210 (11 Dec. 1937): 75; and K-M waffle irons, *SEP*, 210 (11 Dec. 1937): 99.

47. Krementz jewelry, *SEP*, 203 (6 Dec. 1930): 180 (reproduced as illustration 16). For examples of ads that make sweeping generalizations about recipients, see Bondy hairbrushes, *SEP*, 173 (8 Dec. 1900): 16; Barler document file, *SEP*, 173 (8 Dec. 1900): 19; Edgarton suspenders, *SEP*, 173 (20 Dec. 1900): 17; Stevens rifles, *LHJ*, 20 (Dec. 1902): 4; Nut Shell drawings, *LHJ*, 20 (Dec. 1902): 44; Middletown Hat Co., *LHJ*, 20 (Dec. 1902): 47; Lincoln Historical Society [Tarbell's *Lincoln*], *SEP*, 175 (6 Dec. 1902): 30; Crane Linen stationery, *LHJ*, 28 (Dec. 1911): 51; Brown Durrell stockings, *LHJ*, 28 (Dec. 1911): 56; Gillette razors, *LHJ*, 28 (Dec. 1911): 58; Lester lace items, *LHJ*, 28 (Dec. 1911): 63; Lissue handkerchiefs, *LHJ*, 28 (Dec. 1911): 73; Bestyette rainwear, *LHJ*, 28 (Dec. 1911): 80; Bellas and Hess shirtwaists, *LHJ*, 28 (Dec. 1911): 81; Young safety razors, *LHJ*, 28 (Dec. 1911): 82; Shirley suspenders, *SEP*, 184 (2 Dec. 1911): 39; WWW rings, *SEP*, 184 (9 Dec. 1911): 30; Iron Clad socks, *SEP*, 184 (9 Dec. 1911): 50; Keen Kutter tool cabinets, *SEP*, 184 (16 Dec. 1911): 2; Prince Albert pipe tobacco, *SEP*, 184 (16 Dec. 1911): 30; Remington rifles, *SEP*, 184 (16 Dec. 1911): 45; Rochester Stamping appliances, *LHJ*, 29 (Dec. 1912): 47; Brunswick billiard tables, *LHJ*, 29 (Dec. 1912): 60; Gordon silk hosiery, *LHJ*, 29 (Dec. 1912): 66; National carpet sweepers, *LHJ*, 29 (Dec. 1912): 90; Autostrop razors, *SEP*, 185 (Dec 7, 1912): 42; O-Cedar mops, *SEP*, 185 (7 Dec. 1912): 52; Briggs bracelets, *SEP*, 185 (7 Dec. 1912): 77; Royal Rochester appliances, *SEP*, 186 (6 Dec. 1913): 28; Radiopticon projectors, *SEP*, 186 (6 Dec. 1913): 59; Innovation tie holders, *SEP*, 186 (6 Dec. 1913): 62; Stag pipe tobacco, *SEP*, 186 (20 Dec. 1913): 39; Community silver plate, *LHJ*, 37 (Dec. 1920): 92; Liggett chocolates, *SEP*, 193 (4 Dec. 1920): 53; Ever-Ready shaving brushes, razors, *SEP*, 193 (18 Dec. 1920): 37; Wilson's men's furnishings, *SEP*, 193 (18 Dec. 1920): 52; Rid-Jid ironing boards, *SEP*, 193 (18 Dec. 1920): 153; Whiting & Davis mesh bags, *LHJ*, 38 (Dec. 1921): 148; Mendel trunks, *LHJ*, 38 (Dec. 1921): 163; Krementz cuff links, *SEP*, 194 (3 Dec. 1921): 92; Brighton garters, *SEP*, 194 (10 Dec. 1921): 51; Lane cedar chests, *SEP*, 195 (2 Dec. 1922): 54; Paris garters, *SEP*, 195 (2 Dec. 1922): 117; Ingersoll pencils, *SEP*, 195 (9 Dec. 1922): 77; Holmes & Edwards silver plate, *LHJ*, 45 (Dec. 1928): 83; Tootsietoy doll-house furniture, *LHJ*, 45 (Dec. 1928): 103; Lady Seymour wool blankets, *LHJ*, 45 (Dec. 1928): 126; Holeproof hosiery, *SEP*, 201 (8 Dec. 1928): 1; Excel cornpoppers, *SEP*, 201 (8 Dec. 1928): 180; Victor radios, *LHJ*, 46 (Dec. 1929): 202; Ronson lighters, *SEP*, 202 (7 Dec. 1929): 186–87; Knockabout knit jackets, *SEP*, 202 (7 Dec. 1929): 263; Frigidaire refrigerators, *SEP*, 202 (14 Dec. 1929): 93; DuPont boudoir accessories, *SEP*, 203 (6 Dec. 1930): 95; Kaywoodie pipes, *SEP*, 203 (13 Dec. 1930): 96; Spur ties, *SEP*, 203 (13 Dec. 1930): 117; Ingersoll-Waterbury timepieces, *SEP*, 203 (13 Dec. 1930): 124; American Stationery Company, *LHJ*, 53 (Dec. 1936): 131; Sunbeam mixers, *SEP*, 209 (5 Dec. 1936): 78; General Electric refrigerators, *LHJ*, 54 (Dec. 1937): 61; Richard Hudnut cosmetics, *LHJ*, 54 (Dec. 1937): 68; Silex coffee makers, *LHJ*, 54 (Dec. 1937): 92; Whitehall men's shirts and pajamas, *SEP*, 210 (11 Dec. 1937): 99; Gillette gift sets, *SEP*, 210 (18 Dec. 1937): 63; Bourgois toiletries, *LHJ*, 55 (Dec. 1938): 53; Bissell carpet sweepers, *LHJ*, 55 (Dec. 1938): 92; and Rolls razors, *SEP*, 211 (17 Dec. 1938): 71.

48. The quotation is from Conklin fountain pens, *LHJ*, 28 (Dec. 1911): 90 (reproduced

as illustration 17). For ads that picture joyful reception scenes, see Stevens rifles, *LHJ*, 20 (Dec. 1902): 4; Dueber-Hampden watches, *LHJ*, 20 (Dec. 1902): 54; Lissue handkerchiefs, *LHJ*, 28 (Dec. 1911): 73; Larter shirt studs, *LHJ*, 28 (Dec. 1911): 75; Elgin watches, *SEP*, 184 (2 Dec. 1911): 57; Robeson pocket knives, *SEP*, 184 (2 Dec. 1911): 66; Everwear hosiery, *SEP*, 184 (2 Dec. 1911): 73; Shirley suspenders, *LHJ*, 29 (Dec. 1912): 64; National carpet sweepers, *LHJ*, 29 (Dec. 1912): 90; Virtuolo player piano, *SEP*, 185 (7 Dec. 1912): 39; Iver-Johnson bicycles, *SEP*, 185 (7 Dec. 1912): 60; Johnston's chocolates, *SEP*, 185 (7 Dec. 1912): 73; WWW rings, *SEP*, 185 (14 Dec. 1912): 35; Howard watches, *SEP*, 185 (14 Dec. 1912): 42; Waterman's pens, *LHJ*, 30 (Dec. 1913): 57; Winslow ice skates, *LHJ*, 30 (Dec. 1913): 57; Larter shirt studs, *SEP*, 186 (6 Dec. 1913): 65; Waltham watches, *SEP*, 186 (6 Dec. 1913): 69; Whitman's chocolates, *SEP*, 186 (13 Dec. 1913): 23; Hamilton rifles, *SEP*, 186 (13 Dec. 1913): 43; Iron Clad socks, *SEP*, 186 (13 Dec. 1913): 45; S. S. Kresge assorted items, *LHJ*, 27 (Dec. 1920): 39; Apex vacuum cleaners, *LHJ*, 37 (Dec. 1920): 43; Simplex roller ironers, *LHJ*, 37 (Dec. 1920): 49; Kaynee boys' blouses, *LHJ*, 37 (Dec. 1920): 62; Krementz cuff links, *LHJ*, 37 (Dec. 1920): 120; Royal vacuum cleaners, *LHJ*, 37 (Dec. 1920): 137; Bissell carpet sweepers, *LHJ*, 37 (Dec. 1920): 155; La Tausca pearl necklaces, *LHJ*, 37 (Dec. 1920): 163; Nayvee sailor suits, *LHJ*, 37 (Dec. 1920): 167; Nasua wool blankets, *LHJ*, 37 (Dec. 1920): 198; Durham-Duplex razors, *SEP*, 193 (4 Dec. 1920): 62; Westinghouse appliances, *SEP*, 193 (4 Dec. 1920): 120; Educator shoes, *SEP*, 193 (11 Dec. 1920): 127; Town and Country coats, *SEP*, 193 (18 Dec. 1920): 69; Greeting Card trade, *LHJ*, 38 (Dec. 1921): 70; Mendel trunks, *LHJ*, 38 (Dec. 1921): 163; Kum-A-Part cuff buttons, *SEP*, 194 (10 Dec. 1921): 40; Irwin auger bits, *SEP*, 194 (10 Dec. 1921): 85; Rubberset brushes, *SEP*, 194 (10 Dec. 1921): 88; Elasticoat coats, *SEP*, 194 (10 Dec. 1921): 89; Oregon City woolens, *SEP*, 194 (Dec. 1921): 97; Rand McNally's children's books, *LHJ*, 39 (Dec. 1922): 167; Tavannes watches, *SEP*, 195 (2 Dec. 1922): 68; Davenport beds, *SEP*, 195 (2 Dec. 1922): 91; Ward's fruitcakes, *SEP*, 195 (2 Dec. 1922): 122; Dayton tennis racquets, *SEP*, 195 (9 Dec. 1922): 154; Chevrolet automobiles, *SEP*, 195 (16 Dec. 1922): 41; Emery shirts, *SEP*, 195 (16 Dec. 1922): 50; Educator shoes, *SEP*, 195 (16 Dec. 1922): 53; Autostrop razors, *SEP*, 195 (16 Dec. 1922): 71; Whiting and Davis mesh bags, *SEP*, 195 (16 Dec. 1922): 86; Sun-Maid raisins, *SEP*, 195 (16 Dec. 1922): 106; Velvet tobacco, *SEP*, 195 (16 Dec. 1922): 108; President suspenders, *SEP*, 195 (16 Dec. 1922): 116; U.S. Government savings bonds, *SEP*, 195 (23 Dec. 1922): 83; General Electric refrigerators, *LHJ*, 65 (Dec. 1928): 78; Eureka vacuum cleaners, *LHJ*, 65 (Dec. 1928): 114; Puzzle-Peg games, *LHJ*, 65 (Dec. 1928): 148; Street slumber chairs, *LHJ*, 65 (Dec. 1928): 164–66; MacGregor golf equipment, *SEP*, 201 (8 Dec. 1928): 138; Simmons watch chains, *SEP*, 201 (8 Dec. 1928): 149; Nicholson grinding files, *SEP*, 201 (8 Dec. 1928): 154; Ronson lighters, *SEP*, 201 (8 Dec. 1928): 176; Spur ties, *SEP*, 201 (15 Dec. 1928): 90; Van Heusen collars, *SEP*, 201 (15 Dec. 1928): 148; Rogers Bros. silver plate, *LHJ*, 46 (Dec. 1929): 92; L. Vanderbilt toiletries, *LHJ*, 46 (Dec. 1929): 154; Yankee tools, *SEP*, 202 (7 Dec. 1929): 115; Wilson's men's accessories, *SEP*, 202 (7 Dec. 1929): 146; Lane cedar chests, *SEP*, 202 (7 Dec. 1929): 160–61; Winchester assorted items, *SEP*, 202 (7 Dec. 1929): 239; Buick automobiles, *SEP*, 202 (14 Dec. 1929): 57; Bicycle trade, *SEP*, 202 (14 Dec. 1929): 75; Hotpoint electric appliances, *LHJ*, 47 (Dec. 1930): 62; Pequot sheets and pillow cases, *LHJ*, 47 (Dec. 1930): 125; Iver Johnson rifles and bicycles, *SEP*, 203 (6 Dec. 1930): 165; Spur ties, *SEP*, 203 (13 Dec. 1930): 117; Lek-tro-hot car heaters, *SEP*, 203 (13 Dec. 1930): 137; Blue Goose oranges, *SEP*, 203 (20 Dec. 1930): 85; Locktite tobacco pouches, *SEP*, 203 (20 Dec. 1930): 90; Frigidaire refrigerators, *LHJ*, 53 (Dec. 1936): 62; Daniel Green house slippers, *LHJ*, 53 (Dec. 1936): 121; General Electric lamps, *SEP*, 209 (5 Dec. 1936): 40; Ronson lighters, *SEP*, 209 (5 Dec. 1936): 90; Arrow men's clothing, *SEP*, 209 (12 Dec. 1936): 34; Elgin watches, *SEP*, 209 (12 Dec. 1936): 63;

Cheney cravats, *SEP*, 209 (12 Dec. 1936): 76; Union Leader pipes and tobacco, *SEP*, 209 (19 Dec. 1936): 66; Schick electric razors, *SEP*, 209 (19 Dec. 1936): 71; Simoniz car wax, *SEP*, 209 (19 Dec. 1936): 73; Half and Half tobacco, *SEP*, 210 (4 Dec. 1937): 111; Swank men's jewelry, *SEP*, 210 (11 Dec. 1937): 81; Univex movie cameras, *SEP*, 210 (11 Dec. 1937): 83; LaSalle automobiles, *SEP*, 211 (10 Dec. 1938): 28; Hamilton watches, *SEP*, 211 (10 Dec. 1938): 85; TruVal shirts and pajamas, *SEP*, 211 (17 Dec. 1938): 51; and Eversharp pens and pencils, *SEP*, 211 (17 Dec. 1938): 55.

For ads that show recipients explicitly expressing pleasure in the items they received, see Elgin watches, *LHJ*, 28 (Dec. 1911): 76; Hoosier kitchen cabinets, *LHJ*, 30 (Dec. 1913): 45; King air rifles, *SEP*, 186 (20 Dec. 1913): 29; Huyler's chocolates, *SEP*, 186 (20 Dec. 1913): 34; Pneuvac vacuum cleaners, *LHJ*, 37 (Dec. 1920): 45; America electric cleaners, *LHJ*, 37 (Dec. 1920): 46; Kiddie-Kar foot-propelled cars, *LHJ*, 37 (Dec. 1920): 166; Nayvee sailor suits, *LHJ*, 37 (Dec. 1920): 167; Conklin pens, *SEP*, 193 (4 Dec. 1920): 114; Bicycle trade, *SEP*, 193 (11 Dec. 1920): 59; White & Wyckoff stationery, *LHJ*, 39 (Dec. 1922): 134; Ohio Electric cleaners, *LHJ*, 39 (Dec. 1922): 140; Bueschler saxophones, *SEP*, 195 (2 Dec. 1922): 48; Remington pocket knives, *SEP*, 195 (9 Dec. 1922): 51; Thermalware jugs, *SEP*, 195 (9 Dec. 1922): 54; Bull-dog men's accessories, *SEP*, 195 (16 Dec. 1922): 94; Bicycle trade, *SEP*, 201 (1 Dec. 1928): 108; Edgeworth tobacco, *SEP*, 201 (8 Dec. 1928): 134; Hendryx bird cages, *SEP*, 201 (8 Dec. 1928): 171; Iver Johnson bicycles and rifles, *SEP*, 202 (7 Dec. 1929): 262; General Electric refrigerators, *SEP*, 202 (14 Dec. 1929): 38; Hoover vacuum cleaners, *SEP*, 202 (14 Dec. 1929): 98–99; Buick automobiles, *SEP*, 202 (13 Dec. 1930): 41; Royal typewriters, *SEP*, 209 (5 Dec. 1936): 91; Silex coffee makers, *SEP*, 210 (4 Dec. 1937): 92; Velvet tobacco, *SEP*, 210 (11 Dec. 1937): 50; Serval refrigerators, *SEP*, 210 (11 Dec. 1937): 61; and Bendix washers, *SEP*, 211 (10 Dec. 1938): 41.

4. Gimcracks, Appliances, and Silverware

1. For articles that discuss the exchange of gimcracks during the late nineteenth and early twentieth centuries, see Agnes Repplier, "Oppression of Gifts," *L*, 67 (Dec. 1901): 734; John Allen Murphy, "How Manufacturers Are Getting Their Goods into Santa Claus' Pack," *PI*, 121 (2 Nov. 1922): 17; A. L. Townsend, "What Has Christmastide Brought to Another Year of Advertising?" *PI*, 125 (20 Dec. 1923): 104; "Merry Christmas Awaits a Big Retail Outlet," *PI*, 128 (14 Aug. 1924): 33; and G. A. Nichols, "Cold and Fishy Eye for Good Old Santa Claus," *PIM*, 13 (Nov. 1926): 70.

For ads for gimcracks, see illustration 18: Shackman, *LHJ*, 28 (Dec. 1911): 78; illustration 19: Oneida Community, *SEP*, 174 (7 Dec. 1901): 30; and illustration 20: Perry, *LHJ*, 28 (Dec. 1911): 56. See also Crosby, *LHJ*, 19 (Dec. 1901): 34; C. D. Peacock, *LHJ*, 20 (Dec. 1902): 46; Harry A. Merchant, *LHJ*, 20 (Dec. 1902): 46; Dennison, *LHJ*, 20 (Dec. 1902): 48; Baird-North, *LHJ*, 28 (Dec. 1911): 59; National, *LHJ*, 28 (Dec. 1911): 75; and Vantine & Co., *LHJ*, 29 (Dec. 1912): 63. The frequency of ads for gimcracks declined sharply between the period 1911–1913 and the period 1920–1922.

2. For articles that discuss the rise in the popularity of cards vis-à-vis gimcracks, see "Christmas and the Post Office," *Out*, 100 (10 Feb. 1912): 299; Mildred Harrington, "What Can I Give 'Em This Year?" *AMag*, 104 (Dec. 1927): 49; R. W. Hicks, "Advertising Helped Quintuple Greeting Cards Sales," *PI*, 139 (14 April 1927): 160–61 +; Laurence Dale, "Santa Claus Comes Down to Earth," *C&F*, 21 (21 Dec. 1932): 1453; Clementine Paddleford, "The Same To You!" *AHom*, 15 (Dec. 1935): 66ff; Margaret Dana, "Christmas Giving," *At*, 160 (Dec. 1937): 762; and Octavia Goodbar, "Cards," *CH*, 47 (Dec. 1937): 56–58.

For articles that discuss the rise in the popularity of expensive useful items vis-à-vis gimcracks, see Elizabeth Howard Westwood, "Christmas Gifts That Were Gifts," *LHJ*, 27 (Dec. 1911): 32; "Worse-Than-Useless Giving," *Out*, 102 (21 Dec. 1912): 833; Carroll D. Murphy, "American-Made Christmas," *Sys*, 26 (Oct. 1914): 361–62; "The New Christmas," *LD*, 53 (23 Dec. 1916): 1661; "In Defense of Christmas," *Bl*, 25 (27 July 1918): 91–92; M. Hussobee, "Associated Campaign Puts Veils in Christmas Gift Class," *PI*, 113 (23 Dec. 1920): 50–52; Murphy, "How Manufacturers Are Getting Their Goods into Santa Claus' Pack," 17–18+; Townsend, "What Has Christmastide Brought to Another Year of Advertising?" 104; Frank L. Scott, "Sales Arguments That Help Get Christmas Trade," *PI*, 128 (7 Aug. 1924): 3–4+; C. B. Larrabee, "What About Your Christmas Selling Plans?" *PIM*, 10 (May 1925): 20, 122; Nichols, "Cold and Fishy Eye for Good Old Santa Claus," 73; Harrington, "What Can I Give 'Em This Year?" 49; William O. Scroggs, "Christmas and the Payroll," *Out*, 153 (18 Dec. 1929): 621; and Ronald Millar, "Our Billion-Dollar Christmas," *AMag*, 108 (Dec. 1929): 63+.

3. The two ads to which I make specific reference are Utica pliers, *SEP*, 185 (7 Dec. 1912): 58 (reproduced as illustration 22); and Belber luggage, *SEP*, 193 (11 Dec. 1920): 71 (reproduced as illustration 27). For articles that discuss the use of existing useful items as Christmas gifts, see Murphy, "How Manufacturers Are Getting Their Goods in Santa Claus' Pack," 17–18+; "Direct Mail Puts on Its Holiday Apparel," *PI*, 133 (26 Nov. 1925): 33; Larrabee, "What About Your Christmas Selling Plan?" 21; and "Santa Will Carry Towels," *PI*, 161 (10 Nov. 1932): 82.

4. The ad for Bissell carpet sweepers and vacuum cleaners is at *LHJ*, 37 (Dec. 1920): 155. For articles that discuss the use of newly marketed, useful items as Christmas gifts, see Townsend, "What Has Christmastide Brought to Another Year of Advertising?" 104; Scott, "Sales Arguments That Help Get Christmas Trade," 3–4+; "Direct Mail Puts On Its Holiday Apparel," 33–34+; Allen T. Tate, "Some Christmas Copy I Would Rather Not See," *PI*, 136 (2 Sept. 1926): 26; "And Now We Point toward Christmas," *PI*, 19 (Oct. 1929): 40+; S. H. Pittman, " 'Meet the Wife': Introducing—Mrs. Santa Claus," *PI*, 153 (27 Nov. 1930): 97–100; "Now That It's Hot—Let's Think of Christmas," PI, 152 (17 July 1930): 10+; "For Puzzled Husbands," *PI*, 161 (8 Dec. 1932): 48–49; Eloise Davison, "Christmas Presence," *AHom*, 15 (Dec. 1935): 77–79; and "Just What I Wanted," *GH*, 103 (Dec. 1936): 86–87.

5. For articles which note that few manufacturers profited from gimcrack giving, see Hussobee, "Associated Campaign Puts Veils in Christmas Gift Class," 50–52; Murphy, "How Manufacturers Are Getting Their Goods into Santa Claus' Pack," 17–18+; "Direct Mail Puts On Its Holiday Apparel," 33; and Avis D. Carlson, "Our Barbaric Christmas," *NAR*, 231 (Jan. 1931): 68.

6. The quotation is from Martin Hastings, Jr., "Odd Advertising Copy That Brought Christmas Business," *PI*, 121 (28 Dec. 1922): 33. For articles which note that the shift to useful gifts expanded the number of manufacturers who stood to profit from Christmas sales, see Murphy, "How Manufacturers Are Getting Their Goods into Santa Claus' Pack," 17–18+; and Larrabee, "What About Your Christmas Selling Plans?" 20, 122. For evidence of the support of manufacturers for useful items, see Murphy, "How Manufacturers Are Getting Their Goods into Santa Claus' Pack," 17–18+; and Nichols, "Cold and Fishy Eye for Good Old Santa Claus," 70+.

7. The quotation is from Murphy, "How Manufacturers Are Getting Their Goods into Santa Claus' Pack," 18, 177. For additional articles which argue that the shift to useful items increased the number of merchants who enjoyed large Christmas season sales, see Hastings, "Odd Advertising Copy That Brought Christmas Business," 33–34+; "Merry Christmas Awaits a Big Retail Outlet," 33–34+; Scott, "Sales Arguments That Help Get

Christmas Trade," 3–4+; Larrabee, "What About Your Christmas Selling Plans?" 19–21+; and Ed Wolff, "And Now We Point Toward Christmas," *PIM*, 19 (Oct. 1929): 40+.

8. The quotations are from Murphy, "How Manufacturers Are Getting Their Goods into Santa Claus' Pack," 17. For additional articles that discuss the stocking problems of the merchants who sold gimcracks, see "Direct Mail Puts On Its Holiday Apparel," 33–34; Larrabee, "What About Your Christmas Plans?" 21; and Nichols, "Cold and Fishy Eye for Good Old Santa Claus," 70+.

9. For evidence of manufacturers' efforts to package their products in ways that were satisfactory to merchants, see the articles and ads cited in notes 23 and 24 of chapter 3.

10. For discussion of Victorian domestic clutter and the reaction against it, see Russell Lynes, *The Domesticated Americans* (New York, 1957), 138–54, 231–56.

11. The quotations are from John Burt Hardee, "'Twas the Month Before Christmas," *PI*, 149 (28 Nov. 1929): 68; Wolff, "And Now We Point toward Christmas," 40; and Hartwell Chandler, "Book of Christmas Advertising," *PI*, 140 (15 Sept. 1927): 25. For additional articles that criticize useful gift items, see Sydney de Brie, "Beauty Is the Perfect Gift," *CLif*, 49 (Dec. 1925): 122–26; and Walter Morton, "—if You Know What I Mean," *Out*, 155 (12 Dec. 1928): 1315.

12. For evidence of the popularity of luxurious Christmas gifts, see Chandler, "Book of Etiquette for Christmas Advertising," 25; "Prestige and Orders," *PI*, 165 (16 Nov. 1933): 84; "Christmas Gifts," *H&G*, 70 (Dec. 1936): 76–81; and Louise Paine Benjamin, "There's a Beautiful Answer to Your Christmas-Gift Problem," *LHJ*, 57 (Jan. 1940): 24.

The following table gives the percentage of Christmas gift ads from the *Ladies' Home Journal* and *The Saturday Evening Post* that use consumption adjectives to describe their products. Especially note the increase in the 1928–1930 period.

Adjective	1900–02	1911–13	1920–22	1928–30	1936–38
"luxurious"	3%	4%	5%	11%	5%
"new"	4%	5%	5%	24%	16%
"modern"	0%	1%	1%	12%	4%
"smart"	0%	1%	2%	17%	13%

13. For a discussion of the importance of spending in the economy of abundance, see David M. Potter, *People of Plenty* (Chicago, 1954), 173–75.

14. Some examples of ads that characterize the prices of the products they advertise as "reasonable" or "moderate" are Cannon towels, *LHJ*, 45 (Dec. 1928): 173; Simmons watch chains, *SEP*, 201 (8 Dec. 1928): 149; Dresner luggage, *SEP*, 202 (7 Dec. 1929): 203; Buick automobiles, *SEP*, 202 (14 Dec. 1929): 57; Glover pajamas, *SEP*, 203 (6 Dec. 1930): 136–37; and Puritan knit goods, *SEP*, 203 (6 Dec. 1930): 175.

15. The ad for Bissell carpet sweepers is in *LHJ*, 46 (Dec. 1929): 188 (reproduced as illustration 30). For evidence of the increasing use of "new," "modern," and "smart" to describe Christmas gift items, see the table in note 12. For ads that describe their items as "the gift of the year," see Parker pens, *SEP*, 195 (16 Dec. 1922): 105; Conklin pens, *SEP*, 202 (7 Dec. 1929): 209; Manning-Bowman electric clocks, *SEP*, 203 (6 Dec. 1930): 92–93; Toastmaster toasters, *SEP*, 203 (6 Dec. 1930): 97; and Arvin radios, *SEP*, 210 (4 Dec. 1937): 47. For articles that note the new emphasis on style, see "Christmas Sales Show that 1930 Has Bred a New Type of Buyer," *BW*, 17 Dec. 1930), 9: and Dana, "Christmas Giving,"

762–65. For a discussion of the emphasis on "new" in non-Christmas ads, see "A Most Important Word in Present-Day Advertising," *PI*, 126 (20 March 1924): 89–90 + .

5. From Gimcracks to Cards

1. I use the word "friend" to mean a non-kindred adult who is known personally, and with whom the knower has a tie of affection. However, I do not include "sweathearts" in the category of friends as they are treated like the kindred group "wives" and "husbands" and are therefore included in the chapter on exchanges between men and women. The three categories of friends I discuss here are close friends, acquaintances, and business associates.

For discussions of the appearance of gift exchanges among adults, see James H. Barnett, *The American Christmas* (New York, 1954), 80; and Bertha L. Heilbron, "Christmas and New Year's on the Frontier," *MH*, 16 (Dec. 1935): 382–83.

2. For discussions of the early period of Christmas card exchanges in America, see Clementine Paddleford, "Same to You!" *AHom*, 15 (Dec. 1935): 9–11 + ; Octavia Goodbar, "Cards," *CH*, 47 (Dec. 1937): 56–58; George Buday, *The History of the Christmas Card* (London, 1954): 74–80; and Barnett, *The American Christmas*, 18–19.

3. For evidence of the popularity of the gimcracks, see the following gift suggestion lists: "What Shall I Give for Christmas?" *LHJ*, 22 (Dec. 1904): 40; "What Shall I Give for Christmas?" *LHJ*, 23 (Dec. 1905): 42; "Christmas Presents You Can Buy for Your Friends," *LHJ*, 31 (Nov. 1914): 76–80. For ads of gimcracks, see note 1 in chapter 4.

4. The quotation is from Paddleford, "Same to You!" 64. Existing explanations for the decline in Christmas card sales are unpersuasive. They argue that the slump was a result of the refusal of Americans to buy the cheaper imported cards from Germany and Austria. (See, for example, Paddleford, "Same to You!" 62; and Barnett, *The American Christmas*, 18–19.) However, they do not explain why the European cards sold so well in America before the 1890s. Nor do they explain why German and Austrian manufacturers failed to raise the quality of the cards they exported to America when their cheaper cards did not sell. And, finally, they do not explain why American manufacturers did not produce high-quality cards if there was a latent demand for them. What seems more likely is that the demand for Christmas cards of all qualities was very low between 1890 and 1910, and that the-explanation for it lies in the cultural significance of Christmas cards as a type of remembrance.

5. The quotations are from Margaret Deland, "Christmas Giving," *HBaz*, 38 (Dec. 1904): 1158–59; and Minna Thomas Antrim, "A Happier Christmas and a Happier New Year to All," *L*, 84 (Dec. 1909): 764. For objections to the expansion of Christmas gift giving, see Deland, "Save Christmas!" *HBaz*, 46 (Dec. 1912): 593; Eleanor Robson Belmont, "Renaissance of Christmas," *HBaz*, 47 (Jan. 1913): 13; Jacob A. Riis, "The New Christmas That Is Spreading All Over Our Country," *LHJ*, 30 (Dec. 1913): 16; and Edwin Sabin, "Cards or Gifts," *AMag*, 80 (Dec. 1915): 44–45.

Articles that contain criticisms of gimcrack giving are Christine Terhine Herrick, "Selection of Christmas Gifts," *HBaz*, 61 (Dec. 1907): 1220–25; A. L. Gorman, "Home-Made Christmas Gifts," *HBaz*, 42 (Dec. 1908): 1256; R.T.H., "On Reforming Christmas," *L*, 86 (Dec. 1910): 764–65; Sophie Kerr Underwood, "Christmas Fallacy," *WHC*, 38 (Dec. 1911): 46; Elizabeth Atwood, "Christmas Giving," *AHom*, 9 (Dec. 1912): 442–44; "Scientific Management of Christmas," *N*, 97 (Dec. 11, 1913): 559; and Sabin, "Cards or Gifts," 44–45.

6. The quotations are from Antrim, "A Happier Christmas and a Happier New Year to All," 765; and John L. Cowan, "Christmas Giving," *Ov*, n.s., 47 (Dec. 1906): 496. See also

Martha Keeler, "The Girls Who Works," *LHJ*, 30 (Jan. 1913): 38. Somewhat later statements of this same theme are "Curse of Christmas," *I*, 117 (18 Dec. 1926): 697; J. M. Gillis, "Is Christmas Pagan?" *CW*, 130 (Jan. 1930): 486; and Margaret Dana, "Christmas Giving," *At*, 160 (Dec. 1937): 762–65.

7. Charles Ovington's comments are from his interview by Mildred Harrington, "What Can I Give 'Em This Year?" *AMag*, 104 (Dec. 1927): 49. In arguing, as I do here, that the shift from gimcracks to cards was a rational reform, I do not mean to ignore the fact that some changes connected with the shift operated in the opposite direction. For example, a 1926 article in the *Independent* pointed out the connection between the adoption of cards and the total numbers of recipients: "To some extent, the invention of the Christmas card has been a blessing, but it . . . bids fair to become a curse. It is a blessing in so far as it salves a stricken conscience at small expense, cutting down the gift list accordingly; it is a curse in so far as it widens the Christmas circle beyond all previous dimensions ("Curse of Christmas," 697). Thus, while the low cost of cards encouraged givers to prefer them to gimcracks, it also encouraged givers to send cards to a larger circle of recipients. Also, some givers began to prefer to send lower-priced cards to acquaintances and business associates in order to have more money available to spend on gifts for families and close friends. In spite of these aspects of the adoption of the cards, it is, nevertheless, most accurate to view the shift from gimcracks to cards as a rational reform.

8. The quotation is from "Christmas and the Post Office," *Out*, 100 (10 Feb. 1912): 299. Regarding the revival of Christmas card production in America, see R. W. Hicks, "Advertising Helped Quintuple Greeting Card Sales," *PI*, 139 (14 April 1927): 160; Paddleford, "Same to You!" 64; and Goodbar, "Cards," 57.

9. The quotation is from Sydney de Brie, "Beauty Is the Perfect Gift," *CLif*, 49 (Dec. 1925): 124. The general feeling that gimcracks were too substantial a type of remembrance for the relationships they symbolized was reflected in the repeated contentions in periodicals that gift lists were too long and that givers could substantially reduce them if they would send only those gifts that were based on true affection. See, for example, Deland, "Save Christmas!" 593; Atwood, "Christmas Giving," 442–44; R. M. Thompson, "Christmas Gifts," *I*, 73 (26 Dec. 1912): 1486; and "The Spugs and Christmas," *Out*, 105 (13 Dec. 1913): 779.

10. The quotation is from Deland, "Save Christmas!" 593. For other articles that object to the long, wearying hours of shopping required to purchase gimcracks, see Anne Warner, "The Abuse and Perfection of Present-Giving," *Out*, 95 (6 Aug. 1910): 787–88; Walter A. Dyer, "The Spirit of Christmas," *CLif*, 21 (1 Dec. 1911): 35; Nina Bull, "Merry Christmas!" *Sur*, 35 (20 Nov. 1915): 190; and William Rose Benet, "But Once a Year," *Cen*, 95 (Dec. 1917): 314–17.

Of course, one of the reasons that cards required less shopping time was that givers could send copies of a single card design to many recipients rather than having to acquire a different remembrance for each recipient, as givers commonly did in gift-item exchanges. This fact is revealing about cards as a type of remembrance: cards were appropriate for the numerous recipients precisely because they said very little about the relationships they symbolized. They merely signified that the giver regarded the recipient as a friend; they did not define the meaning of that friendship, as a specially selected gift item did.

11. The quoted material is from "The Cloud on Christmas Joy," *Cos*, 50 (Dec. 1913): 19; and Benet, "But Once a Year," 316. For examples of the serious criticisms of the first twenty years of the century, see Agnes Repplier, "Oppression of Gifts," *L*, 68 (Dec. 1901): 734; Deland, "Christmas Giving," 1155–61; and I. McDougall, "The Gift Successful," *HB*, 35 (Dec. 1913): 19.

12. The quoted material is from Deland, "Christmas Giving," 1160, and Will Cuppy, "Christmas is Coming," *Bk*, 64 (Dec. 1926): 450–51.

For articles that criticize the unimaginativeness and inappropriateness of the gimcracks, see Repplier, "Oppression of Gifts," 732–36; Anne O'Hagan, "Gift and the Giver," *HBaz*, 41 (Dec. 1907): 1143–49; "Gifts Which Embarrass," *GH*, 51 (Dec. 1910): 653–58; and Mrs. Woodrow Wilson, "Humors of Christmas," *GH*, 53 (Dec. 1911): 749–52.

Articles which make the same point with humor are Wallace Irwin, "Peace on Earth in the Shopping District," *Cos*, 50 (Jan. 1911): 165–68; "Why Mr. Worldly Wiseman Hates Christmas," *AMag*, 73 (Jan. 1912): 381–84; E. L. McKinney, "My Christmas Presents," *Cen*, 87 (Jan. 1914): 490; Carolyn Wells, "Song of the Gift," *LD*, 52 (1 Jan. 1916): 35; Benet, "But Once a Year," 314–17; F. P. Dunne, "Mr. Dooley on Gifts," *GB*, 2 (Dec. 1925): 753–54; and Corey Ford, "Breaking Even on Christmas," *Col*, 80 (17 Dec. 1927): 49.

13. The display of Christmas cards in the home, although normally lasting only during the holiday season, served important functions, as the distinguished anthropologist Claude Levi-Strauss has observed (see *Elementary Structures of Kinship* [Boston, 1969]: 56). The display of cards exhibited—indeed, boasted—the number of friendship ties that the family unit and its members had. Also, the cards identified the circle of friends because the givers' names were available for perusal on the cards. This identification of givers was a notable difference between cards and gimcracks.

Some writers objected to the pressure on recipients to keep ugly gift items. For example, Margaret Deland suggested that "where any uncertainty exists, let us give as a token of love, or friendship, or human kindness, something that, while expressing these things, will, at least, be harmless. Let it something that does not last;—that brings the meaning and vanishes!—something that will never know the indignity of the top shelf of the spare-room closet!" ("Christmas Giving," 1160). See also Repplier, "Oppression of Gifts," 734.

The pressure on recipients to display the gift items they received after the holidays was a result of two characteristics of those gift items. First, most gift items were intended to last outside the Christmas season, to give more than temporary pleasure or assistance to the recipient. Only a small percentage were short-lived "gifts of the season," such as edible treats or cigars. Second, the gift items symbolized the relationships as conceived by the givers. Therefore, refusing to display gift items after the holiday season symbolically rejected the givers' conception of the relationships.

14. See Hicks, "Advertising Helped Quintuple Greeting Card Sales," 160.

15. Exchanging cards in lieu of gift items received the support of the Council for National Defense. See "In Defense of Christmas," *Bl*, 25 (27 July 1918): 91–92.

16. On the activities of the Greeting Card Association, see Hicks, "Advertising Helped Quintuple Greeting Card Sales," 160. Manufacturers made effective use of war themes in their cards. As Clementine Paddleford noted, "there were cards for the boys at the front, cards for the mothers of soldier sons, cards for families whose loved ones would not come marching home again" ("Same to You!" 64).

17. See Hicks, "Advertising Helped Quintuple Greeting Card Sales," 160–64.

18. All of the quotations are from "Christmas Stocking—and Selling," *BW*, 14 Dec. 1932, 9. See also "Christmas Sales Show That 1930 Has Bred a New Type of Buyer," *BW*, 17 Dec. 1930, 9; "Christmas Shoppers Didn't Buy Less; They Just Paid Less," *BW*, 7 Jan. 1931, 11; and Leslie Roberts, "Reflections on the Christmas Spirit," *HM*, 170 (Dec. 1934): 118–20.

19. The quotation is from Goodbar, "Cards," 58. The sales figures are from Lawrence Dale, "Santa Claus Comes Down to Earth," *C&F*, 21 (21 Dec. 1932): 1453.

20. The quotations are from Donald Argyle, "Christmas Opportunities to Cement

Customer Relations," *PI*, 139 (9 Oct. 1924): 25; and "Christmas Miscellany," *PIM*, 36 (June 1938): 82.
   21. The quotation is from "Say It with Cards!" *PI*, 181 (21 Oct. 1937): 104.
   22. The quotation is from "Say It with Cards!" 104. For additional evidence, see "Christmas Miscellany," 82–83.
   23. The quotation is from Jules Freedman, " 'Merry Christmas,' " *PI*, 142 (5 Jan. 1928): 10.
   24. The quotation is from "Say It with Cards!" 104–5. See also Freedman, " 'Merry Christmas,' " 12; Jerome V. Leary, "And a Happy New Year, Mr. Freedman," *PI*, 142 (2 Feb. 1928): 42; and "Christmas Cards Should Not Have Order Blanks Attached," *PI*, 161 (1 Dec. 1932): 76.
   25. The quotation is from Freedman, " 'Merry Christmas,' " 12. See also Leary, "And a Happy New Year, Mr. Freedman," 41; and "Christmas Cards Should Not Have Order Blanks Attached," 76.
   26. The quotation is from "Say It with Cards!" 104. See also Argyle, "Christmas Opportunities to Cement Customer Relations," 25.

6. The Feminization of Christmas

   1. For a discussion of the sharing of household tasks by husbands and wives prior to industrialization, see Ruth Schwartz Cowan, *More Work for Mother* (New York, c. 1983), 16–31.
   2. For an ad that plays off the heavy work load of women in the modern celebration, see illustration 31: Lorain Oven Heat regulators, *SEP*, 193 (18 Dec. 1920): 155. For articles that note the feminization of Christmas, see Margaret Deland, "Christmas Giving," *HBaz*, 46 (Dec. 1912): 1155–61; Elizabeth Hale Gilman, "The Child's Best Christmas Present," *CLif*, 9 (Dec. 1905): 139; Thomas L. Masson, "Wanted: A New Christmas," *Bk*, 50 (Nov. 1919): 358; Fannie Stearns Gifford, "Spirit of Christmas," *HB*, 48 (Dec. 1920): 461; H. I. Phillips, "I'm Strong for Christmas, But—," *AMag*, 98 (Dec. 1924): 12–13 +; Mildred Harrington, "What Can I Give 'Em This Year?" *AMag*, 104 (Dec. 1927): 49; Avis D. Carlson, "Our Barbaric Christmas," *NAR*, 231 (Jan. 1931): 66–71; and Leslie Roberts, "Reflections on the Christmas Spirit," *HM*, 170 (Dec. 1934): 1117–18.
   The following articles note that men paid the bills for their families' Christmas presents: Harrington, "What Can I Give 'Em This Year?" 49; Ed Wolff, "And Now We Point toward Christmas," *PIM*, 19 (Oct. 1929): 120; and "A Word for Dad," *LD*, 113 (18 June 1932): 19.
   3. The quotation is from Margaret Deland, "Save Christmas!" *HBaz*, 46 (Dec. 1912): 593.
   4. The quotations are from Deland, "Save Christmas!" 593; and Phillips, "I'm Strong for Christmas, But—," 12–13. For additional evidence that women did the vast majority of Christmas shopping, see Margaret Deland, "Christmas Shopping," *HBaz*, 38 (Dec. 1904): 115–61; A. L. Gorman, "Home-Made Christmas Gifts," *HBaz*, 42 (Dec. 1908): 1256; Ronald Millar, "Our Billion Dollar Christmas," *AMag*, 108 (Dec. 1929): 63 +; and Carlson, "Our Barbaric Christmas," 66–71.
   5. The quotation is from Cochran Wilson, "Women and Wage-Spending," *Out*, 84 (13 Oct. 1906): 374. For additional articles that note the predominance of women among year-round shoppers, and that it was a change from previous custom, see Maud Nathan, "Women Who Work and Women Who Spend," *AAA*, 27 (May 1906): 185–86; Belle Squire, "Women and Money Spending," *HBaz*, 39 (Nov. 1905): 1055; Flora McDonald Thompson, "The Work of Wives," *Out*, 111 (24 April 1909): 994; Annette Austin, "When Woman

Buys," *GH*, 49 (Dec. 1909): 624–32; "Advertising and Psychology," *Out*, 113 (11 Sept. 1909): 59; Lucy M. Salmon, "Democracy in the Household," *AJS*, 17 (Jan. 1912): 445; Mrs. Julian Heath, "New Kind of Housekeeping," *LHJ*, 32 (Jan. 1915): 2; "How People Have Been Saving Money," *LD*, 53 (23 Sept. 1916): 806; "Teach Women What Advertising Does," *PI*, 111 (10 June 1920): 177+; John Corbin, "The Forgotten Woman," *NAR*, 216 (Oct. 1922): 456; Ida Bailey Allen, "Helpfulness—the Big Idea in Advertising to Women," *PI*, 123 (14 June 1923): 138; Frances Maule, "The Woman Appeal," *PI*, 126 (31 Jan. 1924): 105–6+; James H. Collins, "All About Women—for Advertisers Only," *PI*, 134 (18 Feb. 1926): 3; "Increasing Sales to Women by Advertising to Men," *PI*, 135 (8 April 1926): 10+; Robert Wilber, "Men's Wear Stores for Women Only," *PI*, 140 (15 Sept. 1927): 162+; Bertha K. Landes, "A Woman—On Women," *PI*, 140 (7 July 1927): 156+; "Healing the Injured Pride of Masculinity," *PI*, 141 (3 Nov. 1927): 10+; B. R. Andrews, "The Home Woman as Buyer and Controller of Consumption," *AAA*, 143 (May 1929): 41–48; Phyllis V. Keyes, "Come to Papa," *PI*, 149 (21 Nov. 1929): 85+; "How About That Man in Your Boudoir?" *PI*, 155 (21 May 1931): 44; Nancy Hale, "What Interests Women—and Why," *A&S*, 27 (21 May 1936): 27; Arthur Hirose, "To the Ladies!" *A&S*, 33 (13 Aug. 1936): 33; and S. E. Gill, "At Least, Males Help Buy," *PI*, 178 (18 Feb. 1937): 81–82.

For articles that mention or discuss the consumer surveys of the early 1920s, see Collins, "All About Women—For Advertisers Only," 3; "Healing the Injured Pride of Masculinity," 11; Keyes, "Come to Papa," 85; Hale, "What Interests Women—and Why," 27; and Hirose, "To the Ladies!" 33.

6. For articles encouraging women to approach shopping in a professional manner, see Nathan, "Women Who Work and Women Who Spend," 646–50; Squire, "Women and Money Spending," 1145; May L. Cheney, "New Science of Home-Making," *Sun*, 24 (March 1910): 280–83; Heath, "New Kind of Housekeeping," 2; and Landes, "A Woman—On Women," 156.

For articles that support the home-economics movement, see "The Return of the Business Woman," *LHJ*, 17 (March 1900): 16; Edward Bok, "Women as Poor Pay," *LHJ*, 18 (June 1901): 14; Mrs. Frederick Schoff, "The Task of the American Mother," *I*, 55 (1 Jan. 1903): 35–37; Josephine Daskam Bacon, "We and Our Daughters," *AMag*, 63 (April 1907): 608–15; Cheney, "New Science of Home-Making," 280–83; Mary L. Read, "What Every Mother Knows," *Out*, 100 (3 Feb. 1912): 274–76; Laura Clarke Rockwood, "Women's Handicap in Efficiency," *AJS*, 19 (Sept. 1913): 229–35; Christine Frederick, "The New Housekeeping," *LHJ*, 32 (Sept. 1915): 21; Marion Chase Baker, "Mothercraft," *Sur*, 46 (24 Sept. 1921): 709–10; Frederick F. Van de Water, "Confessions of a Dub Father," *LHJ*, 42 (May 1925): 25; Mildred Maddocks Bentley, "Schedules Will Help Lighten Housework," *LHJ*, 42 (Nov. 1925): 142+; and Landes, "A Woman—On Women," 156+.

For articles that portray women as the primary savers for their families, see Flora McDonald Thompson, "Domestic Experiment," *HBaz*, 42 (July 1908): 659–63; "Domestic Purse," *HBaz*, 43 (Feb. 1909): 187–88; Martha Bensley Bruere, "The Cost of Children," *Out*, 100 (10 Feb. 1912): 320–24; Frederick, "The New Housekeeping," 21; Flora McDonald Thompson, "The Saving of Waste," *I*, 86 (10 April 1916): 62; "How People Have Been Saving Money," 806; Herbert Hoover, "Thrift and the American Woman," *LHJ*, 37 (Aug. 1920): 3; "Is the Fairer Sex Also the Thriftier Sex?" *LD*, 73 (3 June 1922): 86; Landes, "A Woman—On Women," 156+; Burr Blackburn, "Should the Wife Control the Family Purse?" *AMag*, 116 (Sept. 1933): 106–7; Henrietta Ripperger, "What This Country Needs Is a Woman," *HM*, 172 (Feb. 1936): 373–76; and Norman Krickbaum, "Eve Gets the Razzle-Dazzle," *A&S*, 27 (24 Sept. 1936): 27+.

For a discussion of the movement to professionalize housework, see Susan Strasser, *Never Done: A History of American Housework* (New York, 1982), 202–23.

7. The classic statement of the theory that conspicuous consumption can enhance the status of spenders is Thorstein Veblen, *The Theory of the Leisure Class* (New York, 1934), 68–101.

In all probability, upper-class women shopped according to conspicuous-consumption values, while middle-class women were thrifty. In this regard, see "Is the Fairer Sex Also the Thriftier Sex?" 86.

8. Writers assumed that men would earn the money they spent for their Christmas presents; therefore, most articles that implicitly encouraged gift givers to earn their Christmas shopping money were directed toward women and children. For example, the following two articles contain sympathetic accounts of women's taking seasonal employment in order to earn their holiday spending money: Nina Bull, "Merry Christmas!" *Sur*, 35 (20 Nov. 1915): 190; and "The Christmas Curse," *Cen*, 91 (Dec. 1915): 312–13. Mildred John (in "The Christmas Club Idea in Boston," *BM*, 113 [Dec. 1926]: 841–42) approved of the fact that more Christmas Club depositors in Boston were women than men. The following two articles encouraged parents to suggest to their children ways in which they could earn at least some of their Christmas shopping money: Gilman, "The Child's Best Christmas Present," 139; and Ernestine P. Swallow, "Children's Christmas Giving," *JHE*, 8 (Dec. 1916): 659–60.

9. The classic analysis of givers' spirits as an element of gifts is Marcel Mauss, *The Gift* (New York, 1967), 8–10, 41–45. See also Barry Schwartz, "The Social Psychology of the Gift," *AJS*, 73 (July 1967): 1–11; and Lewis Hyde, *The Gift* (New York, 1983): 3–140.

10. The quotation is from "The Wife and Her Money," *LHJ*, 17 (March 1901): 16. For additional articles that mention wives' humiliation in asking for money, see Helen Churchill Candee, "How to Manage Men," *HBaz*, 33 (29 Dec. 1900): 2268–69; Margaret Hamilton Welch, "The Wife's Share of the Income," *HBaz*, 34 (6 April 1901): 922–23; Susan B. Anthony, "Men and Women: Their Province in the Household," *I*, 54 (8 May 1902): 1126–28; and "Salaried Daughters," *I*, 59 (9 Nov. 1905): 1121–22.

The following articles emphasize that it is important to one's sense of selfhood to own property: William M. Salter, "What Is the Real Emancipation of Woman?" 30; Thompson, "Domestic Experiment," 659; Thompson, "The Work of Wives" *(Out)*, 994–96; Katherine Ferguson, "What Can We Afford? A Christmas Talk," *WHC*, 34 (Dec. 1912): 26; and Earl Barnes, "The Economic Independence of Women," *At*, 110 (Aug. 1912): 260–65.

For articles that emphasize the generosity of American husbands, see "A Better Gift," *Out*, 72 (13 Dec. 1902), 874–75; Anna A. Rogers, "Why American Mothers Fail," *At*, 101 (March 1908): 296; Charles Zueblin, "The Effect on Woman of Economic Dependence," *AJS*, 14 (March 1909): 609; "The Family Income," *GH*, 50 (Feb. 1910): 245–46; and H. I. Phillips, "I'm Strong for Christmas, But—," *AMag*, 98 (Dec. 1924): 12.

According to periodical writers, wives in prosperous families were more likely to have to ask for their shopping money than were wives in either average-income or poor families. See Anthony, "Men and Women: Their Province in the Household," 1126–27; "Money Question between Husband and Wife," *LHJ*, 26 (April 1909): 24; Zueblin, "The Effect on Woman of Economic Dependence," 609; and "Wife's Share, What Proportion of Her Husband's Income Should She Receive?" *HBaz*, 46 (Jan. 1912): 32.

11. During the early twentieth century, periodical writers were highly conscious that women were moving into the work force in large numbers. For examples of articles that describe this movement, see "Working-Women and Chivalry," *HBaz*, 33 (29 Dec. 1900):

2274; Ida Husted Harper, "Women Ought to Work," *I*, 52 (16 May 1901): 1123; Henry T. Finck, "Are Womanly Women Doomed?" *I*, 53 (31 Jan. 1901): 267; Margaret Bisland, "The Curse of Eve," *NAR*, 177 (July 1903): 121; Teresa Billington-Grieg, "The Rebellion of Woman," *CR*, 94 (July 1908): 9; Thompson, "The Work of Wives" *(Out)*, 995–96; U. G. Weatherly, "How Does the Access of Women to Industrial Occupations React on the Family?" *AJS*, 14 (May 1909): 743; Barnes, "The Economic Independence of Women," 264; Inez Milholland, "The Changing Home," *MCl*, 40 (March 1913): 211; Margaret Deland, "Woman in the Market Place," *I*, 86 (22 May 1916: 286; Mary Anderson, "Woman's Place Outside the Home," *I*, 102 (24 April 1920): 123; "The Breadwinning Woman," *NR*, 45 (3 Feb. 1926): 284–85; Helen Glenn Tyson, "The Professional Woman's Baby," *NR*, 46 (7 April 1926): 190; and Helen Glenn Tyson, "Mothers Who Earn," *Sur*, 57 (1 Dec. 1926): 275–76.

    For articles that oppose women's working outside the home, see "The American Woman in the Market-Place," *LHJ*, 17 (April 1900): 19; "The Return of the Business Woman," 16; Mrs. Burton Harrison, "Home Life as a Profession," *HBaz*, 33 (19 May 1900): 148–50; "Mother's Labor Problem," *HBaz*, 33 (11 Aug. 1900): 961; Finck, "Are Womanly Women Doomed?" 267–71; Lavinia Hart, "Motherhood," *Cos*, 32 (March 1902): 463–74; Lilian Bell, "The Management of Husbands," *HBaz*, 36 (March 1902): 203–7; Bisland, "The Curse of Eve," 111–22; "Women as Wage-Earners," *CurL*, 37 (Sept. 1904): 240–42; "Why I Will Not Let My Daughter Go into Business," *LHJ*, 26 (Sept. 1909): 16; Florence Kelley, "The Invasion of Family Life by Industry," *AAA*, 34 (July 1909): 90–96; Elle Morris Kretschmar, "Home-Making and Health," *GH*, 50 (Feb. 1910): 151–53; "How Love Passed Me By; The Confessions of a Business Woman," *HBaz*, 46 (June 1912): 277; Ida M. Tarbell, "Making a Man of Herself," *AMag*, 73 (Feb. 1912): 427–30; Henry Norman, "The Feminine Failure in Business," *Frm*, 63 (April 1920): 455–61; Tyson, "The Professional Woman's Baby," 190–92.

    For articles that favor women's working outside the home, see Miss C. S. Parrish, "The Womanly Woman," *I*, 53 (4 April 1901): 775–78; Harper, "Women Ought to Work," 1123–27; Boyd Winchester, "The New Woman," *Ar*, 27 (April 1902): 367–73; Marion Harland, "The Family versus the 'Solitude of Self,' " *I*, 54 (23 Jan. 1902): 202–7; Salter, "What Is the Real Emancipation of Woman?" 28–35; "Economic Independence of Women," *AJS*, 9 (Sept. 1903): 276–77; "A Father's View of the Home," *I*, 61 (18 Oct. 1906): 911–14; Anne O'Hagan, "Confessions of a Professional Woman," *HBaz*, 41 (Sept. 1907): 848–54; Irene Van Kleeck, "How Women Wage Earners Fare," *WW*, 15 (Dec. 1907): 9683–90; Weatherly, "How Does the Access of Women to Industrial Occupations React on the Family?" 740–52; Lydia Kingsmill Commander, "The Self-Supporting Woman and the Family," *AJS*, 14 (May 1909): 752–57; James E. Hagerty, "How Far Should Members of the Family Be Individualized?" *AJS*, 14 (1909): 797–806; Charlotte Perkins Gilman, "How Home Conditions React Upon the Family," *AJS*, 14 (March 1909): 592–605; Edith B. Speers, "Making a Living," *HBaz*, 46 (May 1912): 262; Milholland, "The Changing Home," 206+; Deland, "Woman in the Market Place," 286–88; "The Breadwinning Woman," 284–85; and Alice Beal Parsons, "Every Woman's Home," *WC*, n.s., 11 (Aug. 1926): 20.

    12. For articles that advocate allowances for housewives, and which make no reference to Christmas, see Welch, "The Wife's Share of the Income," 922–23; "The Wife and Her Money," 16; Harper, "Women Ought to Work," 1123–27; Flora McDonald Thompson, "The Work of Wives," *Ar*, 27 (Jan. 1902): 68–75; Anthony, "Men and Women: Their Province in the Household," 1126–28; "Salaried Daughters," 1121–22; Billington-Grieg, "The Rebellion of Woman," 9; Thompson, "Domestic Experiment," 659–63; "Money Question between Husband and Wife," 24; Zueblin, "The Effect on Women of Economic

Independence," 611–12; Hagerty, "How Far Should Members of the Family Be Individualized?" 798; Barnes, "The Economic Independence of Women," 260–65; and "Man's Financial Grip Slipping," *LD*, 101 (13 April 1929): 13.

13. For articles that are sympathetic to Christmas clubs and do not mention clubs as a solution to wives' having to ask for their Christmas shopping money, see notes 26, 27, 29, 30, and 31 in chapter 3. For articles that encourage women to handmake the items they present at Christmas and make no references to the fact that handmaking the items is appealing because economically dependent women have few other ways to add a true personal content to the gift items they present, see notes 1, 8, and 9 in chapter 3.

7. Within the Marital Bond

1. For examples of Christmas gift ads that portray women in this dignified matronly manner, see illustration 32: Bellas & Hess shirtwaists, *LHJ*, 28 (Dec. 1911): 81; and illustration 33: Peter's chocolates, *SEP*, 184 (23 Dec. 1911): 27. See also Brunswick pool tables, *LHJ*, 18 (Dec. 1900): 43; L. S. Berry, Christmas furs, *LHJ*, 18 (Dec. 1900): 47; Defender Manufacturing Co. bed linen and underwear, *LHJ*, 19 (Dec. 1901): 21; Bedel women's clothes, *LHJ*, 19 (Dec. 1901): 36; Albrecht furs, *LHJ*, 19 (Dec. 1901): 36; Taylor nursery beds, *LHJ*, 28 (Dec. 1911): 37; Lissue handkerchiefs, *LHJ*, 28 (Dec. 1911): 73; Caloric fireless cookstoves, *LHJ*, 28 (Dec. 1911): 80; Brunswick pool tables, *SEP*, 184 (9 Dec. 1911): 33; Ohio Knitting scarves, *SEP*, 184 (9 Dec. 1911): 62; and Hoosier kitchen cabinets, *LHJ*, 29 (Dec. 1912): 51. For a discussion of the home as a refuge from the world, see Kirk Jeffrey, "The Family as a Utopian Retreat from the City," *Sdg*, 55 (1972): 21–41.

2. For advertisements of typical Christmas gifts to women, see Huyler's candies, *LHJ*, 18 (Dec. 1900): 39; Field handkerchiefs, *LHJ*, 18 (Dec. 1900): 43; L. S. Berry Christmas furs, *LHJ*, 18 (Dec. 1900): 47; E. Albrecht furs, *LHJ*, 18 (Dec. 1900): 47; Helman-Taylor pictures and prints, *SEP*, 173 (22 Dec. 1900): 24; Crosby silver and metal novelties, *LHJ*, 19 (Dec. 1901): 34; Bedell women's clothes, *LHJ*, 19 (Dec. 1901): 36; Centemeri & Co. kid gloves, *LHJ*, 19 (Dec. 1901): 36; Regina music boxes, *LHJ*, 19 (Dec. 1901): 44; Libbey glasswear, *LHJ*, 20 (Dec. 1902): inside front cover; Weatherby plate racks, *LHJ*, 20 (Dec. 1902): 21; C. D. Peacock assorted gift items and jewelry, *LHJ*, 20 (Dec. 1902): 46; G. Harry Merchant art and leather novelties, *LHJ*, 20 (Dec. 1902): 46; Shepard Norwell handkerchiefs, *LHJ*, 20 (Dec. 1902): 48; Rosalind Co. longwaists, *LHJ*, 20 (Dec. 1902): 48; Newcomb Endicott handkerchiefs, *LHJ*, 20 (Dec. 1902): 50; Cawson ostrich feathers, *LHJ*, 20 (Dec. 1902): 56; American Electric Novelty Co. clocks and lamps, *LHJ*, 20 (Dec. 1902): 56; Baird-North jewelry, *LHJ*, 28 (Dec. 1911): 59; Lester lace items, *LHJ*, 28 (Dec. 1911): 63; John Davenport handbags, *LHJ*, 28 (Dec. 1911): 66; Reveillon Christmas furs, *LHJ*, 28 (Dec. 1911): 69; Freund & Bros. handbags, *LHJ*, 28 (Dec. 1911): 72; Lissue handkerchiefs, *LHJ*, 28 (Dec. 1911): 73; Wightman and Hough lockets, *LHJ*, 28 (Dec. 1911): 73; National Assorted gifts, *LHJ*, 28 (Dec. 1911): 75; Shackman assorted gifts, *LHJ*, 28 (Dec. 1911): 78; Perry, Dame & Co. furs, *LHJ*, 28 (Dec. 1911): 79; Bellas & Hess shirtwaists, *LHJ*, 28 (Dec. 1911): 81; Ohio Knitting scarves, *SEP*, 184 (9 Dec. 1911): 62; Vantine & Co. Oriental imports, *LHJ*, 29 (Dec. 1912): 63; L. H. Field Co. handkerchiefs, *LHJ*, 29 (Dec. 1912): 72; Phoenix mufflers and hose, *LHJ*, 29 (Dec. 1912): 74; Royal Flower and Feather Co. plumes, *LHJ*, 29 (Dec. 1912): 78; Whitman chocolates, *SEP*, 185 (7 Dec. 1912): 35; Johnston's chocolates, *SEP*, 185 (7 Dec. 1912): 73; Briggs bracelets, *SEP*, 185 (7 Dec. 1912): 77; Gordon & Ferguson furs, *LHJ*, 30 (Dec. 1913): 61; Phillipsborn feminine apparel, *LHJ*, 30 (Dec. 1913): 80; Weil Co. furs and gloves, *LHJ*, 30 (Dec. 1913): 85; Rexall assorted items, *SEP*,

186 (6 Dec. 1913): 36–37; Phoenix scarflers, *SEP*, 186 (13 Dec. 1913): 32; Briggs fobs and lockets, *SEP*, 186 (13 Dec. 1913): 38; and Everwear hosiery, *SEP*, 186 (20 Dec. 1913): 33. For fuller discussions of gimcracks as a type of gift, see chapters 4 and 5.

　　3. For Christmas gift ads that emphasize the daintiness of women and/or the daintiness of gift items intended for them, see Weatherby plate racks, *LHJ*, 20 (Dec. 1902): 21; Shepard Norwell handkerchiefs, *LHJ*, 20 (Dec. 1902): 48; American Electric Novelty Co. clocks and lamps, *LHJ*, 20 (Dec. 1902): 56; J. B. Williams vanity boxes, *LHJ*, 28 (Dec. 1911): 40; Bestyette rainwear, *LHJ*, 28 (Dec. 1911): 80; Bellas & Hess shirtwaists, *LHJ*, 28 (Dec. 1911): 81; Herrick Christmas cards, *LHJ*, 28 (Dec. 1911): 82; Lennox stationery, *SEP*, 184 (2 Dec. 1911): 71; Everwear hosiery, *SEP*, 184 (2 Dec. 1911): 73; Eaton, Crane & Co. stationery, *LHJ*, 29 (Dec. 1912): 55; and Monarch electric toasters, *SEP*, 185 (7 Dec. 1912): 74.

　　The definition for "dainty" is from *Webster's New International Dictionary of the English Language* (Springfield, Mass., 1922).

　　4. For articles that discuss the "servant problem" of the early twentieth century, see Ida Husted Harper, "Women Ought to Work," *I*, 52 (16 May 1901): 1125–26; Goldwyn Smith, "The Passing of the Household," *I*, 59 (24 Aug. 1905): 423–24; Irene Van Kleeck, "How Women Wage Earners Fare," *WW*, 15 (Dec. 1907): 9684–85; Charles Zueblin, "The Effect on Women of Economic Dependence," *AJS*, 14 (March 1909): 614–19; May Ellis Nichols, "Exit the Maid," *Out*, 125 (12 May 1920): 74; C. Frederick, "Teach Women What Advertising Does," *PI*, 111 (10 June 1920): 177 +; John Corbin, "The Forgotten Woman," *NAR*, 216 (Oct. 1922): 456–60; Caroline E. MacGill, "The Importance of Earning a Living," *ScrM*, 74 (Dec. 1923): 743–46; M. S. Dawson, "Housekeeping—A Man's Job," *WC*, n.s., 9 (21 March 1925): 14–15; Amey E. Watson, "The Reorganization of Household Work," *AAA*, 160 (March 1932): 165–77; and Wadsworth H. Mullen, Woman's Leisure Time," *PI*, 170 (17 Jan. 1935): 45 +.

　　For secondary works that discuss domestic servitude in the late nineteenth and early twentieth centuries, see the works cited in notes 1 and 4, chapter 11.

　　As women began to do their own housework, many writers were reminded afresh that housework was very demanding physically. See Christine Terhune Herrick, "The Bowed Back," *HBaz*, 33 (6 Jan. 1900): 23; Harper, "Women Ought to Work," 1125; H. G. Wells, "Anticipations: An Experiment in Prophecy," *NAR*, 173 (July 1901): 58–61; Nichols, "Exit the Maid," 74; E. Davenport, "When Father Helps with the Wash," *LHJ*, 38 (June 1921): 83 +; S. R. Winters, "Housework in the Laboratory," *SA*, 125 (20 Aug. 1921), 130–31 +; G. K. Brown, "Adventure in Housekeeping," *PI*, 111 (17 June 1920): 149–50 +; Corbin, "The Forgotten Woman," 459–61; Ernest R. Groves, "Social Influences Affecting Home Life," *AJS*, 31 (Sept. 1925): 234–35; Allen T. Tate, "Some Christmas Copy I Would Rather Not See," *PI*, 136 (2 Sept. 1926): 26, 28; Graham Pierce, " 'Women Haven't Enough To Do!' " *AMag*, 106 (July 1928): 38–39; and Eloise Davison, "Christmas Presence," *AHom*, 15 (Dec. 1935): 77–79.

　　5. For a fuller discussion of the appearance of the economy of abundance, see chapter 3. See also Inez Milholland, "The Changing Home," *MCl*, 15 (March 1913): 208.

　　For a discussion of appliances that were shelved inventions, see Siegfried Giedion, *Mechanization Takes Command* (New York, 1969), 512–627. For articles that note the popularity of appliances as Christmas gifts to women and their increasing use in American households, see Mary Mortimer Maxwell, "The Lack of Privacy in the American Home," *LA*, 269 (20 May 1911): 451; Nichols, "Exit the Maid," 78–79; Davenport, "When Father Helps with the Wash," 83 +; Brown, "Adventure in Housekeeping," 149–50 +; Frederick, "Teach Women What Advertising Does," 177 +; A. L. Townsend, "What Has Christmastide Brought to Another Year of Advertising?" *PI*, 125 (20 Dec. 1923): 104, 107; Tate, "Some

Christmas Copy I Would Rather Not See," 26, 28; Ed Wolff, "And Now We Point toward Christmas," *PIM*, 19 (Oct. 1929): 40+; and John Burt Hardee, "'Twas the Month before Christmas," *PI*, 149 (28 Nov. 1929): 68+.

For ads that recommend appliances as Christmas gifts, see illustration 34: Universal appliances, *LHJ*, 38 (Dec. 1921): 79. See also Bissell carpet sweepers, *LHJ*, 28 (Dec. 1911): 65; Caloric fireless cookstoves, *LHJ*, 28 (Dec. 1911): 80; Westinghouse appliances, *SEP*, 184 (2 Dec. 1911): 63; Western Electric appliances, *SEP*, 184 (2 Dec. 1911): 68; Rochester Stamping appliances, *LHJ*, 29 (Dec. 1912): 47; Hoosier kitchen cabinets, *LHJ*, 29 (Dec. 1912): 51; Wear-Ever cookwear, *LHJ*, 29 (Dec. 1912): 65; National carpet sweepers, *LHJ*, 29 (Dec. 1912): 90; O-Cedar mops, *SEP*, 185 (7 Dec. 1912): 52; Monarch electric toasters, *SEP*, 185 (7 Dec. 1912): 74; Royal-Rochester percolators, *LHJ*, 30 (Dec. 1913): 61; Duntley carpet sweepers, *LHJ*, 30 (Dec. 1913): 62; Manning-Bowman appliances, *LHJ*, 30 (Dec. 1913): 77; General Electric appliances, *SEP*, 186 (6 Dec. 1913): 47; Frantz Premier vacuum cleaners, *SEP*, 186 (13 Dec. 1913): 51; Apex vacuum cleaners, *LHJ*, 37 (Dec. 1920): 43; Pneuvac vacuum cleaners, *LHJ*, 37 (Dec. 1920): 45; America vacuum cleaners, *LHJ*, 37 (Dec. 1920): 46; Simplex roller ironer, *LHJ*, 37 (Dec. 1920): 49; Pyrex ovenware, *LHJ*, 37 (Dec. 1920): 96; Torrington vacuum cleaners, *LHJ*, 37 (Dec. 1920): 110; Universal appliances, *LHJ*, 37 (Dec. 1920): 114; Royal vacuum cleaners, *LHJ*, 37 (Dec. 1920): 137; Wagner cookware, *LHJ*, 37 (Dec. 1920): 153; ABC clothes washers, *SEP*, 192 (4 Dec. 1920): 43; Hoover vacuum cleaners, *SEP*, 193 (11 Dec. 1920): 39; Lorain oven regulators, *SEP*, 193 (18 Dec. 1920): 115; Rid-Jid ironing boards, *SEP*, 193 (18 Dec. 1920): 153; Eureka vacuum cleaners, *LHJ*, 38 (Dec. 1921): 137; Mirro cookware, *LHJ*, 38 (Dec. 1921): 155; Hotpoint appliances, *LHJ*, 39 (Dec. 1922): 119; Sweeper-Vac vacuum cleaners, *LHJ*, 39 (Dec. 1922): 121; Ohio vacuum cleaners, *LHJ*, 39 (Dec. 1922): 140; Vollrath pans, *LHJ*, 29 (Dec. 1922): 157; Griswold cookware, *LHJ*, 29 (Dec. 1922): 161; Bee-Vac vacuum cleaners, *SEP*, 195 (9 Dec. 1922): 101; and Liberty hot plates, *SEP*, 195 (9 Dec. 1922): 107.

6. Torrington vacuum cleaners, *LHJ*, 37 (Dec. 1920): 110 (reproduced as illustration 35). For other ads that promote appliances because they increase the leisure time of their recipients, see Apex vacuum cleaners, *LHJ*, 37 (Dec. 1920): 43; Simplex roller irons, *LHJ*, 37 (Dec. 1920): 49; Royal vacuum cleaners, *LHJ*, 37 (Dec. 1920): 137; Hoover vacuum cleaners, *SEP*, 193 (11 Dec. 1920): 39; Lorain oven regulators, *SEP*, 193 (18 Dec. 1920): 115; Hoosier kitchen cabinets, *SEP*, 195 (2 Dec. 1922): 58; Eureka vacuum cleaners, *LHJ*, 45 (Dec. 1928): 114; Premier vacuum cleaners, *SEP*, 201 (8 Dec. 1928): 91; Johnson's floor polishers, *SEP*, 201 (8 Dec. 1928): 122; and Robertshaw oven regulators, *LHJ*, 46 (Dec. 1929): 112.

For articles that discuss the leisure provided by appliances, see Nichols, "Exit the Maid," 74–79; Groves, "Social Influences Affecting Home Life," 233–35; Pierce, "Women Haven't Enough To Do!" 38–39; Davison, "Christmas Presence," 77–79. Ruth Schwartz Cohen argues that the appliances raised standards of housekeeping rather than lessened housewives' labor. See her "A Study in Technological Change: The Washing Machine and the Working Wife," in *Clio's Consciousness Raised*, ed. Mary S. Hartman and Lois Banner (New York, 1974), 245–53.

7. For an article that notes the new youthfulness of the women in advertisements, see W. Livingston Larned, "Youth Rides Triumphant in Modern Advertising," *PI*, 140 (1 Sept. 1927): 145–46+. As the ideal of sexual attractiveness moved toward ever younger women during the 1920s, some ad writers even suggested a romantic bond between fathers and their daughters. For their part, mature women began to adopt the clothing styles of younger females. A good discussion of this trend in women's fashions is Kenneth A. Yellis, "Prosperity's Child: Some Thoughts on the Flapper," *AQ*, 21 (Spring 1969): 44–64. For an ad

illustrating the flapper clothing style, see illustration 36: Queen Make dresses, *LHJ*, 38 (Dec. 1921): 168. For an ad that shows a woman wearing a style previously worn only by girls, see illustration 37: Nayvee Middiwear, *LHJ*, 37 (Dec. 1920): 167.

The increased use of the romantic sexual theme in ads generated a debate among advertisers. Some of the articles in this debate are Ruth Leigh, "Do Women Respond to 'Pretty Girl' Pictures?" *PI*, 129 (6 Nov. 1924): 25–26+; "Selling Collars to Men by Pretty Girl Pictures," *PI*, 139 (19 May 1927): 10+; W. Livingston Larned, "When the Skirts of Romance Brush Industry," *PI*, 139 (23 June 1927): 152+; Roy Dickinson, "An Idea Plus Romance as a Copy Formula," *PI*, 114 (5 July 1928): 73–74+; Wilbur Perry, "After All, the Pretty Girls Do Sell Merchandise," *PIM*, 22 (May 1931): 44–45+; Mark O'Dear, "S-s-s-s-sh . . . SEX!" *PI*, 173 (19 Dec. 1935): 45; Frances T. Rowe, "Men in Women's Advertising," *A&S*, 25 (9 May 1935): 27+; and Clarence Fowerbaugh and Norman Krichbaum, "Should Sex Be Dragged In by the Heels?" *A&S*, 28 (3 Dec. 1936): 31–32+.

For an ad showing a playful woman underneath mistletoe with her beau, see illustration 38: Twinplex stroppers, *SEP*, 195 (9 Dec. 1922): 155. For examples of ads that use "cheesecake" illustrations, see illustration 39: Onyx hosiery, *LHJ*, 38 (Dec. 1921): 152; illustration 40: Wolf lingerie, *LHJ*, 37 (Dec. 1920): 179; and illustration 75: CosyToes house slippers, *LHJ*, 38 (Dec. 1921): 165.

8. For an ad that shows husbands presenting Christmas gifts to their ecstatic recipient-wives, see illustration 41: Simplex roller irons, *LHJ*, 37 (Dec. 1920): 49. See also Apex vacuum cleaners, *LHJ*, 37 (Dec. 1920): 43; Pneuvac vacuum cleaners, *LHJ*, 37 (Dec. 1920): 45; America vacuum cleaners, *LHJ*, 37 (Dec. 1920): 46; Royal vacuum cleaners, *LHJ*, 37 (Dec. 1920): 137; Bee-Vac vacuum cleaners, *SEP*, 195 (9 Dec. 1922): 101; and Chevrolet automobiles, *SEP*, 195 (16 Dec. 1922): 41.

9. The best discussion of the advertisers' use of "smart" is Elizabeth Emmett, "This Feminine Character Stuff," *PI*, 135 (8 April 1926): 25–26+. See also Albert Edward Wiggam, "New Styles in American Beauty: Brains and Pulchitrude Now Go Together," *WW*, 56 (Oct. 1928): 648–58; Ernest Elmo Calkins, "Beauty in the Machine Age," *PI*, 152 (25 Sept. 1930): 72–73+; and Sylvia Carewe, "Fashion in Advertising Is Not Spinach," *PIM*, 37 (Nov. 1938): 13+.

For ads that describe either the item advertised or the potential recipient as "smart," see *Ladies' Home Journal* subscriptions, *LHJ*, 45 (Dec. 1928): 118; Daisy luggage, *LHJ*, 45 (Dec. 1928): 122; Dan'l Green Comfy house slippers, *LHJ*, 45 (Dec. 1928): 124; Streit slumber chairs, *LHJ*, 45 (Dec. 1928): 164–66; Parker pens, *SEP*, 201 (1 Dec. 1928): 64; Buxton keytainers, *SEP*, 201 (1 Dec. 1928): 136; Krementz watch bands, *SEP*, 201 (1 Dec. 1928): 149; Glover pajamas, *SEP*, 201 (8 Dec. 1928): 124–25; Travelo knit jackets, *SEP*, 201 (15 Dec. 1928): 151; L. Vanderbilt toiletries, *LHJ*, 46 (Dec. 1929): 154; Maid-Rite house slippers, *LHJ*, 46 (Dec. 1929): 168; Talon zippered items, *SEP*, 202 (7 Dec. 1929): 86–87; Knockabout knit jackets, *SEP*, 202 (7 Dec. 1929): 263; Buick automobiles, *SEP*, 202 (14 Dec. 1929): 57; Pyrex glassware, *LHJ*, 47 (Dec. 1930): 115; Pequot linens, *LHJ*, 47 (Dec. 1930): 125; Munsingwear underwear, *LHJ*, 47 (Dec. 1930): 136; DuPont boudoir accessories, *SEP*, 203 (6 Dec. 1930): 95; Toastmaster toasters, *SEP*, 203 (6 Dec. 1930): 97; Puritan knit goods, *SEP*, 203 (6 Dec. 1930): 175; Ingersoll-Waterbury timepieces, *SEP*, 203 (13 Dec. 1930): 124; Toastmaster waffle irons, *SEP*, 203 (13 Dec. 1930): 131; and Johnston candy, *SEP*, 203 (13 Dec. 1930): inside back cover.

10. By emphasizing the differences between the images of women in the 1920s and 1930s, I do not mean to ignore areas of continuity between the two decades. For example, one of the most common traits of 1920s women—the exhibition of sexual appeal—was still present during the '30s, although with somewhat less frequency than during the '20s.

During the Depression, virtually all Americans looked with disfavor on women who pursued careers. For articles that either reflect or discuss this new consensus, see Jane Allen, "You May Have My Job," *Frm*, 87 (April 1932): 228–31; Philip Curtiss, "The Twilight of the Business Woman," *At*, 153 (Feb. 1934): 167–71; Claire Howe, "Return of the Lady," *NO*, 164 (Oct. 1934): 34–38; Genevieve Parkhurst, "Is Feminism Dead?" *HM*, 170 (May 1935): 154+; and Charlotte Muret, "Marriage as a Career," *HM*, 173 (Aug. 1936): 249–57.

For secondary sources that discuss women's return to the home during the 1930s, see Smith, *Daughters of the Promised Land*, 293–306; Lois Banner, *Women in Modern America* (New York, 1974), 191–96; and William H. Chafe, *The American Woman* (New York, 1972), 101–11.

11. For ads that portray women in this ritzy manner, see illustration 44: Community silver plate, *LHJ*, 53 (Dec. 1936): 93; illustration 45: Cadillac automobiles, *SEP*, 210 (18 Dec. 1937): 35; illustration 46: RCA Victrolas, *SEP*, 211 (10 Dec. 1938): 64; and illustration 47: Rogers Brothers silver plate, *LHJ*, 53 (Dec. 1936): 82. See also Holmes & Edwards silver plate, *LHJ*, 45 (Dec. 1928): 83; Elizabeth Arden beauty preparations, *LHJ*, 45 (Dec. 1928): 138; DuPont boudoir accessories, *SEP*, 203 (6 Dec. 1930): 95; and Elgin watches, *LHJ*, 55 (Dec. 1938): 91.

For articles that discuss the use of the ritzy appeal in ads, see W. Livingston Larned, "A Defense of 'Swank' in Illustration," *PI*, 138 (3 Feb. 1927): 77–78+; "High-Hat Copy," *PI*, 161 (Nov. 10, 1932): 28; and Carewe, "Fashion in Advertising is Not Spinach," 13+.

12. For examples of ads that portray women as aloof, see Martex towels, *LHJ*, 45 (Dec. 1928): 98; Elizabeth Arden beauty preparations, *LHJ*, 45 (Dec. 1928): 138; Community silver plate, *LHJ*, 53 (Dec. 1936): 93; Coty perfume, *LHJ*, 55 (Dec. 1938): 79; and Elgin watches, *LHJ*, 55 (Dec. 1938): 91.

For examples of ads in which the illustration of the woman is separate from that of the item advertised, see DuPont boudoir accessories, *SEP*, 203 (6 Dec. 1930): 95; Community silver plate, *LHJ*, 53 (Dec. 1936): 93; and General Electric appliances, *SEP*, 211 (3 Dec. 1938): 46–47.

13. For ads that suggest luxurious items as gifts for women, see Buick automobiles, *SEP*, 202 (14 Dec. 1929): 57; Rogers Brothers silver plate, *LHJ*, 53 (Dec. 1936): 82; Community silver plate, *LHJ*, 53 (Dec. 1936): 93; Waltham watches, *SEP*, 209 (5 Dec. 1936): 107; Elgin watches, *LHJ*, 54 (Dec. 1937): 80; Cambridge crystal, *LHJ*, 54 (Dec. 1937): 106; Evening in Paris perfume, *LHJ*, 54 (Dec. 1937): back cover; Cadillac automobiles, *SEP*, 210 (18 Dec. 1937): 35; and Fostoria crystal, *LHJ*, 55 (Dec. 1938): 84.

14. For examples of Christmas gift ads that either portray the items as tribute or raise the question of the adequacy of husbands' gifts to their wives, see illustration 48: Community Plate service ware and teapots, *SEP*, 209 (5 Dec. 1936): 72; and illustration 49: Coty perfume, *LHJ*, 55 (Dec. 1938): 79. See also Elizabeth Arden beauty preparations, *LHJ*, 45 (Dec. 1928): 138; Buick automobiles, *SEP*, 202 (14 Dec. 1929): 57; and Community silver plate, *LHJ*, 53 (Dec. 1936): 93.

For articles that discuss the declining authority of fathers within American families, see "Increasing Sales to Women by Advertising to Men," *PI*, 135 (8 April 1926): 162+; Frederick F. Van De Water, "Fathers Are Different," *HM*, 166 (March 1933): 504–8; Hiram Motherwell, "Diary of a Lone Father," *PM*, 8 (Dec. 1933): 24–25+; Dorothy Sabin Butler, "Men Against Women," *Frm*, 94 (Aug. 1935): 81; A. L. Moats, "I Like Men With Money," *SEP*, 208 (9 May 1936): 20–21+; Thomas H. Uzzell and V. E. LeRoy, "The Decline of the Male," *ScrM*, 100 (Dec. 1936): 19–25; Arthur Hirose, "To the Ladies!" *A&S*, 33 (13 Aug. 1936): 33–74; Stewart H. Holbrook, "The Vanishing American Male," *AMer*,

40 (March 1937): 270–79; and Alfred Uhler and Margaret Fishback, "Are Men Mice?" *Frm*, 100 (July 1938): 17–21.

15. For secondary works that discuss the economic advances by women during the 1930s, see Banner, *Women in Modern America*, 171–91; and Dixon Wecter, *The Age of the Great Depression* (New York, 1947), 25–40.

For articles that discuss the increase in female ownership of property, see Henry Morton Robinson, "The Female and the Specie," *R*, 49 (Oct. 1936): 22–24; Nancy Hale, "What Interests Women—and Why," *A&S*, 27 (21 May 1936): 27+; Hirose, "To The Ladies!" 33, 74; Holbrook, "The Vanishing American Male," 273–74; and Issac Marcosson, "Powder-Puff Magnates," *AMag*, 124 (Oct. 1937): 35+. For an opposing view, see Clarissa Wolcott Delaney, "The Myth of Economic Matriarchy," *CH*, 49 (Feb. 1939): 45–46.

16. For works that discuss the intimidating behavior of women during the 1930s, see D. H. Lawrence, "Cocksure Women and Hensure Men," *Frm*, 81 (Jan. 1929): supp. L; Gershon Legman, *Love & Death* (New York, 1949); Philip Wylie, *Generation of Vipers* (New York, 1942); and Ferdinand Lundberg and Marynia Farnham, *Modern Woman, The Lost Sex* (New York, 1947).

This emphasis on men's sexual anxieties during the 1930s is not to ignore the fact that American males, throughout much of the nation's past, have exhibited some concern over their sexual adequacy. Nevertheless, this concern was particularly high in the decades after 1890, as many Americans became convinced that the virility-enhancing frontier had been settled out of existence and as increasing numbers of males assumed nonphysical, white-collar jobs. In spite of the fact that these anxieties concerned adult males, during the early twentieth century the major focus of the concern with male adequacy in periodicals was directed toward boys, as ads repeatedly exhorted boys to be manly and active. However, by the 1930s periodical writers more commonly alluded to the anxieties of the adult males themselves.

For recent secondary works that discuss various aspects of the increase in male sexual anxieties around 1890, see Peter Gabriel Filene, *Him Her Self* (New York, 1976), 68–94; John Higham, "The Reorientation of American Culture in the 1890's," in *Origins of Modern Consciousness*, ed. John Weiss (Detroit, 1965), 25–48; Hendrick M. Ruitenbeek, *The Male Myth* (New York, 1967), passim; Alex Comfort, *The Anxiety Makers* (New York, 1967), passim; and James Harvey Young, *The Medical Messiahs* (Princeton, 1967), passim.

17. For lengthy lists of items that were commonly presented to men during the early twentieth century, see the following two gift-selection articles: H. Taylor, "Gifts for a Man," *LHJ*, 28 (Dec. 1911): 58; and Virginia Hunt, "It's So Hard to Know What to Give a Man," *LHJ*, 30 (Dec. 1913): 46.

18. For advertisements of gift items intended to help husbands in their jobs in minor ways, see Pelouze desk scales, *LHJ*, 18 (Dec. 1900): 42; Barler document files, *SEP*, 173 (8 Dec. 1900): 19; Parker pens, *SEP*, 173 (8 Dec. 1900): 23; Laughlin pens, *SEP*, 173 (8 Dec. 1900): 28; Conklin pens, *SEP*, 174 (7 Dec. 1901): 29 (rather than stressing that Conklin pens would aid the husband in his job, this ad, which is reproduced as illustration 55, stressed that it "would not roll off a slanted desk, will not cause annoyance or violent expressions"); Waterman pens, *SEP*, 174 (21 Dec. 1901): 15; Huebsch year books and diaries, *SEP*, 175 (6 Dec. 1902): 40; and Swan pens, *SEP*, 184 (9 Dec. 1911): 39.

19. For ads showing women picking a single type of gift item for all of their male recipients, see illustration 50: Shirley President suspenders, *LHJ*, 29 (Dec. 1912): 64; and illustration 51: Paris garters, *SEP*, 194 (3 Dec. 1921): 90. For ads of common items presented to men, see illustration 52: Gillette razors, *LHJ*, 29 (Dec. 1912): 57; illustration 53: Bondy

hairbrushes, *SEP*, 173 (8 Dec. 1900): 16; illustration 54: Torrey razor strops, *SEP*, 174 (7 Dec. 1901): 29; and illustration 55: Conklin pens, *SEP*, 174 (7 Dec. 1901): 29.

For advertisements of gift items intended to improve husbands' appearance, see Acme hair brushes, *LHJ*, 19 (Dec. 1901): 43; Middletown hats, *SEP*, 175 (6 Dec. 1902): 30; Hincher suit hangers, *SEP*, 175 (6 Dec. 1902): 36; Larter shirt studs and cuff links, *LHJ*, 28 (Dec. 1911): 75; Simmons watch chains, *LHJ*, 29 (Dec. 1912): 73; and Kerr belts and buckles, *SEP*, 186 (6 Dec. 1913): 44.

For ads for gift items intended to add to husbands' comfort, see Edgarton suspenders, *SEP*, 173 (22 Dec. 1900): 17; Self-closing tobacco pouches, *SEP*, 174 (14 Dec. 1901): 17; Shirley President suspenders, *SEP*, 184 (2 Dec. 1911): 39 (according to this ad, Shirley President suspenders make an ideal Christmas present because they "show that you really thought about his needs and ease and likes; they are comfortable, healthful, and ornamental"); Wickes tobacco pouches, *SEP*, 184 (2 Dec. 1911): 51; Innovation tie holders, *SEP*, 184 (2 Dec. 1911): 71; Prince Albert pipe tobacco, *SEP*, 184 (16 Dec. 1911): 30; George Frost Pad garters, *LHJ*, 29 (Dec. 1912): 65; Boston garters, *SEP*, 185 (7 Dec. 1912): 50; Frank pipes, *SEP*, 185 (14 Dec. 1912): 44; Hardright pipes, *SEP*, 186 (6 Dec. 1913): 57; Old English tobacco, *SEP*, 186 (13 Dec. 1913): 28; Roig and Langsdorf Girard cigars, *SEP*, 186 (13 Dec. 1913): 31; Pioneer garters, *SEP*, 186 (13 Dec. 1913): 50; Stag pipe tobacco, *SEP*, 186 (20 Dec. 1913): 39; and Tuxedo pipe tobacco, *SEP*, 186 (20 Dec. 1913): 45.

For an ad for a watch, see illustration 56: Elgin watches, *LHJ*, 28 (Dec. 1911): 76 (this ads claims that "men of affairs—of power and prestige—own this watch"). See also Howard watches, *SEP*, 185 (14 Dec. 1912): 42 (this ad states explicitly that the Howard watch is the symbol of the successful man).

For discussions of gimcracks as a type of Christmas gift, see chapters 4 and 5.

20. The quotation is from Kin Hubbard, "Paw's Christmas Present," *Cos*, 50 (Jan. 1911): 63; H. I. Phillips, "I'm Strong for Christmas, But—," *AMag*, 98 (Dec. 1924): 178–79. See also Errol Flynn, "Not That I'm Ungrateful," *WHC*, 65 (Jan. 1938): 64.

21. For articles that note that gifts to men became more expensive during the 1920s, see William O. Scroggs, "Christmas and the Payroll," *Out*, 153 (18 Dec. 1929): 621 (this article notes that "at the beginning of the present century, . . . the highly ornamental case made to hold a single handkerchief was deemed an appropriate gift for a young man, while dad got a lovely hand-embroidered thingumajig in which he was supposed to lay away his suspenders every night before retiring. Tastes have changed since then. . . . Christmas goods have become more costly and more luxurious"); and Avis D. Carlson, "Our Barbaric Christmas," *NAR*, 231 (Jan. 1931): 66–71.

For ads for men's Christmas gifts from the early 1920s that stress the luxuriousness or high quality of the items, see illustration 57: Bond Street spats, *SEP*, 202 (21 Dec. 1929): 84; and illustration 58: Emery shirts, *SEP*, 194 (17 Dec. 1921): 90. See also Ever-Ready razors, *SEP*, 194 (10 Dec. 1921): 1; Robert Burns cigars, *SEP*, 194 (24 Dec. 1921): 25; Tavannes watches, *SEP*, 195 (2 Dec. 1922): 68; Autostrop razors, *SEP*, 195 (16 Dec. 1922): 71; and Parker pens, *SEP*, 195 (16 Dec. 1922): 105.

22. The heightened concern of men with their personal appearance following World War I is reflected in the content of Christmas gift ads in *The Saturday Evening Post* and the *Ladies' Home Journal*. Between two three-year periods, 1911–1913 and 1920–1922, the percentage of men's Christmas gifts ads that promoted articles of clothing rose from 22 percent to 42 percent.

For ads that suggest expensive garments for presentation to men, see Pelter coats, *SEP*, 193 (18 Dec. 1920): 47; Wilson furnishings, *SEP*, 193 (18 Dec. 1920): 52; Town and Country coats, *SEP*, 193 (18 Dec. 1920): 69; Emery shirts, *SEP*, 194 (17 Dec. 1921): 90; Hart, Schaffner, and Marx overcoats, *SEP*, 195 (16 Dec. 1922): 2; Bull-dog men's accessories, *SEP*, 195 (16 Dec. 1922): 94; Travelo knit jackets, *SEP*, 201 (15 Dec. 1928): 151; Knockabout knit jackets, *SEP*, 202 (7 Dec. 1929): 263; and Arrow shirts, *SEP*, 202 (14 Dec. 1929): 204.

For ads that suggest toiletries for presentation to men, see Yardley toiletries, *LHJ*, 45 (Dec. 1928): 116; and Mennen toiletries, *SEP*, 201 (15 Dec. 1928): 51.

For ads that suggest grooming aids for presentation to men, see Durham-Duplex razors, *SEP*, 193 (4 Dec. 1920): 62; Ever-Ready brushes and razors, *SEP*, 193 (18 Dec. 1920): 37; Rubberset brushes, *SEP*, 194 (10 Dec. 1921): 88; Gillette razors, *SEP*, 195 (9 Dec. 1922): 109; Twinplex stroppers, *SEP*, 195 (9 Dec. 1922): 115; Rubberset shaving brushes, *SEP*, 195 (16 Dec. 1922): 48; Autostrop razors, *SEP*, 195 (16 Dec. 1922): 71; Gillette razor blades, *SEP*, 201 (8 Dec. 1928): 147; Gem nail clippers, *SEP*, 201 (15 Dec. 1928): 157; Rolls razors, *SEP*, 202 (21 Dec. 1929): 68; Puritan knit goods, *SEP*, 203 (6 Dec. 1930): 175; and Enders razors, *SEP*, 203 (20 Dec. 1930): 77.

For articles that indicate the changes in men's clothing styles during the 1920s, see M. Olds, "Can Advertising Stick to Fundamental Motives?" *PI*, 112 (12 Aug. 1920): 73–74+; Frank E. Fehlman, "Are Men Interested in Style?" *PIM*, 20 (June 1930): 46+; and Norman Levy, "The Sartorial Revolution," *HM*, 173 (June 1936): 100–5.

For a discussion of men's "great renunciation" of display in their clothing toward the end of the eighteenth century, see J. C. Flugal, *The Psychology of Clothes* (New York, 1969), 103–17.

Ads for men's Christmas gifts from the early 1920s which argue that the items will improve the appearance of recipients are Hickock belts, *LHJ*, 38 (Dec. 1921): 175; Kum-A-Part cuff buttons, *SEP*, 194 (10 Dec. 1921): 40; Kuppenheimer clothes, *SEP*, 195 (2 Dec. 1922): inside front cover; and Tavanes watches, *SEP*, 195 (2 Dec. 1922): 68.

For an ad showing a man in the Arrow Collar mold, see Kuppenheimer clothes, *SEP*, 195 (2 Dec. 1922): inside front cover.

23. Ads for men's Christmas gifts from the early 1920s which stress the stylishness of the items are Wadsworth watch cases, *SEP*, 194 (3 Dec. 1921): 60–61; Krementz cuff links, *SEP*, 194 (3 Dec. 1921): 92; Kum-A-Part cuff buttons, *SEP*, 194 (10 Dec. 1921): 40; Emery shirts, *SEP*, 194 (17 Dec. 1921): 90; Spur ties, *SEP*, 195 (2 Dec. 1922): 86; Dunn-Pen pens, *SEP*, 195 (16 Dec. 1922): 86; Wahl pens, *SEP*, 195 (9 Dec. 1922): 96–97; Hickock belts and buckles, *SEP*, 195 (9 Dec. 1922): 104–5; Hart, Schaffner, and Marx overcoats, *SEP*, 195 (16 Dec. 1922): 2; and Bull-dog men's accessories, *SEP*, 195 (16 Dec. 1922): 94.

For secondary works that discuss the appearance of consumption values in American culture, see Leo Lowenthal, *Literature, Popular Culture, and Society* (Palo Alto, Calif., 1961), 109–36; and Walter A. Weisskopf, *The Psychology of Economics* (Chicago, 1954), 243–53.

The appearance of consumption values in men's Christmas gift ads following World War I coincided with the appearance of those same values in women's Christmas gift ads. Generally, husbands received items to improve their personal appearance during the 1920s, whereas their wives received gifts that, it was hoped, would contribute to their leisure-time activities. In particular, wives received household appliances that enabled them to finish their chores more quickly than before.

24. For articles that note the increased practicality of Christmas gifts during the 1930s, see "Christmas Sales Show That 1930 Has Bred a New Type of Buyer," *BW*, 17 Dec. 1930, 9–10; and "Christmas Shoppers Didn't Buy Less; They Just Paid Less," *BW*, 7 Jan. 1931, 11–12.

For examples of men's Christmas gift ads of the 1930s that stress the practicality of suggested items, see Ronson lighters, *SEP*, 209 (5 Dec. 1936): 90; Bulova watches, *SEP*, 209

(19 Dec. 1936): 65; Taylor instruments, *SEP*, 209 (19 Dec. 1936): 81; Waterman's pens, *SEP*, 210 (4 Dec. 1937): 109; Buxton leather goods, *SEP*, 210 (11 Dec. 1937): 85; R. J. Reynolds tobacco, *SEP*, 210 (18 Dec. 1937): 39; Cheney cravats, *SEP*, 211 (3 Dec. 1938): 51; Eversharp pens and pencils, *SEP*, 211 (17 Dec. 1938): 55; and Paris garters, *SEP*, 211 (17 Dec. 1938): 64.

For examples of men's Christmas gift ads of the 1930s that stress that the items will last into the distant future, see Ronson lighters, *SEP*, 209 (5 Dec. 1936): 90; Central watches, *SEP*, 209 (5 Dec. 1936): 95; Waltham watches, *SEP*, 209 (5 Dec. 1936): 107; Gillette blade packages, *SEP*, 209 (12 Dec. 1936): 79; Buxton leather accessories, *SEP*, 209 (12 Dec. 1936), 111; Bulova watches, *SEP*, 209 (19 Dec. 1936): 65; Conklin pens, *SEP*, 210 (4 Dec. 1937): 91; Univex cameras, *SEP*, 210 (4 Dec. 1937): 98; Waterman's pens, *SEP*, 210 (4 Dec. 1937): 109; Half and Half pipe tobacco, *SEP*, 210 (4 Dec. 1937): 111; Sheaffer pens, *SEP*, 210 (11 Dec. 1937): inside front cover; Univex movie cameras, *SEP*, 210 (11 Dec. 1937): 83; Taylor instruments, *SEP*, 210 (11 Dec. 1937): 84; Parker pens, *SEP*, 211 (10 Dec. 1938): inside front cover; Hamilton watches, *SEP*, 211 (10 Dec. 1938): 85; and Eversharp pens and pencils, *SEP*, 211 (17 Dec. 1938): 55.

25. For articles which note that, during the 1930s, gift givers began to present less expensive items at Christmas, see "Christmas Sales Show that 1930 Has Bred a New Type of Buyer," 9–10; "Christmas Shoppers Didn't Buy Less; They Just Paid Less," 11–12; "Christmas Stocking—and Selling," *BW*, 14 Dec. 1932, 9–10; and "Stores Re-Order Christmas Goods," *BW*, 17 Dec. 1938, 30–31.

My content analysis of the Christmas gift ads in the *Ladies' Home Journal* and *The Saturday Evening Post* in two three-year periods, 1928–1930 and 1936–1938, reveals that the percentage of ads for gifts to men that suggested high-priced items for presentation declined between the two periods (see table A).

TABLE A

Years	Low ($0–$10)	Moderate ($10–$25)	High (Over $25)
1928–1930	68%	14%	18%
1936–1938	80%	16%	4%

This trend contrasts with the slight rise in the percentage of women's ads which suggested high-priced items (see table B).

TABLE B

Years	Low ($0–$10)	Moderate ($10–$25)	High (Over $25)
1928–1930	40%	20%	40%
1936–1938	29%	25%	46%

Examples of ads for the most common types of men's items are Cheney cravats, *SEP*, 209 (12 Dec. 1936): 76; Real Silk ties, *LHJ*, 55 (Dec. 1938): 60; Arrow ties, *SEP*, 211 (3 Dec. 1938): 85; Paris garters, *SEP*, 209 (12 Dec. 1936): 96; Paris suspenders, *SEP*, 209 (12 Dec. 1936): 96; Schick razors, *SEP*, 209 (12 Dec. 1936): 112; Gillette gift sets, *SEP*, 210 (18 Dec. 1937): 63; Rolls razors, *SEP*, 210 (18 Dec. 1937): 86; Edgeworth tobacco, *SEP*, 209 (5 Dec. 1936): 100; Prince Albert tobacco, *SEP*, 209 (12 Dec. 1936): 42; Sir Walter Raleigh tobacco,

SEP, 209 (19 Dec. 1936): 61; Union Leader tobacco, *SEP*, 209 (19 Dec. 1936): 66; Half and Half tobacco, *SEP*, 210 (4 Dec. 1937): 111; Velvet tobacco, *SEP*, 210 (11 Dec. 1937): 50; Interwoven socks, *SEP*, 209 (19 Dec. 1936): 85; Real Silk socks, *LHJ*, 55 (Dec. 1938): 60; and Pacer socks, *SEP*, 211 (10 Dec. 1938): 83.

For examples of men's Christmas gift ads of the 1930s which stress that the items are sensibly priced, see Waltham watches, *SEP*, 209 (5 Dec. 1936): 107; Parker pens, *SEP*, 209 (19 Dec. 1936): 1; Union Leader tobacco, *SEP*, 209 (19 Dec. 1936): 66; and Elgin watches, *LHJ*, 55 (Dec. 1938): 91.

For articles that advocate rationality and "sensible spending" as a response to the Depression, see Royal Wilbur France, "Which Way Prosperity?" *RR*, 82 (Dec. 1930): 82; William Trufant Foster and Waddill Catchings, "Riotous Saving," *At*, 146 (Nov. 1930): 667–72; "World on a Saving Spree," *LD*, 108 (7 March 1931): 44; Henry Pratt Fairchild, "Exit the Gospel of Work," *HM*, 162 (April 1931): 566–73; "Is Wise Spending a Part of Thrift?" *RR*, 84 (Oct. 1931): 82; "Hoarding: A New Symptom," *RR*, 84 (Nov. 1931): 84–86; "A Time to Save and a Time to Spend," *LD*, 110 (12 Sept. 1931): 42; Samuel Chowther, "Why Traitor Dollars Prolong Depression," *LHJ*, 49 (Feb. 1932): 21+; "Coaxing Slacker Dollars Back to Work," *LD*, 112 (20 Feb. 1932): 11; Henry Kittredge Norton, "America's Overstuffed Nest Egg," *NO*, 161 (June 1933): 36–38; and Stephen M. Foster, "Money: Active and Static," *NR*, 76 (23 Aug. 1933): 39–40.

8. *"Something for the Kid"*

1. For works that discuss the lessened parental authority over children during the Christmas season, see James H. Barnett, *The American Christmas* (New York, 1954), 10, 31–32; Clement A. Miles, *Christmas in Ritual and Tradition* (London, 1912), 223–24, 306–308; and "Christmas a Hundred Years Ago," *Cen*, 103 (1921–22): 287.

Works that discuss the nineteenth-century celebration are Barnett, *The American Christmas*, 6–9; Harnett T. Kane, *The Southern Christmas Book* (New York, 1958), passim; John Esten Cooke, "Christmas Time in Old Virginia," *MAH*, 10 (Dec. 1883): 443–59; Norman M. Walker, "The Holidays in Early Louisiana," *MAH*, 10 (Dec. 1883): 46–66; George William Curtis, "Christmas," *HNMW*, 68 (Dec. 1883): 15–16; Phil Weaver, Jr., "Christmases and Christmases," *OM*, 21 (Jan. 1893): 32–44; Florence Whiting Lee, "Christmas in Virginia before the War," *SW*, 37 (1908): 686–89; "Christmas a Hundred Years Ago," 81–89; "Holidays in Old St. Louis," *GP*, 1 (Dec. 1933): 1–6; Bertha L. Heilbron, "Christmas and New Year's on the Frontier," *MH*, 16 (Dec. 1935): 281–83; and Walter Prescott Webb, "Christmas and New Year in Texas," *SHQ*, 44 (July 1940): 357–79.

New England was the only section of the country in which Christmas gifts to children were not popular. This lack of popularity was only one facet of a general opposition to the holiday there, which did not diminish significantly until the second half of the nineteenth century. This attitude had begun with the Puritan contention that the day should not be celebrated because there were no biblical commands to do so. For works that describe the unpopularity of Christmas in New England, see Barnett, *The American Christmas*, 2–4; Curtis, "Christmas," 5–15; Edward E. Hale, "Christmas in Boston," *NEM*, 1 (Dec. 1889): 355–56; Abram English Brown, "The Ups and Downs of Christmas in New England," *NEM*, 29 (Dec. 1903): 479–84; Frida Davidson, "How Our Christmas Customs Came," *NH*, 28 (11 Nov. 1928), 625; and Dorothy Neuhoff, "Christmas in Colonial America," *SS*, 40 (Dec. 1949): 339–41.

2. For articles that describe the most common types of gift items presented to children before 1880, see Cooke, "Christmas Time in Old Virginia," 453–55; Edward Bok, "Are We

Fair to Our Children at Christmas," *LHJ*, 20 (Dec. 1902): 18; John Burroughs, "Corrupting the Innocents," *I*, 61 (13 Dec. 1906): 1424–25; Lee, "Christmas in Virginia before the War," 688; Carl Werner, "Christmas When We Were Kids," *Out*, 102 (23 Nov. 1912): 678–83; "Old-Fashioned Christmas," *SRL*, 10 (23 Dec. 1933): 368; Heilbron, "Christmas and New Year's on the Frontier," 381–83; Lois Lenski, "Christmas Is What You Make It," *PM*, 10 (Dec. 1935): 13; Webb, "Christmas and New Year in Texas," 361–373, 377; Alexander J. Wall, Jr., "St. Nicholas and the Society," *NYHSQB*, 25 (Jan. 1941): 10–16. Two books that describe these early gifts to children are Barnett, *The American Christmas*, 80–81; and Kane, *The Southern Christmas Book*, 17, 70–71, 172, 232, 251–52.

3. The reversal of normal positions of authority at Christmas is an old aspect of the holidays. For discussions of this holiday theme in the antebellum South, see Kenneth M. Stampp, *The Peculiar Institution* (New York: Vintage Books, 1956), 166, 169–70, 365, 368; Kane, *The Southern Christmas Book*, 63–76; Cooke, "Christmas Time in Old Virginia," 447–48; Lee, "Christmas in Virginia before the War," 687–88; and Webb, "Christmas and New Year in Texas," 374–75. For discussions of other aspects of the reversal of authority at Christmas, see Barnett, *The American Christmas*, 70–78, 92–95; O. M. Spencer, "Christmas throughout Christendon," *HNMM*, 46 (Dec. 1872): 241–42, 254; and "Christmas a Hundred Years Ago," 289.

4. The quotation is from Eugene Wood, "A Christmas Thought," *Ev*, 15 (Dec. 1906): 805–6. For secondary works that discuss the rewarding and punishing sides of the early nineteenth-century Santa Claus, see Barnett, *The American Christmas*, 26, 44–45; Kane, *The Southern Christmas Book*, 41–42; and Alexander J. Wall, Jr., "St. Nicholas at the Society," *NYHSQB*, 25 (Jan. 1941): 13–14.

5. Weir's painting of Santa Claus is reproduced as illustration 60. It is currently owned by the New-York Historical Society. For discussions of it, see R.W.G. Vail, "Santa Claus Visits the Hudson," *NYHSQB*, 35 (Oct. 1951): 337–43; and Charles W. Jones, "Knickerbocker Santa Claus," *NYHSQB*, 38 (Oct. 1954): 382–83.

6. For works that discuss the Pelznickel figure, see Barnett, *The American Christmas*, 11, 26–27; Miles, *Christmas in Ritual and Tradition*, 219–20; Kane, *The Southern Christmas Book*, 41–42; Spencer, "Christmas Throughout Christendom," 246–51; Wood, "A Christmas Thought," 806; J.E.G. de Montmorency, "Saint Nicholas," *CR*, 104 (Dec. 1913): 888; Davidson, "How Our Christmas Customs Came," 625; Wall, "St. Nicholas at the Society," 11; and Neuhoff, "Christmas in Colonial America," 344.

Two articles that note the punishing side of the European St. Nicholas are D.J.D., "Santa Claus' Family Tree," *Men*, 15 (Dec. 1927): 59; and "Certainly It's True," *LD*, 103 (28 Dec. 1929): 21.

For works that discuss the St. Nicholas cult in Europe, see Barnett, *The American Christmas*, 25–26; Miles, *Christmas in Ritual and Tradition*, 218–21, 229–32; Spencer, "Christmas throughout Christendom," 246–51; Franklin B. Wiley, "What Christmas Really Means," *LHJ*, 20 (Dec. 1902): 6; Albert Schinz, "The Good Bishop Saint Nicholas," *Ov*, n.s., 54 (Dec. 1909): 537–43; de Montmorency, "Saint Nicholas," 885–88; "Do You Believe in Santa Claus?" *I*, 115 (19 Dec. 1925): 705–8; John Macy, "The True Story of Santa Claus," *Bk*, 66 (Dec. 1927): 350–56; "The Inside Story of Santa Claus," *RR*, 77 (Jan. 1928): 96–97; D.J.D., "Santa Claus' Family Tree," 59; "Certainly It's True," 21; W. Branch Johnson, "Santa Claus Comes to Life," *CR*, 140 (Dec. 1931): 771–76; W. Branch Johnson, "Santa Claus and the Children," *CW*, 134 (Dec. 1931): 257–65; Wall, "St. Nicholas at the Society," 10–11; and Jones, "Knickerbocker Santa Claus," 357–59.

The following works discuss the life of the historical figure St. Nicholas (Bishop of Myra in the fourth century): Barnett, *The American Christmas*, 537–43; de Montmorency, "Saint

Nicholas," 886–88; Charles Johnson, "From Saint Nicholas to Santa Claus," *Out*, 105 (20 Dec. 1913): 842–45; Macy, "The True Story of Santy Claus," 350–52; Davidson, "How Our Christmas Customs Came," 625; "The Inside Story of Santy Claus," 96; W. Branch Johnson, "Santa Claus in Strange Guises," *CW*, 132 (Dec. 1930): 266–75; and Johnson, "Santa Claus and the Children," 257–62.

7. For an analysis of the shift from handmade to manufactured gift items, see chapter 3. For articles that note this shift as manifested in presents from parents to their children, see Edward Bok, "Are We Fair to Our Children at Christmas?" *LHJ*, 20 (Dec. 1902): 18; John Burroughs, "Corrupting the Innocents," *I*, 61 (13 Dec. 1906): 1424–25; Ellis Parker Butler, "Something for the Kid," *Cos*, 50 (Jan. 1911): 168–70; Sophia E. Delavan, "Did You Ever Buy a Toy for a Child?" *AMag*, 92 (Dec. 1921): 41–43; and "Old-Fashioned Christmas," 368.

8. The two articles by Bok are "Are We Fair to Our Children at Christmas?" 18, and "Giving Children Mechanical Toys," *LHJ*, 23 (Dec. 1905): 18. For additional articles that object to the mechanical toys' encouragement of passivity, see "The Question of Christmas Observance," *LHJ*, 24 (Dec. 1906): 5; Emelyn Lincoln Coolidge, "Young Mother at Christmastime," *LHJ*, 29 (Dec. 1912): 54; Carl Werner, "Christmas When We Were Kids," *Out*, 102 (23 Nov. 1912): 681; Delevan, "Did You Ever Buy a Toy for a Child?" 41; and Ruth Leigh, "Christmas Gifts for the Children," *PM*, 4 (Dec. 1929): 68. For an ad for a mechanical gift for a child, see illustration 61: Ives toys, *SEP*, 184 (2 Dec. 1911): 56.

9. The quotation is from Burroughs, "Corrupting the Innocents," 1424–25. Two other articles which agreed with Burroughs that modern mechanical toys left children jaded are "The Spectator," *Out*, 72 (29 Nov. 1902): 722–23; and "The Curse of Christmas," *I*, 117 (18 Dec. 1926): 697.

10. The quotation is from Butler, "Something for the Kid," 168–70. For examples of articles which argue that parents give their children too many Christmas gifts, see Bok, "Are We Fair to Our Children at Christmas," 18; Friedrich Paulsen, "Old and New Fashioned Notions about Education," *ER*, 35 (May 1908): 483–84; Elizabeth Hale Gilman, "The Child's Best Christmas Present," *CLif*, 9 (Dec. 1905): 139; and Burroughs, "Corrupting the Innocents," 1424–25.

11. For discussions of the totally rewarding Santa Claus and his plumper physiognomy, see Barnett, *The American Christmas*, 30–33; Wood, "A Christmas Thought," 805–6; "The Curse of Christmas," 697; and Richardson Wright, "Why Is Christmas Always Symbolized by a Stout Elderly Man in Whiskers?" *H&G*, 64 (Dec. 1933): 25.

12. The articles from which I quote are "Do You Believe in Santa Claus?" 705; Thomas L. Masson, "Wanted: A New Christmas," *Bk*, 50 (Nov. 1919): 358; and E. Douglas Branch, "Jingle Bells," *SRL*, 17 (4 Dec. 1937): 3.

Moore drew on the description of Santa in Washington Irving's *Knickerbocker History* (1809), although Moore was the first to stress the modern characteristics of plumpness and joviality. For discussions of the importance of Irving's book to the development of the Santa Claus myth in America, see Jones, "Knickerbocker Santa Claus," 372–77; Barnett, *The American Christmas*, 27; and D.J.D., "Santa Claus' Family Tree," 59.

For other discussions of Moore, see Jones, "Knickerbocker Santa Claus," 377–82; Barnett, *The American Christmas*, 27–28; Gamaliel Bradford, "Santa Claus: A Psychograph," *Bk*, 62 (Dec. 1925): 403; Macy, "The True Story of Santy Claus," 354–56; and D.J.D., "Santa Claus' Family Tree," 59.

13. For an example of a Nast Santa, see illustration 62. It also appears in the convenient collection, *Thomas Nast's Christmas Drawings* (New York, 1978), 43. While Nast drew some short, plump, genial Santas, he is most important for the tall Santas he created.

For discussions of Nast's influence on the development of the Santa Claus icon, see Barnett, *The American Christmas*, 28–29; James H. Barnett, "Christmas in American Culture," *P*, 9 (Feb. 1946): 53; and Daniel J. Boorstin, *The Americans: The Democratic Experience* (New York, 1973), 160.

14. For an account of a family's celebration that includes a visit to the home by Santa, see A. Radclyffe Dugmore, "Santa Claus and His Reindeer," *CLif*, 11 (Dec. 1906): 154–56. One article not only contained instructions for making Santa Claus suits, but also assured the reader that "anyone—Grandfather, Grandmother, Father, Mother, Big Sister or Brother, or you yourself—can assume the character of this live little saint" (L. Beard, "Home-Made Santa Claus and a Christmas Tree," *LHJ*, 25 [Dec. 1907]: 35).

See Dugmore, "Santa Claus and His Reindeer," 154–56, for photographs of a home celebration in which the suit and mask are clearly visible. One of the best sources of information on the costumes of domestic Santas is the Sears, Roebuck, and Company catalogues. With regard to the use of the togas, Sears did not offer pants with their Santa Claus suits until the early 1920s. See also William Allen White, "Science, St. Skinflint, and Santa Claus," *AMag*, 63 (Dec. 1906): 182; and Beard, "Home-Made Santa Claus and a Christmas Tree," 35.

15. For articles that discuss the street-corner Santas of the early twentieth century, see Magner White, "Experiences of a Department Store Santa Claus," *AMag*, 100 (Dec. 1925): 45 +; "The Curse of Christmas," 697; P. K. Crocker, "Some Christmas Ideas to Pass on to Retailers," *PI*, 137 (7 Oct. 1926): 97–100; "This Xmas Spirit," *I*, 120 (7 Jan. 1928): 4; Archibald Stone, "The Day of Gifts," *HB*, 64 (Dec. 1928): 708; Lawrence Dale, "This Christmas Business," *C&F*, 17 (19 Dec. 1928): 2687; Betty Thornley, "A Morning Off with Santa Claus," *CLif*, 57 (Dec. 1929): 35–36; "Standard Santas," *Ftn*, 16 (Dec. 1937): 12; and "Santa Supply," *LD*, 124 (11 Dec. 1937): 18–19.

16. The reference to the existence of the three Santa Claus schools in New York City is in Jones, "Knickerbocker Santa Claus," 360. For other discussions of these schools, see Barnett, *The American Christmas*, 34; Boorstin, *The Americans: The Democratic Experience*, 160; "Standard Santas," 12; and "Santa Supply," 18–19.

17. For evidence of the higher quality and greater realism of the street-corner Santas' costumes, see White, "Experiences of a Department Store Santa Claus," 45 +; C. W. Steffler, "Where Christmas Comes Every Day in the Year," *C&F*, 16 (21 Dec. 1927): 2613–14; "Standard Santas," 12; and "Santa Supply," 18–19.

18. Accounts of the actions by the Salvation Army, the Boston City Council, and the department store are from Dale, "This Christmas Business," 2687; "Santa Supply," 19; and Boorstin, *The Americans: The Democratic Experience*, 160–61. Three articles which concur that there were too many professional Santas are White, "Experiences of a Department Store Santa Claus," 90; Stone, "Day of Gifts," 708; and "Standard Santas," 12.

19. Riis's description is in his "Is There a Santa Claus?" *I*, 52 (20 Dec. 1900): 3055. For other articles that express deep reservations about the perpetuation of the Santa Claus myth, see E. L. Hermance, "Christmas Declaration of Independence," *LHJ*, 26 (Dec. 1908): 24; "The Belief in Santa Claus," *Out*, 99 (16 Sept. 1911): 140; Charlotte Perkins Gilman, "Cross-Examining Santa Claus," *Cen*, 105 (Dec. 1922): 169–74; "The Curse of Christmas," 697; Heywood Broun, "It Seems to Heywood Broun," *N*, 125 (28 Dec. 1927): 728; "This Xmas $pirit," 4; and Helen Perry Curtis, "Making the Christmas Story Live," *PM*, 7 (Dec. 1932): 20–21 +.

20. For articles that favor the perpetuation of a modified Santa Claus myth, see "Is There a Santa Claus?" and "The Troubled Parent at Christmas," both of which may be found at *LHJ*, 23 (Dec. 1905): 18; Gilman, "The Child's Best Christmas Present," 104; "The

Question of Christmas Observance," 5–6; Edward S. Martin, "Is There Really a Santa Claus?" *LHJ*, 27 (15 Dec. 1910): 7; "Fact, Fiction, and the Truth," *Out*, 106 (4 April 1914): 746–49; Mildred W. Stillman, "What to Tell the Children?" *Frm*, 74 (Aug. 1925): 216; Lenski, "Christmas Is What You Make It," 13; Louise Price Bell, "There is a Santa Claus!" *AHom*, 15 (Dec. 1935): 43+; "The Truth about Santa," *PM*, 12 (Dec. 1937): 69; and Branch, "Jingle Bells," 24. See also Barnett, *The American Christmas*, 29–30.

21. For articles that favor perpetuating an unchanged Santa Claus myth, see R. C. Lewis, "New Kind of Santa Claus," *LHJ*, 23 (Nov. 1906): 24; Eugene Wood, "Old Santy," *Ev*, 31 (Dec. 1914): 850–57; White, "Experiences of a Department Store Santa Claus," 45+; and "Santa Supply," 18–19.

22. For discussions of the Santa Claus Association, see "Immortal Santa Claus," *Out*, 112 (12 Jan. 1916): 66; Barnett, *The American Christmas*, 32–33; and Boorstin, *The Americans: The Democratic Experience*, 160.

23. For ads for boys' gift items that reflect the vigorous, manly ideal, see illustration 63: Winslow's ice skates, *SEP*, 185 (14 Dec. 1912): 29; and illustration 64: Iver-Johnson bicycles, *SEP*, 185 (7 Dec. 1912): 60. See also Stevens rifles, *LHJ*, 20 (Dec. 1902): 4; George Horace Lorimer's *Letters from a Self-Made Merchant to His Son*, *SEP*, 175 (20 Dec. 1902): 18; Book Supply Co. Christmas books, *LHJ*, 28 (Dec. 1911): 49; *American Boy Magazine* ad in *LHJ*, 28 (Dec. 1911): 71; Worthington tricycles and bicycles, *LHJ*, 28 (Dec. 1911): 76; Flexible Flyer sleds, *LHJ*, 28 (Dec. 1911): 90; Maxim gun silencers, *SEP*, 184 (2 Dec. 1911): 53; Robeson pocket knives, *SEP*, 184 (2 Dec. 1911): 66; Brunswick pool tables, *SEP*, 184 (9 Dec. 1911): 33; Daisy air rifles, *SEP*, 184 (9 Dec. 1911): 41; Winchester guns, *SEP*, 184 (9 Dec. 1911): 53; Remington rifles, *SEP*, 184 (16 Dec. 1911): 45; Winslow's ice skates, *LHJ*, 29 (Dec. 1912): 75; U.S. ice skates, *SEP*, 185 (7 Dec. 1912): 70; King air rifles, *SEP*, 186 (6 Dec. 1913): 32; and Hamilton rifles, *SEP*, 186 (13 Dec. 1913): 43.

For articles that favor this same ideal, see "When a Girl Became a Girl to My Boy," *LHJ*, 24 (Feb. 1907): 14; Wyllys Rede, "A New Method of Making Character," *I*, 71 (26 Oct. 1911): 914–19; Gerald Stanley Lee, "A Christmas for Cities," *Ev*, 29 (Dec. 1913): 771–86; and Lemuel Standish, "My Boy," *AMag*, 84 (Nov. 1917): 14+.

24. The Howard watch ad may be found at *SEP*, 186 (13 Dec. 1913): 34 (reproduced as illustration 65). Ads for Christmas gifts for boys that encourage the recipients to adopt a mature demeanor are American School of Correspondence courses, *LHJ*, 19 (Dec. 1901): 45; Ingersoll watches, *SEP*, 174 (7 Dec. 1901): 32; American typewriters, *SEP*, 175 (6 Dec. 1902): 38; George Horace Lorimer's *Letters from a Self-Made Merchant to His Son*, *SEP*, 175 (20 Dec. 1902): 18; Waltham watches, *LHJ*, 28 (Dec. 1911): 78; Cecilian pianos, *SEP*, 184 (2 Dec. 1911): 53; Bestyette raincoats, *LHJ*, 29 (Dec. 1912): 79; Gruen watches, *SEP*, 185 (7 Dec. 1912): 32; American Model Builders models, *SEP*, 185 (7 Dec. 1912): 57; Hallet and Davis pianos, *LHJ*, 30 (Dec. 1913): 48; Snellenburg Clothing Co. suits, *LHJ*, 30 (Dec. 1913): 64; Parker pens, *LHJ*, 30 (Dec. 1913): 66; Larter shirt studs, *SEP*, 186 (6 Dec. 1913): 65; and Elgin watches, *SEP*, 186 (13 Dec. 1913): 38.

25. For discussions of the heightened concern with virility after 1890, see the works cited in note 16, chapter 7.

26. The three ads to which I specifically refer are Stevens rifles, *LHJ*, 20 (Dec. 1902): 4 (reproduced as illustration 73); Remington rifles, *SEP*, 184 (16 Dec. 1911): 45 (reproduced as illustration 66); and Daisy air rifles, *SEP*, 184 (9 Dec. 1911): 41 (reproduced as illustration 67).

27. The advertisement for Maxim silencers may be found at *SEP*, 184 (2 Dec. 1911): 53 (reproduced as illustration 68).

28. The two ads to which I specifically refer are *The American Boy Magazine* ad in *LHJ*,

29 (Dec. 1912): 73; and Brunswick billiard tables, *LHJ*, 18 (Dec. 1900): 43 (reproduced as illustration 69). See also *The American Boy Magazine* ads in *LHJ*, 28 (Dec. 1911): 71; *LHJ*, 30 (Dec. 1913): 77; *SEP*, 186 (6 Dec. 1913): 69; *SEP*, 186 (13 Dec. 1913): 39; and the Brunswick billiard table ads at *SEP*, 185 (7 Dec. 1912): 68; and *LHJ*, 29 (Dec. 1912): 60. For additional ads that encourage boys to develop a morally upright character, see the *Boy's Magazine* ads in *LHJ*, 29 (Dec. 1912): 76; *SEP*, 185 (7 Dec. 1912): 74; *SEP*, 186 (6 Dec. 1913): 38; and *SEP*, 186 (13 Dec. 1913): 34.

For articles that make this same point, see "Spoiling the Home Brood," *LD*, 70 (27 Aug. 1921): 29; and William Byron Forbush, "Home Training as Citizenship Insurance," *MR*, 46 (July 1923): 533–35.

29. For examples of articles on raising boys that were published between 1920 and 1940, see Edgar Guest, "My Job as a Father," *AMag*, 94 (Aug. 1922): 13–15; Frederick F. Van de Water, "Confessions of a Dub Father," *LHJ*, 42 (May 1925): 25; Isabel F. Bellows, "Be a Good Boy," *ER*, 69 (Feb. 1925): 86–87; Clarence Budington Kelland, "It's Fun Being a Father," *AMag*, 103 (Jan. 1927): 54–55; G. N. Fletcher, "Bringing Up Father," *LHJ*, 44 (Sept. 1927): 35 +; W. O. Saunders, "The Last Hope for Freedom Has Flown," *AMag*, 106 (Oct. 1928): 50–51; Henry C. Fulcher, "My Son and I Go Fishing," *PM*, 5 (May 1930): 32–33; Henry B. Lent, "I Am a Week-end Father," *PM*, 6 (Sept. 1931): 17 +; Lewis Gaston Leary, "The Fine Art of Letting Go," *ScrM*, 91 (June 1932): 358–60; John Hudson McMurtrie, "For Fathers Only," *PM*, 7 (Aug. 1932): 9; Frederick Van de Water, "Fathers Are Different," *HM*, 166 (March 1933): 504–8; Christian Gauss, "What I've Found Out About Fathers and Sons," *PM*, 8 (July 1933): 23 +; and E. F. DuTeau, "Father to His Son," *R*, 55 (Aug. 1939): 45.

30. The statistics on the output of domestic toys are from C. W. Steffler, "Where Christmas Comes Every Day in the Year," 2613. For other discussions of the importation of toys before 1914 and the effects of World War I on the American toy industry, see Carroll D. Murphy, "American-made Christmas," *Sys*, 26 (Oct. 1914): 358–62; Marion Clinch Calkins, "Toys and Tears," *Sur*, 45 (25 Dec. 1920): 455; and James L. Fri, "This Business of Christmas," *CH*, 47 (Dec. 1937): 54–55.

31. The quotation is from Fri, "This Business of Christmas," 54–55. For other articles that emphasize the practical, educational nature of American toys, see Murphy, "American-made Christmas," 361–62; Delavan, "Did You Ever Buy a Toy for a Child?" 41–43; Steffler, "Where Christmas Comes Every Day in the Year," 2613; and Dale, "This Christmas Business," 2688.

For an ad for this type of toy, see illustration 70: Meccano Company model sets, *SEP*, 186 (20 Dec. 1913): 28; illustration 71: American Mechanical Toy Co. model sets, *SEP*, 185 (7 Dec. 1912): 57; and illustration 72: Holgate Educational toys, *LHJ*, 55 (Dec. 1938): 97. See also Lincoln Logs, *LHJ*, 46 (Dec. 1929): 148.

32. For articles that refer to the continued high cost of Christmas gifts to children during the 1920s and 1930s, see G. A. Nichols, "Cold and Fishy Eye for Good Old Santa Claus," *PIM*, 13 (Nov. 1926): 73; Lawrence Dale, "Santa Claus Comes Down to Earth," *C&F*, 21 (21 Dec. 1932): 1453; C. S. Hough, "The Boy Market Is Depression Proof," *PI*, 164 (Aug. 10, 1933): 41 +; and Rose G. Anderson, "Our Overprivileged Children," *RD*, 34 (Feb. 1939): 44–46. For articles that make closely related points, see Charles G. Muller, "Don't Overlook the Sons and Daughters of Mr. and Mrs. Consumer," *PI*, 155 (21 May 1931): 57–58 +; M. Harrington, "Assistant to Santa Claus," *GH*, 97 (Dec. 1933): 39 +; Grace E. Batchelder, "Gifts for Older Boys and Girls," *PM*, 9 (Dec. 1934): 24 +; "Guide to Giving," *PM*, 13 (Dec. 1938): 90–95; and "Stores Re-Order Christmas Goods," *BW*, 17 Dec. 1938, 30–31.

244 8. "SOMETHING FOR THE KID"

There was a decline of interest in child rearing on the part of periodical writers, as Agnes Repplier noted in 1923: "Children were less popular in fiction than they were a few years ago. Bad, clever little boys; sensitive, dreamy, ghost-seeing little boys; amatory little boys, who at nine or eleven have enrolled themselves in 'the great cruising brotherhood of the Pilgrims of Love,' no longer fill our magazines to the exclusion of grown-up people. It almost seems as though the harmless, necessary adult were coming into his own again. There is also something resembling a lull in the counsels of experts who instruct mothers in the bringing up of their offspring, and teachers in the art of education" ("Concerning Children," *I*, 110 [17 Mar. 1923]: 183). Moreover, the percentage of Christmas gift ads in the *Ladies' Home Journal* and *The Saturday Evening Post* suggesting items for presentation to boys declined from 13 percent (1911–1913) to 10 percent (1920–1922) to 8 percent (1928–1930) to 6 percent (1936–1938).

33. Two examples of ads that recommend "housekeeping" toys for presentation to girls at Christmas are Old Hickory Chairs, *LHJ*, 19 (Dec. 1901): 40; and Royal toy laundry wringers, *LHJ*, 20 (Dec. 1902): 42.

For examples of ads in which writers portray girls as young and dependent, see Brunswick pool tables, *LHJ*, 18 (Dec. 1900): 43; Stevens rifles, *LHJ*, 20 (Dec. 1902): 4; Equitable endowment policies, *SEP*, 175 (6 Dec. 1902): 33; Elgin watches, *SEP*, 184 (2 Dec. 1911): 57; Caloric stoves, *SEP*, 184 (2 Dec. 1911): 60; Detroit electric cars, *SEP*, 184 (9 Dec. 1911): 70; Baldwin player pianos, *SEP*, 185 (7 Dec. 1912): 34; Virtuolo player pianos, *SEP*, 185 (7 Dec. 1912): 39; Smith & Wesson revolvers, *SEP*, 185 (7 Dec. 1912): 59; Hoosier kitchen cabinets, *LHJ*, 30 (Dec. 1913): 45; Victrolo record players, *LHJ*, 30 (Dec. 1913): 88; Baldwin Manuolo pianos, *SEP*, 186 (6 Dec. 1913): 29; and Globe-Wernicke bookcases, *SEP*, 186 (6 Dec. 1913): 30.

34. Stevens rifles, *LHJ*, 20 (Dec. 1902): 4 (reproduced as illustration 73).

35. For ads that portray older and/or sexy girls, see illustration 74: Buick automobiles, *SEP*, 203 (13 Dec. 1930): 41; illustration 75: CosyToes feltwear, *LHJ*, 38 (Dec. 1921): 165; and illustration 76: Paul Jones Sailor suits, *LHJ*, 37 (Dec. 1920): 185. See also Bicycle Trade, *SEP*, 193 (11 Dec. 1920): 59; Miss Saratoga middy suits and blouses, *LHJ*, 38 (Dec. 1921): 143; De Benoise brassieres, *LHJ*, 39 (Dec. 1922): 176; Whiting & Davis mesh bags, *SEP*, 195 (16 Dec. 1922): 86; Bulova watches, *SEP*, 195 (16 Dec. 1922): 112; Frigidaire refrigerators, *LHJ*, 46 (Dec. 1929): 70; Van Heusen collars, *SEP*, 201 (15 Dec. 1928): 148; Royal portable typewriters, *SEP*, 209 (5 Dec. 1936): 91; Prince Albert tobacco, *SEP*, 209 (12 Dec. 1936): 42; and Underwood portable typewriters, *SEP*, 210 (11 Dec. 1937): 103. See also the discussion in W. Livingston Larned, "Youth Rides Triumphant in Modern Advertising," *PI*, 140 (1 Sept. 1927), 145–46+.

For a good account of the appearance of the flapper style, see Kenneth A. Yellis, "Prosperity's Child: Some Thoughts on the Flapper," *AQ*, 21 (Spring 1969): 44–64.

36. For ads in which girls participate in the central action, see Campbell soups, *LHJ*, 37 (Dec. 1920): 33; Kiddie-Kar foot-propelled cars, *LHJ*, 37 (Dec. 1920): 166; Paul Jones sailor suits, *LHJ*, 37 (Dec. 1920): 185; Nasua wool blankets, *LHJ*, 37 (Dec. 1920): 198; Bicycle Trade, *SEP*, 193 (11 Dec. 1920): 59; Bissell carpet sweepers, *LHJ*, 38 (Dec. 1921): 159; Faultless rubber goods, *LHJ*, 39 (Dec. 1922): 193; Whiting & Davis mesh bags, *SEP*, 195 (16 Dec. 1922): 86; Majestic radios, *SEP*, 202 (21 Dec. 1929): 28; Van Heusen collars, *SEP*, 201 (15 Dec. 1928): 148; Prince Albert tobacco, *SEP*, 209 (12 Dec. 1936): 42; and Dan'l Green house slippers, *LHJ*, 210 (Dec. 1937): 63.

For ads for gift items with which girls could get exercise, see Kiddie-Kar foot-propelled cars, *LHJ*, 37 (Dec. 1920): 166; Bicycle Trade, *SEP*, 193 (11 Dec. 1920): 59; Flexible Flyer sleds, *LHJ*, 38 (Dec. 1921): 166; Gendron children's vehicles, *LHJ*, 39 (Dec. 1922): 199;

Whiting & Davis mesh bags, *SEP*, 195 (16 Dec. 1922): 86; Kangru-Springshus, *SEP*, 202 (14 Dec. 1929): 185; and Iver Johnson bicycles, *SEP*, 209 (12 Dec. 1936): 108.

Regarding active gift items, a writer of 1921 noted that "from [age ten] until . . . fifteen, athletic toys are particularly acceptable to both boys and girls. Young America now wants sleds, bicycles, roller skates, baseball outfits, croquet sets, and magic-lantern or 'movie' outfits, as well as the things that go with fishing and camping. The same thing applies to both sexes, although girls are more partial to croquet sets and boys have pretty much of monopoly on baseballs, bats, and gloves" (Delevan, "Did You Ever Buy a Toy for a Child?" 42). See also the suggestions of Charlotte Ross Mochrie, "Gifts for Eight to Sixteen," *PM*, 10 (Dec. 1935): 20 + .

37. For a 1930s ad that emphasizes the age difference between a mother and her daughter, see illustration 77: Daniel Green Comfy slippers, *LHJ*, 54 (Dec. 1937): 63.

9. The Ever Wider Horizon

1. My conception of community stems from Robert Redfield's conception of an ideal folk society. He concisely describes this type of society in the opening paragraph of his seminal essay "The Folk Society": "Understanding of society may be gained through construction of an ideal type of primitive or folk society as contrasted with modern urbanized society. Such a society is small, isolated, non-literate, and homogeneous, with a strong sense of group solidarity. The ways of living are conventionalized into that coherent system which we call a 'culture.' Behavior is traditional, spontaneous, uncritical, and personal; there is no legislation or habit of experiment and reflection for intellectual ends. Kinship, its relationships and institutions are the type categories of experience and the familial group is the unit of action. The sacred prevails over the secular; the economy is one of status rather than of the market. These and related characterizations may be restated in terms of 'folk mentality' *(Classic Essays on the Culture of Cities*, ed. Richard Sennett [New York, 1969], 180). See also Louis Wirth, "Urbanism as a Way of Life," ibid., 143–64; Georg Simmel, "The Metropolis and Mental Life," in *The Sociology of Georg Simmel*, trans. and ed. Kurt H. Wolff (New York, 1964), 409–24; and Horace Miner, "The Folk-Urban Continuum," in *Cities and Society*, ed. Paul K. Hiatt and Albert J. Reiss, Jr. (Glencoe, Ill., 1957), 22–34.

A strong sense of community membership and identification characterized not only the pronouncedly communitarian settlements of the seventeenth century, but also the more secular, commercial cities of the eighteenth century. For discussions of the sense of community in preindustrial cities, see Michael Zuckerman, *Peaceable Kingdoms* (New York, 1970); Carl Bridenbaugh, *Cities in the Wilderness* (New York, 1971); Zane L. Miller, *The Urbanization of Modern America* (New York, 1973), 3–24; Sam Bass Warner, Jr., *The Urban Wilderness* (New York, 1972), 7–14; Howard P. Chudacoff, *The Evolution of American Urban Society* (Englewood Cliffs, N.J., 1975), 1–13; and Charles N. Glaab and A. Theodore Brown, *A History of Urban American* (New York, 1967), 1–24.

For discussions of the effects of the industrial revolution on cities, see Lewis Mumford, *The City in History* (New York, 1961), 446–81; Chudacoff, *Evolution of American Urban Society*, 48–50; Miller, *Urbanization of Modern America*, 25–34; and George Rogers Taylor, *The Transportation Revolution* (New York, 1951), 3–14, 132–52, 384–98.

For discussions of the changes in urban life during the last quarter of the nineteenth century, see Sam Bass Warner, Jr., *Streetcar Suburbs* (New York, 1969), 153–66; Glaab and Brown, *History of Urban America*, 133–66; Miller, *Urbanization of Modern America*, 35–45; Chudacoff, *Evolution of American Urban Society*, 64–89; Blake McKelvey, *The Urbanization of*

America: 1860–1915 (New Brunswick, N.J., 1963), 51–52, 61–85; Mumford, *The City in History*, 487–513; and Robert H. Weibe, *The Search for Order* (New York, 1967), 44–75.

2. For a discussion of the attachment of metropolitan leaders to the characteristics of small-town life, see Jean Quandt, *From the Small Town to the Great Community* (New Brunswick, N.J., 1970). See also B. O. Flower, "Christmas Spirit," *Ar*, 38 (Dec. 1907): 705–6.

3. On the initiating role of the New York City festival organizers, see Sonya Levien, "Sentimental New York," *Sur*, 29 (4 Jan. 1913): 416; and "A Saner Merry Christmas," *Out*, 103 (4 Jan. 1913): 1. The quotation is from G. M. Johnston, "Joyeux Noel," *Sur*, 35 (27 Nov. 1915): 205–7.

4. Regarding the anonymity of the organizers, see "A Saner Merry Christmas," 1; "What the Tree in the Square Heard," *LHJ*, 30 (Dec. 1913): 11; "Night before Christmas in the City Square," *Sur*, 33 (5 Dec. 1914): 260.

The quotation is from Harry Lee, "Why Not a Community Christmas?" *CLif*, 37 (Dec. 1919): 54.

5. The fullest account of the fund-raising effort is Levien, "Sentimental New York," 415–16. See also "Night before Christmas in the City Square," 258–60; and Lee, "Why Not a Community Christmas?" 54.

6. On the lack of prior publicity for the celebration, see Levien, "Sentimental New York," 416.

For the attendance figures, see "What the Tree in the Square Heard," 11; "Community Christmas Tree," *Out*, 106 (3 Jan. 1914): 4; and Riis, "The New Christmas That Is Spreading All Over Our Country," *LHJ*, 30 (Dec. 1913): 16.

7. Regarding the spread of the celebration, see Levien, "Sentimental New York," 416; Riis, "The New Christmas That Is Spreading All Over Our Country," 16; "Community Christmas Tree," 4; "Night before Christmas in the City Square," 258–60; "The New 'Community' Christmas," *LD*, 51 (25 Dec. 1915): 1482; Johnston, "Joyeux Noel," 205–7; and Lee, "Why Not a Community Christmas?" 54.

8. For a classic statement of the point that the size of cities necessarily makes them impersonal, see Wirth, "Urbanism as a Way of Life," 152–53.

9. The standard discussion of nativism in the late nineteenth and early twentieth centuries is in John Higham, *Strangers in the Land* (New York, 1969).

The quoted material is from "What the Tree in the Square Heard," 11; "Community Christmas Tree," 4; "Night before Christmas in the City Square," 260; and G. M. Johnston, "Joyeux Noel," 205.

Just as organizers recognized and accepted the diverse nature of the cities, they were also keenly aware of economic class differences. For example, the periodicals make constant reference to the fact that both rich and poor attended the celebrations. Although they saw the existence of economic classes clearly, the community Christmas organizers were interested only in creating a climate in which the problems of poverty could be discussed with understanding and compassion; they did not have a plan for dealing with disparities of wealth directly. There was no explicit encouragement of charity at the festivals, nor did the celebrations commonly involve many spontaneous exchanges of property. But there were several approving accounts of coins being slipped from "gloved hands to bare hands," and there were other examples of the increased good will fostered by the tree.

The small role of gift exchanges at the community Christmas celebrations raises the question of whether a discussion of the community festivals should be included in this study of Christmas gift exchanges. Even though the celebrations did not center around actual gift exchanges, they must be analyzed in this study because, throughout history, community members have used gifts to reaffirm their ties and to redistribute available resources. With this in mind, the important questions become why Americans did not exchange gifts in their efforts to reaffirm various communities between 1900 and 1940, and what alternative rituals they employed to reaffirm community bonds.

10. The play is described in "New York's Christmas Fantasy," *I*, 85 (24 Jan. 1916): 127.

11. Wiebe, *The Search for Order*. See also John Higham, "The Reorientation of American Culture in the 1890's," in *The Origins of Modern Consciousness*, ed. John Weiss (Detroit, 1965), 25–48. The quotation is from "What the Tree in the Square Heard," 11.

12. The traditional Christmas theme of returning to a golden age, of avoiding all social conflicts during the holidays, did not produce any widespread objection to the major social conflict of the period—the war itself—in December periodicals. To the contrary, most writers saw the war as an expression of the true Christmas spirit. For example, one writer in 1917 argued that "never has America celebrated any Christmas more fitly than in the way in which she will celebrate Christmas, 1917. We are not to think of this coming Christmas Day as a brief interlude in the war; but, rather as a day that can be reverently observed by the very sounding of artillery" ("Bearers of the Message of Christmas," *Out*, 117 [19 Dec. 1917]: 635). See also Royal B. Farnum, "Three Christmas Activities," *IAM*, 7 (Dec. 1918): 459–60.

For discussions of the Liberty Bond sales, see Frederic L. Paxson, *America at War* (Boston, 1939), 14–18, 137–42, 270–71, 432–33; George Soule, *Prosperity Decade* (New York, 1968), 49; Preston W. Slosson, *The Great Crusade and After* (Chicago, 1971), 60–62; John Bach McMaster, *The United States in the World War* (New York, 1918), 380–83, 415–17; and Ida Clyde Clarke, *American Women and the World War* (New York, 1918), 107–17.

13. For examples of the sentiment to rationalize Christmas shopping, see "The New Christmas," *LD*, 53 (23 Dec. 1916): 1661; "Christmas Giving," *Out*, 127 (5 Dec. 1917): 553; and "In Defense of Christmas," *Bl*, 25 (July 27, 1918): 91–92. See also Roy G. Blakey, "America's New Conception of Thrift," *AAA*, 87 (Jan. 1920): 1–3; and William Mather Lewis, "Freedom Bought Through Thrift," *AAA*, 87 (Jan. 1920): 9–10.

14. For discussions of charitable fund-raising activities during the war, see Paxon, *America at War*, 361–62; Roy Lubove, *The Professional Altruist* (New York, 1972), 189–92; F. J. Bruno, *Trends in Social Work, 1874–1956* (New York, 1957), 230–38; and Robert Bremner, *American Philanthropy* (Chicago, 1960), 129–40. For a listing and brief descriptions of the many organizations through which women could send items to Europe, see Clarke, *American Women and the World War*, 411–511. See also "The New Christmas," 1661. For a discussion of the women's movement during the war, see William L. O'Neill, *Everyone Was Brave* (Chicago, 1971), 169–224. One effort of some Y.M.C.A. representatives to obtain Christmas gifts for soldiers and to make possible a traditional holiday celebration is recounted in Katherine Mayo, "*That Dam Y*" (Boston, 1920), 59–65.

15. For an analysis of gift exchanges in which the parties do not know one another, see Richard M. Titmuss, *The Gift Relationship* (New York, 1971), 70–75, 88–89, 212–16.

16. I am concerned with what American gift givers received in return from those in Europe—not with the social esteem they may have received from their communities or with any personal reasons that may have motivated their gifts.

17. For a discussion of the national Christmas tree, see "Christmas Good-will Offering to the Nation," *PI*, 133 (10 Dec. 1925): 148–53.

18. For articles advocating thrift in postwar America, see "What We Can Afford to Give," *N*, 102 (3 Feb. 1916): 125–26; "Learning to Give," *Bl*, 23 (17 Nov. 1917): 538–39; Charles S. Ward, "How to Make the Stingy Generous," *AMag*, 87 (March 1919): 14–15; and A. A. Hyde, "Shall We Accumulate or Distribute?" *MR*, 42 (Jan. 1919): 11–12.

19. The quotation is from Lewis, "Freedom Bought through Thrift," 9. See also Blakey, "America's New Conception of Thrift," 1–3. Immediately after World War I there was an increase in the number of periodical articles on thrift. For example, the number of citations under "thrift" in the *Readers' Guide to Periodical Literature* rose dramatically, and an entire issue of the *Annals of the American Academy* was devoted to the subject. In addition to these articles, educators made efforts to establish courses on thrift in public schools.

20. For Christmas gift ads which suggest that the item advertised is typically American, see Whiting and Davis mesh bags, *LHJ*, 45 (Dec. 1928): 92; Martex towels, *LHJ* (Dec. 1928): 98; Yardley toiletries, *LHJ*, 45 (Dec. 1928): 116; Daniel Green Comfy slippers, *LHJ*, 45 (Dec. 1928): 124; Community Plate silver, *LHJ*, 46 (Dec. 1929): 103; Elgin watches, *LHJ*, 46 (Dec. 1929): 147; Furniture trade, *LHJ*, 46 (Dec. 1929): 179; White sewing machines, *LHJ*, 47 (Dec. 1930): 58; and Bissell carpet sweepers, *LHJ*, 47 (Dec. 1930): 124. See also Marshall McLuhan, *The Mechanical Bride* (New York, 1951), 116–18.

For discussions of the shift from production orientation to consumption orientation, see Leo Lowenthal, "The Triumph of Mass Idols," in *Literature, Popular Culture, and Society* (Palo Alto, Calif., 1961), 109–36; and David M. Potter, *People of Plenty* (Chicago, 1954), 166–88. For a penetrating analysis of consumption as a motivation for purchasing, see Walter A. Weisskopf, *The Psychology of Economics* (Chicago, 1954).

21. The quotation is from Charles Edward Jefferson, "The Christmas Gift the World Needs," *I*, 104 (25 Dec. 1920): 426. For other examples of the emphasis on the community of mankind at Christmas, see S. Adele Shaw, "The Americanization of Christmas," *NR*, 33 (10 Jan. 1923): 171; Edward S. Martin, "Thoughts Proper for Christmas," *HM*, 150 (Dec. 1924): 28–29; "Spirit of Christmas," *CW*, 124 (Dec. 1926): 396–97; Henry C. Link, "Heart of Christmas," *PM*, 11 (Dec. 1936): 9; "Christmas Sanctuary," *Et*, 54 (Dec. 1936): 753; Regina Scott Wieman, "The Spirit of Giving, *PM*, 12 (Dec. 1937): 11; and Anne Bryan McCall, "Spirit of Giving," *WHC*, 64 (Dec. 1937): 6.

The attention periodical writers gave to the community of mankind did not preclude a concern with smaller communities. However, writers increasingly viewed the smaller communities as interrelated constituent elements of larger communities rather than as isolated independent entities. As one writer in 1929 argued, "The new conception of the community is that it is a segment of a larger integrated unit. Under existing circumstances, the successful cooperation of the older community ideal would be possible only in connection with a policy of segregation [of the community from outside contacts] inconsistent with our social and political traditions. It might possibly have succeeded fifty years ago, but today with the open doors of the world before us we chose the alternative of wider association. The community movement of the future must adjust itself to changing conditions—which involves the conception of a wider and more flexible unit inseparably interrelated with surrounding areas" (Jesse F. Steiner, "Whither the Community Movement?" *Sur*, 62 [15 April 1929]: 130).

22. For discussions of the transportation and communication developments of the 1920s, see Frederick Lewis Allen, *Only Yesterday* (New York, 1931), 161–67; George E. Mowry, *The Urban Nation* (New York, 1965), 111–17; Soule, *Prosperity Decade*, 147, 164–70, 182; John D. Hicks, *Republican Ascendancy* (New York, 1960), 111–14; and William E. Leuchtenburg, *The Perils of Prosperity* (Chicago, 1958), 185–87.

10. The Rationalization of Charity

1. For penetrating analyses of various "golden ages," see the following four books by Mircea Eliade: *Myths, Dreams, and Mysteries* (New York, 1967), 39–72; *Myth and Reality* (New

York, 1968), 21–55, 75–91; *Cosmos and History* (New York, 1959), 49–92; and *Patterns in Comparative Religion* (Cleveland, 1963), 388–409.

2. For a brief discussion of the increased importance of charity in the American Christmas celebration after the mid–nineteenth century, see James H. Barnett, *The American Christmas* (New York, 1954), 70–72. See pages 14–18 of Barnett's book for a discussion of the influence of Dickens on Christmas charity.

3. The crest in concern with the poor at Christmas during the early twentieth century was, to a large degree, a facet of the general interest in all aspects of poverty around the turn of the century. For analyses of this public concern, see Robert H. Bremner, *From the Depths* (New York, 1956), 123–98; Roy Lubove, *The Professional Altruist* (New York, 1972), passim; Frank J. Bruno, *Trends in Social Work* (New York, 1948), 133–238; Nathan Edward Cohen, *Social Work in the American Tradition* (New York, 1958), 86–96; and Walter I. Trattner, *From Poor Law to Welfare State* (New York, 1974), 179–92.

For discussions of the heightened concern over the family during the early twentieth century, see William L. O'Neill, *Divorce in the Progressive Era* (New York, 1973), passim; and Aileen S. Kraditor, *The Ideas of the Woman Suffrage Movement, 1890–1920* (New York, 1971), 82–104.

For discussions of the appropriation of traditional household tasks by outside institutions, see George Rogers Taylor, *The Transportation Revolution* (New York, 1968), 207–34; Andrew Sinclair, *The Emancipation of the American Woman* (New York, 1966), 139–43; and Michael B. Katz, *The Irony of Early School Reform* (Boston, 1968), 5–17, 213–18. On this subject, the reader may also find informative the following works, although they are not about America: Ivy Pinchbeck, *Women Workers and the Industrial Revolution* (London, 1930), 306–16; Vern L. Bullough, *The Subordinate Sex* (Baltimore, 1974), 277–84; and Philippe Aries, *Centuries of Childhood* (New York, 1962), 137–336.

For discussions by Gilman of the functions of the home, see "The Passing of the Home in Great American Cities," *Cos*, 38 (Dec. 1904), 137–41; and *The Home* (New York, 1903), passim.

4. See Owen Kildare, "Christmas with Us in the Tenements," *LHJ*, 24 (Dec. 1906): 26; Samuel McChord Crothers, "Christmas and the Spirit of Democracy," *Ev*, 17 (Dec. 1907): 794–99; "How We Can Have a Happy Christmas," *LHJ*, 26 (Dec. 1908): 28; John Allen Murphy, "How Manufacturers Are Getting Their Goods into Santa Claus' Pack," *PI*, 121 (2 Nov. 1922): 182; "Merry Christmas Awaits a Big Retail Outlet," *PI*, 128 (14 Aug. 1924): 33–34; Ralph F. Linder, "Groceries for Christmas Gifts," *PI*, 165 (7 Dec. 1933): 68–69; and "A Christmas Miscellany," *PIM*, 36 (June 1938), 23. For anthropological perspectives on the significance of food as a gift item, see Eliade, *Patterns in Comparative Religion*, 331–66; and Claude Levi-Strauss, *The Elementary Structures of Kinship* (Boston, 1969), 32–36.

Anthropologists have encountered various ritual meals in their investigations. See Philip Drucker, *Cultures of the North Pacific Coast* (Scranton, Pa., 1965): 55–66; Moses I. Finley, *The World of Odysseus* (rev. ed.; New York, 1965), 133–36; Eliade, *Patterns in Comparative Religion*, 331–52; and the controversial, provocative analysis in Sigmund Freud, *Totem and Taboo* (New York, 1960), 26–84.

5. For discussions of the grocery industry campaign, see Murphy, "How Manufacturers Are Getting Their Goods into Santa Claus' Pack," 182; "Merry Christmas Awaits a Big Retail Outlet," 33–34; Ralph F. Lindner, "Groceries for Christmas Gifts," 68–69; and "A Christmas Miscellany," 23.

6. For a discussion of the reduction of parental authority over children, see chapter 8.

For articles that reflect the heightened concern of periodical writers for poor children at Christmas during the early twentieth century, see "Hints on Christmas Giving," *LHJ*, 22

(Dec. 1904): 57; A. Preston, "Christmas Ideals of Girls," *LHJ*, 23 (Dec. 1905): 26; Mary Humphrey, "What Christmas Means to Some," *LHJ*, 23 (Dec. 1905): 62; R. C. Lewis, "New Kind of Santa Claus," *LHJ*, 23 (Nov. 1906): 24; Minna Thomas Antrim, "A Happier Christmas and a Happier New Year to All," *L*, 84 (Dec. 1909): 764–66; and "Christmas Editorial," *LHJ*, 27 (Dec. 1910): 5.

7. For discussions of the concern for children in the late nineteenth and early twentieth centuries, see Bernard Wishy, *The Child and the Republic* (Philadelphia, 1972), 85, 94–181; Gilman Ostrander, *American Civilization in the First Machine Age: 1890–1940* (New York, 1972), 121–56; Anthony M. Platt, *The Child Savers* (Chicago, 1969), passim; Walter I. Trattner, *Crusade for the Children* (Chicago, 1970), 21–160; Trattner, *From Poor Law to Welfare State*, 96–115; Bruno, *Trends in Social Work*, 152–76; Bremner, *From the Depths*, 212–29; Lawrence A. Cremin, *The Transformation of the School* (New York, 1961), 58–126; and Richard Hofstadter, *Anti-Intellectualism in American Life* (New York, 1962), 323–90.

8. The description of Miss Phillips's activities and the quotation are from R. C. Lewis, "New Kind of Santa Claus," *LHJ*, 23 (Nov. 1906): 24.

For additional articles that advocate getting a Christmas present to every child, see Humphrey, "What Christmas Means to Some," 62; "What Other Women Have Found Out about Christmas," *LHJ*, 24 (Dec. 1906): 41; and Charlotte Reeve Conover, "Playing at Santa Claus," *Sur*, 23 (25 Dec. 1909): 422.

9. See, "Hints on Christmas Giving," 57; "Helping the Poor at Christmastide," *LHJ*, 27 (Dec. 1909): 44; Mary E. Richmond, "Of Christmas Gifts," *Sur*, 25 (24 Dec. 1910): 499; and "Five Principles of Christmas Giving," *C&F*, 16 (21 Dec. 1927): 2613.

10. The quotation is from Nathaniel Fowler, Jr., "Unchristian Christmas," *Out*, 91 (9 Jan. 1909): 68. For additional articles on this theme, see Humphrey, "What Christmas Means to Some," 62; "What Other Women Have Found Out About Christmas," 41; E. L. Coolidge, "Young Mother at Christmas Time," *LHJ*, 25 (Dec. 1907): 62; "Christmas Ideas That Have Made Others Happy," *LHJ*, 25 (Dec. 1907): 30; E. L. Heermance, "Christmas Declaration of Independence," *LHJ*, 26 (Dec. 1908): 24; "How We Can Have a Happy Christmas," 28; "Helping the Poor at Christmastide," 44; "Christmas Editorial," 5; and Selene Armstrong, "Giving Poor Children What They Want at Christmas," *LHJ*, 28 (Dec. 1911): 37.

11. The quotation is from Humphrey, "What Christmas Means to Some," 62.

12. The quotation is from "How We Can Have a Happy Christmas," 28. For other articles that advocate in-person, direct charitable gifts to known recipients, see "Hints on Christmas Giving," 57; "What Other Women Have Found Out about Christmas," 41; "Christmas Ideas That Have Made Others Happy," 30; "Helping the Poor at Christmastide," 44; and Leslie Roberts, "Reflections on the Christmas Spirit," *HM*, 170 (Dec. 1934): 118.

13. See "Hints on Christmas Giving," 57; Humphrey, "What Christmas Means to Some," 62; Emma E. Walker, "Christmas Giving That Is Worth While," *LHJ*, 23 (Dec. 1905): 29; Conover, "Playing at Santa Claus," 423; and Armstrong, "Giving Poor Children What They Want at Christmas," 37.

14. The quotation is from "Helping the Poor at Christmastide," 44. For additional examples of articles that advocate giving the poor a mixture of useful and pleasure-giving items, see Evelyn Crawford, "Charitable Organizations," *Ov*, n.s., 48 (Dec. 1906): 484; Conover, "Playing at Santa Claus," 422; and R.T.H., "On Reforming Christmas," *L*, 86 (Dec. 1910): 765.

15. The quotations are from Antrim, "A Happier Christmas and a Happier New Year," 765. For other articles that encourage the prosperous to redirect gifts they were presenting

to their prosperous friends to the poor, see "Hints on Christmas Giving," 57; "How They Simplified Their Christmas," *LHJ*, 23 (Nov. 1906): 42; "How We Can Have a Happy Christmas," 28; and Martha Keeler, "The Girl Who Works," *LHJ*, 30 (Jan. 1913): 38.

16. For articles that encourage these redistributive efforts, see "Christmas Ideas That Have Made Others Happy," 30; "Helping the Poor at Christmastide," 44; Conover, "Playing at Santa Claus," 422–23; Armstrong, "Giving Poor Children What They Want at Christmas," 37; Keeler, "The Girl Who Works," 38; and Claudia Cranston, "Girl Who Plays Santa Claus," *GH*, 65 (Dec. 1917): 35 +.

17. Cranston, "Girl Who Plays Santa Claus," 35.

18. For discussions of the adoption of bureaucratic values by leaders of non-Christmas charities during the late nineteenth century, see Lubove, *The Professional Altruist*, 1–21; Bremner, *From the Depths*, 46–66; Samuel Mencher, *From Poor Law to Poverty Program* (Pittsburgh, 1967), 279–309; Bruno, *Trends in Social Work*, 96–111; Bremner, *American Philanthropy* (Chicago, 1960), 89–104; and Trattner, *From Poor Law to Welfare State*, 75–95.

19. For articles that suggest the competitiveness between charities, see Louise de Koven Bowen, "Chicago's Christmas Tree," *Sur*, 31 (29 Nov. 1913): 229; and "Night before Christmas in the City Square," *Sur*, 33 (5 Dec. 1914): 258.

20. One significant group that favored collective giving to the poor was the Society for the Prevention of Useless Giving (SPUG), an organization discussed at greater length in chapter 11. See also J. Edwin Murphy, "Yearly Pensions as a Substitute for Christmas Baskets," *Sur*, 31 (13 Dec. 1913): 298–99. Murphy noted a distinct decrease in what he called desultory Christmas giving between 1909 and 1913.

The account of sales of "stock" in Cleveland is in "Night before Christmas in the City Square," 258. See also "Christmas Common Sense," *Sur*, 67 (15 Dec. 1931): 315.

For discussions of the use of the community chest idea by non-Christmas charities, see Lubove, *The Professional Altruist*, 183–219; and Bruno, *Trends in Social Work*, 199–206.

21. For evidence of the duplication of assistance under the old style of Christmas charity, see Owen Kildare, "Christmas with Us in the Tenements," *LHJ*, 24 (Dec. 1906): 26; "How We Can Have a Happy Christmas," 28; and "Night before Christmas in the City Square," 258.

The Orange, New Jersey, file is described in "Night before Christmas in the City Square," 258.

22. The quotation is from Nina Bull, "Merry Christmas!" *Sur*, 35 (20 Nov. 1915): 190. For additional articles that criticize one-day-a-year charity, see Bowen, "Chicago's Christmas Tree," 229; Murphy, "Yearly Pensions as a Substitute for Christmas Baskets," 298–99; "Christmas Baskets," *Sur*, 47 (17 Dec. 1921): 430; and "Five Principles of Christmas Giving," 2613.

23. For discussions of attitudes toward charitable giving during the 1920s, see Lubove, *The Professional Altruist*, 157–219; Clarke A. Chambers, *Seedtime of Reform* (Ann Arbor, Mich., 1967), passim; Trattner, *From Poor Law to Welfare State*, 212–27; and Cohen, *Social Work in the American Tradition*, 138–55.

24. Murphy, "Yearly Pensions as a Substitute for Christmas Baskets," 298–99, notes the appearance of plans for monthly assistance in several cities. See also "Christmas Baskets," 430.

25. See "Selfishness of Rich Givers," *LD*, 51 (30 Oct. 1915), 962–63.

26. For the increase in contributions to domestic charities, see "What We Can Afford to Give," *N*, 102 (3 Feb. 1916): 125–26.

For expressions of the hope that Americans had learned to give during the war, see "What We Can Afford to Give," 125–26; "Learning to Give," *Bl*, 23 (17 Nov. 1917): 538–

39; Charles S. Ward, "How to Make the Stingy Generous," *AMag*, 87 (March 1919): 14–15; and A. A. Hyde, "Shall We Accumulate or Distribute," *MR*, 42 (Jan. 1919): 11–12.

27. The high level of charitable donations during the 1920s is discussed in Bremner, *American Philanthropy*, 139–41. The increasing popularity of community chests during the postwar decade is discussed in Lubove, *The Professional Altruist*, 183–219.

28. For a discussion of the high level of technological unemployment during the 1920s, see Irving Bernstein, *The Lean Years* (Baltimore, 1966): 52–63.

For discussions of the support among charity leaders, the public, and government officials for government action in the welfare field during the Depression, see Bremner, *American Philanthropy*, 143–64; Chambers, *Seedtime of Reform*, 183–207; Trattner, *From Poor Law to Welfare State*, 228–45; and Cohen, *Social Work in the American Tradition*, 180–83.

29. For a contemporary description of the increased role of the government in the welfare field, along with an analysis of the government's use of bureaucratic forms, see Robert E. Speer, "New Day in Giving," *MR*, 57 (July 1934): 343–44. For a secondary article on this topic, see Gerald D. Shuttles and David Street, "Aid to the Poor and Social Exchange," in *The Logic of Social Hierarchies*, ed. Edward O. Laumann, Paul M. Siegel, and Robert W. Hodge (Chicago, 1970), 744–55.

30. I do not intend to imply that there is some intrinsic connection between governmental action and the use of bureaucratic forms. The prevalence of the distinctly unbureaucratic spoils systems in the federal government before the 1880s and the equally unbureaucratic dispensation of favors by city bosses between 1865 and 1930 indicates that a variety of forms are available to governments besides highly rationalized ones. What I do suggest is that the fashion in administrative thinking during the 1930s strongly favored the use of bureaucratic forms and that, given this preference, it would have been surprising had the government adopted less rationalized forms. In addition to this factor of administrative "fashion," the material realities of the decade—the widespread economic distress requiring large-scale substantive reponses—pushed the government to use the most efficient (that is, bureaucratic) forms to dispense aid.

31. See "Let's Make It a Real American Christmas," *LHJ*, 49 (Dec. 1932): 26–29; and Charlotte Montgomery, "Better to Give," *AHom*, 19 (Dec. 1937): 13 + .

For articles that emphasize the smallness of the gifts of the 1930s, see "Let's Make It a Real American Christmas," 26–29; Montgomery, "Better to Give," pp. 13 + ; and Corinne Updegraff Wells, "Philanthropy without Money," *R*, 57 (Aug. 1940): 30–32 + .

For articles that recommend thoughtful acts, see Henry C. Link, "Heart of Christmas," *PM*, 11 (Dec. 1936): 9; Montgomery, "Better to Give," 13 + ; and Wells, "Philanthropy without Money," 30–32 + . (The article by Wells is informative on this general question, although it is not exclusively concerned with charity at Christmas.)

32. Mrs. Edison's article is "Share Your Christmas," *PM*, 9 (Dec. 1934): 11. The 1936 article is Link, "Heart of Christmas," 9. See also Montgomery, "Better to Give," pp. 13 + ; and Anne Bryan McCall, "Spirit of Giving," *WHC*, 74 (Dec. 1937): 6.

The following articles are informative on this general issue, although not exclusively concerned with charity at Christmas: Newton D. Baker, "Human Factors in a Depression," *NO*, 161 (Nov. 1932): 19–20; Lyford, "Relief," 114; and Wells, "Philanthropy Without Money," 30–32 + .

33. Marcel Mauss, *The Gift* (New York, 1967), 8–12. See also Lewis Hyde, *The Gift* (New York, 1983), 3–140.

11. The Rationalization of Christmas Bonuses

1. Writers became concerned with servants in the early twentieth century for two major reasons. First, they became more interested in workers in general; thus, the interest in domestic workers increased. Second, the number of domestics had increased significantly during the second half of the nineteenth century as a consequence of the arrival of millions of immigrants who needed employment at the same time that a well-salaried, white-collar employer class also expanded.

For surveys of domestic service in America, see Russell Lynes, *The Domesticated Americans* (New York, 1963), 155–74; Ruth Schwartz Cowan, *More Work for Mother* (New York, c.1983), 119–27; Susan Strasser, *Never Done: A History of American Housework* (New York, 1982), 162–79; and Lois W. Banner, *Women in Modern America* (New York, 1974), 30–32. For a discussion of the appearance of white-collar workers, see C. Wright Mills, *White Collar* (New York, 1951), 63–76. For a discussion of the importance of domestic servants to the middle-class life-style, the reader may find informative J. A. and Olive Banks, *Feminism and Family Planning* (New York, 1964), 62–74, even though it is about English society rather than American.

2. For a list of twenty-seven items suggested as Christmas gifts for "those who help us keep house" and "our outside helpers," see "What Shall I Give for Christmas?" *LHJ*, 22 (Dec. 1904): 40.

For an article that contains a collection of advice from numerous people about the treatment of household workers at Christmas, see F. A. Kellor, "Housewife at Christmas," *LHJ*, 24 (Dec. 1906): 48.

3. The comments are from Kellor, "Housewife at Christmas," 48.

4. For a discussion of the decline in the number of domestic servants, see Lynes, *Domesticated Americans*, 169–75. See also Cowan, *More Work for Mother*, 121–22; Strasser, *Never Done: A History of American Housework*, 163–64; and John W. Dodds, *Everyday Life in Twentieth Century America* (New York, 1965), 137–38; Page Smith, *Daughters of the Promised Land* (Boston, 1970): 207–8; and Arthur M. Schlesinger, *The Rise of the City* (New York, 1933): pp. 138–39.

For a provocative analysis of the adoption of appliances in American homes, see Siegfried Giedion, *Mechanization Takes Command* (New York, 1969): 512–95. Ruth Schwartz Cowan challenges the notion that appliances have reduced housework in her "A Case Study in Technological Change: The Washing Machine and the Working Wife," in *Clio's Consciousness Raised*, ed. Mary S. Hartman and Lois Banner (New York, 1974), 245–53.

5. For evidence of the expansion of Christmas gift giving during the late nineteenth and early twentieth centuries, see Margaret Deland, "Christmas Giving," *HBaz*, 28 (Dec. 1904): 1158–59; Margaret Deland, "Save Christmas!" *HBaz*, 46 (Dec. 1912): 593; Eleanor Robson Belmont, "Renaissance of Christmas," *HBaz*, 47 (Jan. 1913): 26; Carolyn Wells, "Givers and Receivers," *HBaz*, 47 (Jan. 1913): 13; Jacob A. Riis, "The New Christmas That Is Spreading All Over Our Country," *LHJ*, 30 (Dec. 1913): 16; and Edwin L. Sabin, "Cards or Gifts," *AMag*, 80 (Dec. 1915): 44–45.

Writers also discussed workers who delivered gift items—store delivery boys and postal employees—but at less length than they did factory workers and clerks.

6. The quotation is from Rheta Childe Dorr, "Christmas from Behind the Counter," *I*, 63 (5 Dec. 1907): 1344–45.

7. The quotation is from Edwin Markham, "Grind Behind the Holidays," *Cos*, 42 (Dec. 1906): 148. For additional articles that criticize the long Christmas season workdays, see "A Dark Side of Christmas," *WW*, 13 (Dec. 1906): 8264; Dorr, "Christmas from Behind the

Counter," 1341; "Two Christmas Reforms," *Out*, 105 (13 Dec. 1913): 779; and "The Christmas Curse," *Cen*, 111 (Dec. 1915): 312–13.

A particularly maddening policy of many employers was their refusal to pay their employees overtime for the extra hours they required them to work during the holiday season. While in some cases they provided them with supper allowances, the allowances merely indicated the employers' awareness that the workdays they required during the Christmas season were unusually long—yet they still did not pay employees for the additional hours. For evidence on this point, see Dorr, "Christmas from Behind the Counter," 1341; and "The Christmas Curse," 312–13.

8. The description of factory conditions is from "A Dark Side of Christmas," 8264. The description of clerking conditions is from "Question of Christmas Observance," *LHJ*, 24 (Dec. 1906): 6. For additional evidence on this point, see Markham, "Grind Behind the Holidays," 143–50; "Two Christmas Reforms," 650; Nathaniel C. Fowler, Jr., "Unchristian Christmas," *Out*, 91 (9 Jan. 1909): 68; Patch, "Other Side of Christmas," 24; and "The Christmas Curse," 312–13.

9. The quotation is from "The Cloud on the Christmas Joy," *Cos*, 50 (Dec. 1910): 145. See also Dorr, "Christmas from Behind the Counter," 1344–45; and "Christmas and the Shoppers," 779.

10. There has been some concern with male adequacy throughout the American past, but it was particularly intense around 1900. For discussions of this heightened concern, see Peter Gabriel Filene, *Him Her Self* (New York, 1976), 68–94; John Higham, "The Reorientation of American Culture in the 1890's," in *The Origins of Modern Consciousness*, ed. John Weiss (Detroit, 1965), 25–48; and Hendrick M. Ruitenbeek, *The Male Myth* (New York, 1967), passim.

11. The quotations are from Fowler, "Unchristian Christmas," 68; and Dorr, "Christmas from Behind the Counter," p. 1343. The temple analogy was drawn by Nina Bull in her "Merry Christmas!" *Sur*, 35 (20 Nov. 1915): 190. See also Charlotte Perkins Gilman, "Cross-Examining Santa Claus," *Cen*, 105 (Dec. 1922): 173–74.

12. The quotation is from B. O. Flower, "The Christmas Spirit," *Ar*, 38 (Dec. 1907): 705–6. See also E. L. Coolidge, "Young Mother at Christmas Time," *LHJ*, 25 (Dec. 1907): 62; and "Christmas in the Shops," *Out*, 96 (26 Nov. 1910): 662.

13. The quotation is from "The Cloud on Christmas Joy," *Cos*, 50 (Dec. 1910): 144. See also Markham, "Grind Behind the Holidays," 50; Patch, "Other Side of Christmas," 24; Deland, "Save Christmas!" 593; "Christmas and the Shoppers," 779; and "Christmas Spirit," *At*, 128 (Dec. 1921): 860.

14. The quotation is from "Spugs and Christmas," *Out*, 105 (13 Dec. 1913): 779. See also "Worse Than Useless Giving," *Out*, 102 (21 Dec. 1912): 833; Eleanor Robson Belmont, "Renaissance of Christmas," *HBaz*, 47 (Jan. 1913): 26; and Jacob A. Riis, "New Christmas That Is Spreading All Over Our Country," *LHJ*, 30 (Dec. 1913): 16.

15. For the role of the Consumer's League in leading the Shop Early campaign, see Dorr, "Christmas Behind the Counter," 1340; "Two Christmas Reforms," 650; "The Cloud on the Christmas Joy," 145; "Christmas and the Shoppers," 779; and "The Christmas Curse," 312–13. For additional statements of sentiment in favor of shopping early, see "Questions of Christmas Observance," 6; Kellor, "Housewife at Christmas," 48; Patch, "Other Side of Christmas," 24; "Whom Can I Make at Christmas," *LHJ*, 30 (Dec. 1913): 30; and Bull, "Merry Christmas!" 190.

16. For articles supporting the elimination of extra holiday shopping hours, see Dorr, "Christmas from Behind the Counter," 1344; "The Cloud on the Christmas Joy," 145; "Christmas and the Shoppers," 779; and "The Christmas Curse," 312–13.

17. Regarding geographical support for the campaign, see "Two Christmas Reforms," 650; and "The Cloud on Christmas Joy," 145. For a recent discussion, see William L. O'Neill, *Everyone Was Brave* (Chicago, 1971), 96.

Regarding the support of "better" stores for the Shop Early campaign, see Dorr, "Christmas from Behind the Counter," 1340–47; and K. W. Patch, "Other Side of Christmas," 24.

18. The quotation is from "The Christmas Curse," 313. See also "The Cloud on the Christmas Joy," 145; "Christmas and the Shoppers," 779; and O'Neill, *Everyone Was Brave*, 96.

19. Regarding the reliance on public opinion, see "A Dark Side of Christmas," 8264; "Question of Christmas Observance," 6; "The Cloud on the Christmas Joy," 145; "Christmas in the Shops," 662; and "The Christmas Curse," 312–13.

20. The quotation is from Ralph D. Paine, "Christmas in Business Life," *WW*, 7 (Dec. 1903): 4243. For evidence of the use of gift forms in rewarding employees, see Paine, "Christmas in Business Life," 4242–45; William Allen White, "Science, St. Skinflint and Santa Claus," *AMag*, 63 (Dec. 1906): 182–84; Samuel McChord Crothers, "Christmas and the Spirit of Democracy," *Ev*, 17 (Dec. 1907): 794–99; and "Scrooge's Ghost," *At*, 102 (Dec. 1908): 850–51.

An author in 1903 described a yearly Christmas party in a large department store in which "1,000 employees, from managers to cash-boys, meet on equal footing for one night of the year" (Paine, "Christmas is Business Life," 4243).

21. For an article that describes the appearance of the more rational forms, see Crothers, "Christmas and the Spirit of Democracy," 794–99. See also James H. Barnett, *The American Christmas* (New York, 1954), 93–95.

22. For an early statement that the bonuses were in some cases beginning to be thought of as wages, see Paine, "Christmas in Business Life," 4243. See also Barnett, *The American Christmas*, 93–95.

23. A writer in 1930 listed the following companies as having produced special assortments for Christmas: American Sugar Refining, Borden, Colgate-Palmolive-Peet, Beech-Nut, and American Chicle (Don Masson, "Stockholders and the Family of Products Meet at Christmas," *PI*, 153 [11 Dec. 1930]: 96). A writer in 1933 mentioned the following companies as having assortments: Carnation-Albers, Crosse & Blackwell, Duff & Sons, Welch's, H. J. Heinz, Kraft-Phoenix, Snider, National Biscuit, Libby, and Swift (Ralph F. Lindner, "Groceries for Christmas Gifts," *PI*, 165 [7 Dec. 1933]: 68–69).

For discussions of the special assortments, see Donald Argyle, "Christmas Opportunities to Cement Customer Relations," *PI*, 129 (9 Oct. 1924): 25; Don Masson, "Stockholders and the Family of Products Meet at Christmas," 96 (the special assortments were usually made available to stockholders in addition to workers); Lindner, "Groceries for Christmas Gifts," 68–69; "Check-Points for Christmas," *PI*, 176 (3 Sept. 1936): 84–85; and "Christmas Miscellany," *PIM*, 36 (June 1938): 80–81.

12. Riches and Uncertainty

1. For discussions of the expansion of the productive capacity of American factories during World War II, see Peter D'A. Jones, *The Consumer Society* (Baltimore, 1965), 328–37; and Francis G. Walett, *Economic History of the United States* (New York, 1954), 228–35.

For discussions of the fear of another depression among postwar policymakers, and the strategies they devised to lessen that possibility, see Eric F. Goldman, *The Crucial Decade—*

and After (New York, 1960), 19–28, 46–57; and Cabell Phillips, *The Truman Presidency* (Baltimore, 1969), 101–25.

2. For articles that express retailers' befuddlement and frustration at their inability to predict Christmas buying patterns, see "Stores Bank on Next Two Weeks," *BW*, 15 Dec. 1951, 22; "Uneasy Retailers Wait, Worry," *BW*, 17 Nov. 1956, 34–35; "Stores Wait for a Miracle," *BW*, 7 Dec. 1957, 25–26; "Buyers Turning Cautious?" *USNWR*, 43 (6 Dec. 1957), 70–72; "Late Shoppers Turned the Tide," *BW*, 4 Jan. 1958, 28; "Sales Get into the Xmas Spirit," *BW*, 20 Dec. 1958, 17–18; "Not Much Cheer for Retailers," *BW*, 24 Dec. 1960, 22; "When Buyers Swamped Stores: The Biggest Christmas Boom," *USNWR*, 69 (27 Dec. 1965): 65–66; "What Christmas Trade Shows," *USNWR*, 67 (22 Dec. 1969): 30–32; "Christmas Trade: The Outlook around U.S.," *USNWR*, 67 (20 Oct. 1969): 45–46; "Christmas Prices Take the Down Escalator," *BW*, 26 Dec. 1970, 14; "It's Christmas or Never for the Big Stores," *BW*, 5 Dec. 1970, 25; "Good Year for Christmas Trade," *USNWR*, 69 (21 Dec. 1970): 16–18; "As Prices Skyrocket, a Buyers' Strike Threatens," *USNWR*, 77 (2 Dec. 1974): 21–22 +; and "Stores Wait for the Last Moment," *BW*, 20 Dec. 1976, 23 +.

3. For articles that indicate the concern of retailers over which general price ranges of items would be preferred by Christmas shoppers, see "Pockets Afire with War Money," *NW*, 24 (11 Dec. 1944): 70 +; "Once a Year: 1947," *T*, 50 (15 Dec. 1947): 21; "Christmas Specials Trim Stocks, Build Sales," *BW*, 1 Jan. 1949, 42–43; "Christmas Trade: Off to a Slow Start," *USNWR*, 35 (4 Dec. 1953): 68–72; "It's Fast, It's Frantic, It's 1955's Xmas," *BW*, 17 Dec. 1955, 32–34; "Stores Wait for a Miracle," 25–26; "Sales Get into the Xmas Spirit," 17–18; "Buying Mood Is Back," *BW*, 2 Dec. 1961, 37–38; "Holiday Hail of Cash," *BW*, 30 Dec. 1961, 17–18; "Christmas Trade: Record Boom?" *USNWR*, 49 (8 Nov. 1965): 37–39; "When Buyers Swamped Stores—The Biggest Christmas Boom," 65–66; "Christmas Trade: Better, But . . . ," *USNWR*, 63 (25 Dec. 1967): 15–17; "Chrismas Trade to Break Records," *USNWR*, 65 (16 Dec. 1968): 58–60; "What Christmas Trade Shows," 30–32; "Good Year for Christmas Trade," 16–18; "Christmas Trade: A Blockbuster," *USNWR*, 71 (27 Dec. 1971): 13–15; "Merry Christmas: Survey of Holiday Buying," *USNWR*, 73 (25 Dec. 1972): 26–28; "As Prices Skyrocket, a Buyers' Strike Threatens," 21–22 +; "More Confident Countdown," *BW*, 8 Dec. 1975, 22–23; "Last-Minute Solace from the Shoppers," *BW*, 13 Jan. 1975, 32–33; and "Christmas Splurging Starts Early," *BW*, 19 Dec. 1977, 24–25.

For articles that indicate the concern of retailers over which general types of items would be preferred by Christmas shoppers, see "Merry Christmas," *BW*, 15 Nov. 1941, 57–58; "Pockets Afire with War Money," 70 +; "Yule Sales Peak," *BW*, 16 Dec. 1944, 96 +; "Christmas Brings Record Sales," *BW*, 1 Dec. 1945, 83–84; "New High in Christmas Retail Trade," *USNWR*, 21 (20 Dec. 1946): 30–31; "Retailers Ride Buying Wave," *BW*, 10 Jan. 1948, 19–20; "Merry Xmas for Retailers," *BW*, 3 Dec. 1949, 68–70; "Trend of Christmas Shopping," *USNWR*, 27 (16 Dec. 1949): 13–14; "Big Christmas, and Then—," *USNWR*, 31 (30 Nov. 1951): 23–24; "Christmas Sales Came Through," *BW*, 5 Jan. 1952, 22; "Retailers Hope for Merriest Christmas," *BW*, 10 Oct. 1953, 31; "Busy Christmas for Retailers," *BW*, 20 Nov. 1954, 30–31; "Nothing's Too Good," *NW*, 46 (19 Dec. 1955): 72 +; "Sales Add Up but Add No Joy," *BW*, 19 Jan. 1957, 133–36; "Stores Wait for a Miracle," 25–26; "Buyers Turning Cautious?" 70–72; "It Looks Like a Merry Xmas for . . . ," *BW*, 15 Nov. 1958, 25; "Nippy Air Perks Retailers' Hopes for Yule," *BW*, 3 Dec. 1960, 30–32; "Buying Mood Is Back," 37–38; "Christmas '63: Best Sales Ever," *BW*, 21 Dec. 1963, 15–16; "It's a Real Boom in Christmas Shopping," *USNWR*, 55 (23 Dec. 1963): 23–24; "No Mink, Just a New Living Room Set," *BW*, 21 Nov. 1964; 139 +; "Christmas Trade: Record Boom?" 37–39; "Christmas Tune Is a Bit Off Key," *BW*, 3 Dec. 1966, 33–35; "Christmas Trade, 1966:

It's Good, But—," *USNWR*, 61 (19 Dec. 1966): 76–77; "There's Less Reason to Be Jolly," *BW*, 27 Dec. 1969, 14–15; "Christmas Trade: The Outlook Around U.S.," 45–46; "Uncertain Season: Merchants Have Fingers Crossed," *USNWR*, 75 (3 Dec. 1973): 30+; "As Prices Skyrocket, a Buyers' Strike Threatens," *USNWR*, 77 (2 Dec. 1974), 21–22+; "Wary Approach to Christmas," *BW*, 29 Sept. 1975, 26–27; "Last-Minute Solace from the Shopper," 32–33; "Stores Wait for the Last Moment," 23+; "It's Beginning to Look Like a Record in Christmas Sales, But . . . ," *USNWR*, 81 (22 Nov. 1976): 52–53; and "Christmas Splurging Starts Early," 24–25.

For articles that suggest the concern of retailers over which specific types of items would be preferred by Christmas shoppers, see "Nothing's Too Good," 72+; "It's Fast, It's Frantic, It's 1955's Xmas," 32–34; "Trade at Xmas to Break Records," *USNWR*, 39 (28 Oct. 1955): 26–28; "Yule Sales Head for a Record," *BW*, 12 Dec. 1959, 25–26; "Not Much Cheer for Retailers," *BW*, 24 Dec. 1960, 22; "Buying Mood Is Back," 37–38; "But Once a Year," *T*, 78 (15 Dec. 1961), 56–58+; "Shoppers Back to Resume Buying," *BW*, 30 Nov. 1963, 89–90; "Christmas '63: Best Sales Ever," 15–16; "It's a Real Boom in Christmas Shopping," 23–24; "Retailers Ringing Up Merriest Season Ever," *BW*, 18 Dec. 1965, 28–29; "Christmas Trade: Record Boom?" 37–39; "When Buyers Swamped Stores—The Biggest Christmas Boom," *USNWR*, 59 (27 Dec. 1965): 65–66; "Santa '66: Fattest of All," *NW*, 67 (5 Dec. 1966): 86–88; "Christmas Trade: Better, But . . . ," 15–17; "Good Year for Christmas," 16–18; "Christmas Trade: A Blockbuster," 13–15; "Merry Christmas: Survey of Holiday Buying," 26–28; "Shoppers in a Mood to Splurge," *USNWR*, 73 (13 Nov. 1972): 69–70; "More Confident Countdown," 22–23; "Christmas Buying Breaking Records," *USNWR*, 79 (15 Dec. 1975): 31–33; "Stores Wait for the Last Moment," 23+; "Christmas Shoppers: Big Spenders but Picky, Too," *USNWR*, 83 (28 Nov. 1977): 59–61; and "Stores Expect Muted Holiday Jingle," *USNWR*, 85 (13 Nov. 1978): 95–97.

4. For articles that note retailers' concern over which types of stores shoppers would favor, see "Christmas Brings Record Sales," 83–84; "Xmas Sales Hitting New High," *BW*, 13 Dec. 1947, 26; "Christmas Specials Trim Stocks, Build Sales," 42–43; "Trend of Christmas Shipping," 13–14; "Christmas Sales Came Through," 22; "Best Christmas Ever," *BW*, 7 Jan. 1956, 28; Elizabeth Browne, "Christmas Is More Than Santa Claus and Holly," *Am*, 100 (22 Nov. 1958): 242–43; "Sales Get into the Christmas Spirit," 17–18; "Yule Sales Head for a Record," 25–26; "Not Much Cheer for Retailers," 22; "In Stores across the Country: Biggest Season Ever, But . . . ," *USNWR*, 49 (19 Dec. 1960): 46–48; "Buying Mood Is Back," 37–38; "Holiday Hail of Cash," 17–18; "Merry Christmas to All," *BW*, 8 Dec. 1962, 29–30; "Retailers Set Their Sights Still Higher," *BW*, 2 Jan. 1965, 14–15; "There's Reason to be Jolly," 14–15; and "Uncertain Ring of Christmas," *BW*, 6 Dec. 1969, 59–60.

For articles that discuss the appearance of discount houses, see "Christmas Shopping," *BW*, 1 Jan. 1955, 18–20; "Trade at Christmas to Break Records," 26–28; "For Retailers, Is There a Santa?" *BW*, 22 Dec. 1956, 25; "Sales Add Up but Add No Joy," 133–36; "It Looks Like a Merry Christmas for . . . ," 25; "Nippy Air Perks Retailers' Hopes for Yule," 30–32; "Not Much Cheer for Retailers," 22; "Buying Mood is Back," 37–38; "Holiday Hail of Cash," 17–18; "Plenty to Spend, and Ready to Buy," *BW*, 21 Nov. 1964, 25–27.

5. For articles that discuss the appearance of suburban branches of department stores, see "Retailers Have Merriest Christmas," *BW*, 10 Jan. 1953, 25–26; "Christmas Shopping," 18–20; "Fast Start on Biggest Xmas Yet," *BW*, 26 Nov. 1955, 42+; "Best Christmas Ever," 28; "For Retailers, Is There a Santa?" 25; "Sales Add Up but Add No Joy," 133–36; and "Buying Mood is Back," 37–38.

For articles that express the retailers' concern over which parts of cities consumers would choose to shop in, or over which sections of the country would have the most vigorous holiday business, see "Xmas Sales Hitting New High," 26; "Once a Year: 1947," 21; "Retailers Ride Buying Wave," 19–20; "Late Buying Rush Did It," *BW*, 7 Jan. 1950, 23–24; "Toy Departments Busiest with Near-Record Sales," *NW*, 36 (25 Dec. 1950): 54–55; "Santa Claus Slump," *NW*, 38 (17 Dec. 1951): 75; "Stores Bank on Next Two Weeks," 22; "Christmas Sales Came Through," 22; "Never, Never Underestimate the Power of a Man," *NW*, 42 (14 Dec. 1953): 67; "It's Fast, It's Frantic, It's 1955's Christmas," 32–34; "Best Christmas Ever," 28; Uneasy Retailers Wait, Worry," 34–35; "Christmas Dollar: Going to Exurbia," *NW*, 48 (31 Dec. 1956): 47; "For Retailers, Is There a Santa?" 25; "Late Shoppers Turned the Tide," 28; "Yule Sales Head for a Record," 25–26; "Not Much Cheer for Retailers," 22; "Better Christmas Giving, Better Year Round Living," *CB*, 48 (Dec. 1965): 18–19; "Christmas Trade: Better, But . . . ," 15–17; "Merchants Count Blessings," *BW*, 28 Dec. 1968, 17–19; "Christmas Trade: A Blockbuster," 13–15; and Merry Christmas: Survey of Christmas Buying," 26–28.

6. For articles that note retailers' concern over the timing of holiday purchases within the Yule season, see "Pockets Afire with War Money," 70+; "Yule Sales Peak," 96+; "Santa Delivered," *BW*, 5 Jan. 1946, 80–81+; "Christmas Specials Trim Stocks, Build Sales," 42–43; "Christmas Sales: Same as '47," *BW*, 8 Jan. 1949, 21; "Christmas Sales, *Ftn*, 41 (Jan. 1950): 12–14; "Late Buying Rush Did It," 23–24; "Santa Claus Slump," 75; "Stores Bank on Next Two Weeks," 22; "Uneasy Retailers Wait, Worry," 34–35; "Christmas Dollar: Going to Exurbia?" 47; "Stores Wait for a Miracle," 25–26; "Late Shoppers Turned the Tide," 28; "It Looks Like a Merry Christmas for . . . ," 25; "Sales Get into the Christmas Spirit," 17–18; "Made-to-order Yule for Stores," *BW*, 3 Jan. 1959, 11; "Yule Sales Head for a Record," 25–26; "Nippy Air Perks Retailers' Hopes for Yule," 30–32; "Xmas Sales Ring Up a Record," *BW*, 29 Dec. 1962, 21; "Retailers Set Their Sights Still Higher," 14–15; "Merchants Count Blessings," 17–19; "Practical Look to Holiday Buying," *BW*, 22 Dec. 1973, 29–30; "Shoppers Trim the Christmas List," *BW*, 7 Dec. 1974, 26–27; and "Stores Wait for the Last Moment," 23+.

7. For articles that express retailers' concern over such factors as weather, strikes, and governmental policies, see "Christmas Sales," 12–14; "Santa Claus Slump," 75; "Christmas Opens U.S. Hearts," *NW*, 38 (24 Dec. 1951): 13; "Stores Bank on Next Two Weeks," 22; "Christmas Trade: Off to a Slow Start," 68–72; "Never Better," *NW*, 45 (10 Jan. 1955): 70; "Uneasy Retailers Wait, Worry," 34–35+; "Christmas Dollar: Going to Exurbia?" 47; "Sales Add Up but Add No Joy," 133–36; "Sales Get into the Christmas Spirit," 17–18; "Stores Count the Days to Yule," *BW*, 7 Nov. 1959, 34; "Yule Sales Head for a Record," 25–26; "Nippy Air Perks Retailers' Hopes for Yule," 30–32; "Not Much Cheer for Retailers," 22; "Stores Have Green Christmas," *BW*, 2 Jan. 1960, 29; "Winter's Chill," *T*, 76 (12 Dec. 1960): 88; "In Stores across the Country: Biggest Season Ever, But . . . ," 46–48; "Holiday Hail of Cash," 17–18; "Merry Christmas to All," 29–30; "Xmas Sales Ring Up a Record," 21; "Shoppers Flock Back to Resume Buying," 89–90; "Christmas '63: Best Sales Ever," 15–16; "It's a Real Boom in Christmas Shopping," *USNWR*, 55 (23 Dec. 1963): 23–24+; "Plenty to Spend and Ready to Buy," 25–27; "Bell Ringer," 73; "Retailers Set Their Sights Still Higher," 14–15; "When Buyers Swamped Stores: The Biggest Christmas Boom," 65–66; "Jingle Just Wasn't Quite So Loud," 16–17; "Christmas Tune is a Bit Off Key," 33–35; "Can the Consumer Carry the Ball?" *BW*, 25 Nov. 1967, 42+; "Christmas Trade: Better But . . . ," 15–17; "Merchants Count Blessings," 17–19; "Happy Holidays," *T*, 92 (29 Nov. 1968): 96; "There's Less Reason to be Jolly," 14–15; "Christmas Trade: Hurt by Flu and Rising Taxes?" *USNWR*, 66 (6 Jan. 1969): 6; "What Christmas Trade Shows," 30–32; "Christmas Trade: The Outlook Around U.S.," 45–46; "Shoppers Signal

a So-So Christmas," *USNWR*, 69 (2 Nov. 1970): 50–52; "Christmas Consumer as Scrooge," *T*, 96 (28 Dec. 1970): 54–55; "This Year Santa Is Really Packing Them In," *BW*, 4 Dec. 1971, 24–25; "Christmas Trade: A Blockbuster," 13–15; "Christmas Shopping: Biggest Ever," *USNWR*, 71 (29 Nov. 1971): 26–28; "Stores Add Up a Merry Selling Season," *BW*, 1 Jan. 1972, 18–19; "Sales Will Brighten a Dimmer Christmas," *BW*, 1 Dec. 1973, 23; "Uncertain Season: Merchants Have Fingers Crossed," 30+; "Shoppers Trim the Christmas List," 26–27; "As Prices Skyrocket, a Buyers' Strike Threatens," 21–22+; "Wary Approach to Christmas," 26–27; "More Confident Countdown," 22–23; "It's Beginning to Look Like a Record in Christmas Sales, But . . . ," 52–53; "Christmas Splurging Starts Early," 24–25; and "Christmas Shoppers: Big Spenders but Picky, Too," 59–61.

8. For articles which mention that Christmas sales were satisfactory during World War II even though materials were requisitioned, see F. W. McDonough, "Has Merry Christmas Become a Mockery?" *BH&G*, 19 (Dec. 1940): 6; "American Christmas," *HB*, 82 (Dec. 1940): 43; Selma Robinson, "It's the Gift," *Col*, 106 (21 Dec. 1940): 46; "Merry Christmas," 57–58; "Greetings to All," *BW*, 21 Nov. 1942, 92+; "Pockets Afire with War Money," 70+; "Yule Sales Peak," 96+; and "Christmas Brings Record Sales," 83–84.

For articles which suggest that continuing to celebrate Christmas during the war was an act of patriotism, see "American Christmas," 43; Gladys Denny Shultz, "Christmas as Usual, Please!" *BH&G*, 20 (Dec. 1941): 58; Algernon D. Black, "What Christmas Means," *IW*, 21 (Dec. 1942): 353; "Merry Christmas," *NW*, 22 (25 Oct. 1943): 80+; Grace B. Lally, "The War's First Christmas," *AMag*, 139 (Jan. 1945): 108; and "Guide for Holiday Givers," *H&G*, 88 (Nov. 1945): 92–99.

9. For evidence of the euphoria among Christmas retailers in the immediate postwar period, see "Wrap It Up," *T*, 46 (31 Dec. 1945): 84; "Santa Delivered," 80–81+; "Christmas Rush," *Lf*, 21 (23 Dec. 1946): 33–34; "New High in Christmas Retail Trade," 30–31; "Xmas Sales Hitting New High," 26; "Jingle Sales, Jingle Sales," *NW*, 30 (22 Dec. 1947): 62; and "Retailers Ride Buying Wave," 19–20.

The quotation is from "The Old-Fashioned Way," *T*, 52 (6 Dec. 1948): 93. For additional evidence of the slow sales of 1948, see "Christmas Sales: Same as '47," 21; and "Trend of Christmas Shopping," 13–14.

10. The quotation is from "Christmas Sales: Same as '47," 21. For additional articles that note the apprehensiveness and self-doubt of business people following the Christmas of 1948, see "The Old-Fashioned Way," 93; "Christmas Specials Trim Stocks, Build Sales," 42–43; "Merry Xmas for Retailers," 68–70; "Christmas Sales Came Through," 22; "Retailers Have Merriest Christmas," 25–26; "Business Outlook," *BW*, 28 Nov. 1953, 17; "Christmas Trade: Off to a Slow Start," 68–72; and "Busy Christmas for Retailers," 30–31.

11. For articles that note the general cautiousness of retailers after 1948, in particular, their careful stocking for the holiday season, see "Christmas Sales: Same as '47," 21; "Merry Xmas for Retailers," 68–70; "Trend of Christmas Shopping," 13–14; "Stores Bank on Next Two Weeks," *BW*, 15 Dec. 1951, 22; and "Fast Start on Biggest Xmas Yet," *BW*, 26 Nov. 1955, 42+.

12. For discussions of the 1952 and 1953 Christmases, see "Retailers Have Merriest Christmas," 25–26; and "Christmas Trade: Off to a Slow Start," 68–72. See also "Christmas Sales," 12–14; and "Toy Departments Busiest with Near-Record Sales," 54–55.

13. For articles that discuss the uneven Christmas sales of the late 1950s, see "It's Fast, It's Frantic, It's 1955's Xmas," 32–34; "$6 Billion Christmas," *Lf*, 39 (19 Dec. 1955): 14–23; "Trade at Xmas to Break Records," 26–28; "Uneasy Retailers Wait, Worry," 34–35; "For Retailers, Is There a Santa?" 25; "Christmas Sales Finish Strong," *BW*, 5 Jan. 1957, 38; "Sales Add Up but Add No Joy," 133–36; "Stores Wait for a Miracle," 25–26; "Buyers

Turning Cautious?" 70–72; "Made-to-Order Yule for Stores," 11; "Yule Sales Head for a Record," 25–26; "Not Much Cheer for Retailers," 22; "Winter's Chill," 88; and "In Stores across the Country: Biggest Season Ever, But—," 46–48.

For articles that discuss the string of good years in the early 1960s, see "Buying Mood Is Back," 37–38; "Holiday Hail of Cash," 17–18; "Merry Christmas to All," 29–30; "Xmas Sales Ring Up a Record," 21; "Shoppers Flock Back to Resume Buying," 89–90; "Christmas '63: Best Sales Ever," 15–16; "It Was the Biggest Spending Binge Ever," *BW*, 28 Dec. 1963, 18; "It's a Real Boom in Christmas Shopping," 23–24; "Bell Ringer," 73; "It's a Record Boom in Christmas Shopping," 94–95; "Retailers Set Their Sights Still Higher," 14–15; "Stores Load Shelves, Brace for Record Yule," *BW*, 6 Nov. 1965, 30–31; "Retailers Ring Up Merriest Season Ever," 28–29; and "When Buyers Swamped Stores—The Biggest Christmas Boom," 65–66.

For evidence of the increased emphasis on fashion and fads during the Christmas seasons of the 1960s, see "Buying Mood Is Back," 37–38; "Holiday Hail of Cash," 17–18; "When the Needless is Essential," *BW*, 15 Dec. 1962, 50–52; "Christmas '63: Best Sales Ever," 15–16; "Plenty to Spend, and Ready to Buy," 25–27; "It's a Record Boom in Christmas Shopping," 94–95; "Retailers Set Their Sights Still Higher," 14–15; "Stores Load Shelves, Brace for Record Yule," 30–31; "Christmas Trade: Record Boom?" 37–39; "When Buyers Swamped Stores—The Biggest Christmas Boom," 65–66; "Santa '66: Fattest of All," 86–88; "Jingle Just Wasn't Quite So Loud," 16–17; "Christmas Tune Is a Bit Off Key," 33–35; "Can the Consumer Carry the Ball?" 42+; "Christmas Trade: Better, But . . . ," 15–17; "Merchants Count Blessings," 17–19; "Happy Holidays," 96; "Christmas Trade to Break Records," 58–60; "Uncertain Ring of Christmas," 59–60; "What Christmas Trade Shows," 30–32; and "Christmas Trade: The Outlook Around U.S.," 45–46.

14. For evidence of the uneven holiday sales of the late 1960s, see "Santa '66: Fattest of All," 86–88; "Jingle Just Wasn't Quite So Loud," 16–17; "Christmas Tune Is a Bit Off Key," 33–35; "More for More," *T*, 87 (7 Jan. 1966): 81–82; "Christmas Trade, 1966: It's Good, But—," *USNWR*, 61 (19 Dec. 1966): 76–77; "Can the Consumer Carry the Ball?" 42+; "Christmas Trade: Better, But . . . ," 15–17; "Merchants Count Blessings," 17–19; "Christmas Trade to Break Records," 58–60; "There's Less Reason to be Jolly," 14–15; "Uncertain Ring of Christmas," 59–60; "What Christmas Trade Shows," 30–32; "Christmas Trade: The Outlook Around U.S.," 45–46; "Christmas Prices Take the Down Escalator," 14; and "Christmas Consumer as Scrooge," 54–55.

15. For evidence of the retailers' attitude of resignation about the complexity of Christmas marketing decisions in the 1970s, see "It's Christmas or Never for the Big Stores," 25; "Shoppers Signal a So-So Christmas," 50–52; "Good Year for Christmas Trade," 16–18; "This Year Santa Is Really Packing Them In," 24–25; "Christmas Trade: A Blockbuster," 13–15; "Christmas Shopping: Biggest Ever," 26–28; "Shoppers Trim the Christmas List," 26–27; "As Prices Skyrocket, a Buyers' Strike Threatens," 21–22+; "Wary Approach to Christmas," 26–27; "More Confident Countdown," 22–23; "Christmas Buying Breaking Records," 31–33; "Stores Wait for the Last Moment," 23+; "Retailing: An Unexpectedly Happy Holiday," *BW*, 19 Jan. 1976, 18; "It's Beginning to Look Like a Record in Christmas Sales, But . . . ," 52–53; "Waiting for Some Christmas Cheer," *Ftn*, 96 (Nov. 1977): 19+; and "Stores Expect Muted Holiday Jingle," 95–97.

16. For articles that discuss the expansion of consumer services during the 1970s, see "There's Less Reason to be Jolly," 14–15; "What Christmas Trade Shows," 30–32; "Christmas Trade: The Outlook Around U.S.," 45–46; "Christmas Prices Take the Down Escalator," *BW*, 26 Dec. 1970, 14; "It's Christmas or Never for the Big Stores," 25; "Good Year for Christmas Trade," 16–18; "Christmas Consumer as Scrooge," *T*, 96 (28 Dec. 1970): 54–

55; "This Year Santa Is Really Packing Them In," 24–25; "Christmas Trade: A Blockbuster," 13–15; "Merry Pre-Christmas at the Counters," *BW*, 2 Dec. 1972, 21–22; "Shoppers in a Mood to Splurge," 69–70; "Shoppers Trim the Christmas List," 26–27; "Wary Approach to Christmas," 26–27; "More Confident Countdown," 22–23; "Last Minute Solace from Shoppers," 32–33; "Stores Wait for the Last Moment," 23+; and "Stores Expect Muted Holiday Jingle," 95–97.

Index